D1266915

The Limits
of
Administration

The Limits
of
Administration

Christopher C. Hood

Department of Politics,
Glasgow University

JOHN WILEY & SONS

London · New York · Sydney · Toronto

Library of Congress Cataloging in Publication Data:

Hood, Christopher C.
  The limits of administration.

  1., Public administration. 2. Policy sciences.
I. Title.
JF1411.H65   350   75-37850

ISBN 0 471 01652 7

Typeset in IBM Journal by Preface Ltd, Salisbury, Wilts and printed by
The Pitman Press Ltd., Bath

Preface

This book marks the end of about ten years of thought about the role of administration in the policy process. The book is intended to fill two closely related gaps. One gap is in the theory of public administration, the other is in the developing study of 'policy analysis'. One might suppose that policy analysis and public administration are simply different titles for the same thing, but in fact these terms denote fields of study which are illogically distinct. In this book I am attempting to show how administrative analysis can make a contribution to policy studies.

The gap which needs to be filled in policy studies is the neglect of the administrative element. In our increasingly bureaucratic society, more and more writing appears on the subject of the philosophy and politics of public policy and of the new 'managerial' styles of rational decision and planning. But 'administration', in the more prosaic sense of control, surveillance and policy implementation, has somehow received much less attention from the policy analysts. Indeed, the 'old-fashioned' concerns with the nuts and bolts of administration have been submerged to a large extent under a wave of fashionable technological fixes for better decision-making which in fact assume away the real problems of administration.

Why should there be a relative neglect of the 'administrative' element in policy studies? Is it that administration is too trivial, or too difficult, to be worth writing about in a serious way? Some people still tend to assume that administration is very simple, and to be impatient with those who see the need for 'theories' of any kind; perhaps this is a legacy of the old 'cookery book' approach to administrative science, in which successful public officials or industrialists tended to lay down universal maxims of administrative success as self-evident truths. This over-simple approach has long been discredited in academic circles, but it is surprisingly resilient among practitioners. This book purports to show that administration is not a trivial element in the policy process (or, to put it another way, that the trivia are important); to offer a framework for analysing the administrative element, and to show that such analysis deserves a more central place in policy analysis than it has received up to now. The importance of administration in the policy process is amply testified in folk-lore and satire; but there is no general theoretical framework, or even a coherent vocabulary, for discussing the problem in a general way. Many academic writers have lamented this deficiency.

In fact, the analysis of the role of administration in the policy process is now beginning to be developed from a number of disciplinary angles, and this book is no more than one of a number of sighting shots which have been fired in recent years. It stresses a number of key themes or limits of administration, each of which deserves a book on its own and some of which have been very neglected in conventional theories of public administration. Deficiencies in public administration theory constitute the second gap which this book is trying to fill. Traditionally, public administration has tended to be intellectually parochial in two senses. One is an implicit, but mistaken, attempt to treat public administration as a 'pure' subject, or at least as a pure social science like economics or psychology. But public administration cannot be a pure science in this sense. It can only come to life as a hybrid or applied science, importing concepts and insights from other social sciences. Indeed, it is beginning to be accepted that an adequate theory of policy implementation by public agencies would have to borrow its vocabulary or concepts from political science, law, economics and organizational sociology (some would add other disciplines), and in this book public administration is approached from a more interdisciplinary viewpoint than is customary.

The other sense in which public administration has tended to be parochial lies in the concentration on case-study research and the steady breakdown of the field into separate policy-area specialisms, leaving a theoretical vacuum at the centre. I am not arguing that such area specialisms ought not to exist, only that administration in many different contexts often shares important common features which may be obscured by the academic barriers which have been erected within the subject of 'administration'. The case-study approach also has disadvantages. Typically, the conclusions which can be drawn from the experience of a single case, rather than from a comparative study, are rather limited. I have experienced these limitations in my own past work, and so in this book I have attempted to construct a fairly general analysis drawing on a wide range of fields of administration and from several case studies. Obviously, this approach has its limitations too: one cannot achieve breadth and depth at the same time.

Although this book is written in a non-technical style which should be comprehensible to the general reader, it should be made clear that this is not a textbook setting out the conventional wisdom in administrative theory, but that it represents a particular point of view and a particular line of analysis. The plan of the book is as follows. Part 1 sets out the general problem, shows some of the complexities involved in identifying 'administrative limits' in the policy process, offers a model of 'perfect administration', and shows some of the types of administrative limits which are revealed by relaxing the conditions of the perfect model. Parts 2 and 3 examine each of these types of limits (categorization problems, adaptation problems and control problems) in more detail. A case study ends each Part, and if any reader finds some of the chapters difficult to follow, he might be well advised to read the case studies first and to work outwards to the analytical chapters from those.

My chief debt of gratitude is to Professor W. J. M. Mackenzie and to Andrew Dunsire, who between them taught me most of what I know about administration and who both read some of the chapters of this book. In addition to these, I must thank Richard Mowbray and Ted Kitchen for reading individual chapters and sections of this book. Professor Geraint Parry read the whole draft at a late stage and offered some very useful advice. Naturally, the responsibility for error and confusion is my own.

I am indebted to the Controller of HM Stationery Office, to HM Customs and Excise and to the Keeper of the Public Records Office, London, for permission to use materials in publication. Thanks are due to the editor of *Public Administration* for permission to reproduce the substance of articles published in that journal in Summer 1972 and Winter 1974.

Glasgow
September, 1975

Contents

PART 2: ADAPTATION AND CATEGORIZATION

PART 3: AUTHORITY AND CONTROL

Part 1

Introduction

'In practice, the State is a collection of officials and inspectors, sometimes wise, sometimes foolish, with no more omniscience than the individuals they propose to coerce.' Joad, C. E. M., *Introduction to Modern Political Theory*, Clarendon, Oxford, 1924, p. 29.

Chapter 1

Perfect Administration

'No contemporary tyrant . . . can govern by mere *fiat*.' J. H. Meisel,
Counterrevolution, Atherton Press, New York, 1966, p. 203.

The Problem

There is a calculable limit to which the thickening of lenses increases magnification.
Very thick lenses behave like prisms, splitting light up into its constituent colours
and preventing the image from forming at one spot.

Can we speak in a similar way about limits of 'administration'?

This is the question which forms the subject of this book. It is not a simple
question. In fact, it triggers off a round of difficulties. What do we mean by
'administration'? What do we mean by 'limits'? Such problems have to be tackled
before the question can be accurately framed.

The practical man may be impatient with such academic niceties. He knows
pretty well what 'administration' is; and he may know something about its limits
from common sense and common experience. Indeed, he lives in an age of big
organizations and of 'big government', where grandiose administrative schemes all
too often achieve nothing, or, worse, achieve results contrary to those which were
desired. To illustrate such problems, let us look briefly at a few well-known cases
where policy implementation, instead of moving nearer to a target, goes sideways,
backwards or nowhere at all.

The pursuit of social welfare policies provides many illustrations of the problem.
Everyone has heard of 'planning blight', the aggravation rather than the mitigation
of urban squalor which can be produced by town-planning decisions. Similarly,
conventional prisons have long been said to aggravate the problems which they are
supposed to solve by acting as breeding-grounds for a criminal sub-culture.[1] Slum
clearance programmes may be ineffective because of delays in rebuilding and higher
rents charged for new houses, which cause displaced slum-dwellers to move to other
slum areas, already overcrowded, leaving the new houses to be occupied by more
well-to-do people.[2] Problems of unforeseen developments and unexpected responses are very general in the urban setting; indeed, sophisticated computerized
modelling of large-scale social systems has led to the conclusion that 'counter-
intuitive behaviour' is a basic property of such systems, contriving to defeat
simple-minded policy measures.[3]

Military operations are another area in which effective policy implementation is
particularly difficult to achieve. Every ex-serviceman can relate tales of administrative chaos, horrifying or humorous. Defence contracting is full of notorious

cases like the quick £1 m project which turns in to £5 m worth of scrap iron and orders for overseas weapons instead (as with the British Mark 31 Torpedo project).[4] Military operations themselves are very often counter-productive. A well-known example is the doctrine of 'strategic bombing' which was followed by the United States forces in the Vietnam War. In a simple agricultural economy such as Vietnam there are few, if any, points whose destruction by bombing could paralyse the whole economy, so a strategy of selective bombing could not be very effective. The alternative strategy of 'carpet bombing', that is, laying down a barrage of bombs indiscriminately over wide areas, was worse, because it destroyed potential support for the United States' cause as much as it weakened the insurgents.[5] In fact, military measures to put down rebellions, particularly of a guerilla kind, can very easily be self-defeating. Measures such as internment, the forcible relocation of populations and physical barriers sealing off one area from another, often fan the flames of discontent.[6]

As a final example, we can turn to the folk-lore of business administration, particularly in big corporations. Here too, we find tales of elaborate blunders, of snarl-ups between production, sales, design and stock control departments, and of the unexpected, often counter-productive, effects of seemingly 'rational' management strategies such as financial targets or wage systems based on output.[7] It is the everyday experiences represented by such stories which help to shape the popular image of 'administration' as muddle, confusion, delay and expensive, self-destructive mistakes.

It seems clear from such examples that there *is* a problem about administration and its limits; and this problem has become more obvious with recent failures to implement ambitious social programmes, particularly the United States' poverty programmes in the 1960s. But the problem is too complex to be adequately tackled by a common-sense approach which avoids definition and careful analysis. There are several reasons for this. One is that, unlike the example of magnifying lenses with which we began, there may be many different types of administrative failures and limits. Very often the 'practical man' tends to emphasize only one administrative problem or solution which has been important in his own experience, excluding other types of problem. In the same vein, there is a good deal of semi-satirical analysis of administrative problems, such as *Parkinson's Law*[8] and *The Peter Principle*,[9] which offer easily-grasped and simple explanations of 'why things always go wrong' in large-scale administrative enterprise. Analysis of this kind certainly offers valuable insight, but the range of examples which was given above was chosen to illustrate a variety of processes which cannot easily be reduced to a single explanation. Indeed, throughout this book we will tend to stress the variety of administrative limits which can occur, rather than concentrating on any single type.

The second reason why definition and analysis is necessary is that, as one author has remarked, important arguments develop about what is and what is not 'administration'; and indeed, many supposed cases of administrative 'failure' turn out to be highly ambiguous on closer examination. This applies to many of the examples which were given above; and to take an even more extreme case, consider the failure of the Nazi regime in Germany either to centralize or to co-ordinate its administrative machinery. Here, one might think, is a pure case of administrative limits, since this was a regime which was supposed to be all-powerful and monolithic and which was willing to use the most bloodthirsty of possible means in order to achieve its objectives. On the other hand, did this failure *really* lie with inherent administrative defects or with Hitler's characteristic indecision in the face of conflicts between his subordinates?[10] It all depends, of course, on what you mean by 'administration'.

'Administration' and 'Limits'

For both of these reasons, some elaboration and definition of terms is required. Let us look first at 'administration'. It is an ambiguous word: Andrew Dunsire has identified no less than 22 different meanings of 'administration',[11] and even that may not exhaust the possibilities. For the purposes of this book, the meaning of administration can be defined as 'deliberate processes of implementation and control' and loosely distinguished from policy-making and decision. The traditional legal definition of administration as *imperare, vetare, permittere, punire* (command, prohibition, permission and punishment) covers most of the processes which are involved, though it does not quite catch the modern meaning of administration as 'implementation', a broad strategic activity of 'making things happen',[12] as opposed to simply giving out orders or meting out punishment. Moreover, the emphasis here is on public administration, but much of the analysis which is applicable to public administration is also applicable to administration as a generic social process.

Note the term 'deliberate' in our definition. We wish to distinguish administration from relatively spontaneous forms of 'social control' (such as parental control over children), except insofar as such types of control are deliberately harnessed or initiated for administrative purposes. This is important, because, as we will see later on, there is only a very fine line between administrative control and social control in a wider sense, and many types of administrative control operate by harnessing social controls of a more spontaneous type.

Let us now turn to the question of 'limits'. In the example from optics with which we began, we are dealing with a *calculable* limit. But we do not actually need to be able to calculate a limit precisely in order to establish that it exists. A famous example of this point was given by Thomas Malthus, the eighteenth-century economist. Malthus observed that no-one can calculate precisely what the maximum possible size of a carnation would be. Nevertheless, we know that there *is* a maximum size, and we know why: no carnation could grow as large as a cabbage, for example, because of the mechanical stresses to which the stalk would be subjected.[13] Administrative analysis is typically restricted to this level of precision. The restriction arises because in many matters we have to rely on circumstantial rather than on systematic evidence. We may not be able to say exactly where the point will fall in any given case, but we may be able to establish some of the mechanisms which operate the limits.

The example with which we began also concerned a *single* type of limit, as has already been mentioned. But we will be identifying a multiplicity of types of limit as the book proceeds. For example, we have to distinguish 'administrative limits' proper from other kinds of policy limits. 'Administerability' is not the only element which limits the outcomes of policy. Some policies cannot be carried out because the available resources are insufficient. Other policies cannot be carried out because they are unacceptable for political reasons. Any workable policy must involve both resource availability and political acceptability as well as 'administerability'.

Apart from the distinction of external and internal limits, we will be distinguishing dilemmas and 'non-linearities', ineffectiveness and negative effectiveness, 'economic' and absolute limits. The first two of these pairs will be elaborated in later chapters, and the last distinction is almost self-explanatory. Absolute limits are physical and unambiguous, such as the point at which a structure breaks or at which resources are exhausted. The other type of limit is relative, referring to balance of advantage. For example, there is typically a point at which crime has been reduced to a satisfactory level, such that it is no longer *worth-while* to devote extra resources to catching criminals, even though some crime is still going on. The rewards are too small to justify the effort. It is the difference between maximum capacity and optimum activity. The second type of limit is familiar to economists, the first type more familiar to engineers. In discussing administration it is clearly important to distinguish economic-type limits from engineering-type limits.

Perfect Administration

One way of analysing implementation problems is to begin by thinking about what 'perfect administration' would be like, comparable to the way in which economists employ the model of perfect competition. Perfect administration could be defined as a condition in which 'external' elements of resource availability and political acceptability combine with 'administration' to produce perfect policy implementation.

We will be discussing the 'external' conditions in the next section. But what are the 'internal' conditions of perfect administration? Several writers have thought about what perfect planning and administrative machinery would be like, particularly in terms of the information capacity which would be needed for complete co-ordination of all activities in a large-scale system.[14] Indeed, there is almost a ready-made model of perfect administration in the form of conditions for a 'total surveillance society' devised by J. B. Rule (in order to show that such a society could not really exist).[15]

Five major conditions can be identified here as the 'internal' components of perfect administration, defined as a condition in which administration proper would have no limiting effect on policy outcomes. Several of these conditions are closely similar to J. B. Rule's conditions for 'total surveillance'.

(1) The first condition overlaps slightly with the 'external' conditions of perfect administration. This is that the administrative system has to be unitary, like a huge army with a single line of authority. This is because any conflict of authority might potentially weaken administrative control. Two of Rule's conditions for total surveillance are similar to this: he requires a single system of surveillance and control covering everybody, and that all information be collated at a single point, to avoid compartmentalism in the system.

(2) The second condition can be borrowed directly from Rule: the norms or rules enforced by the system would have to be uniform. Even if the administrative

system was unitary, the objectives of its various sub-units would not necessarily be, and so we must require 'given' and uniform objectives. These objectives must also be clearly ascertainable to the officials, even if they are kept secret from the population at large.

(3) Third, it is not sufficient to have clear and authoritative objectives. The objectives must be implemented. There are two possible conditions which could provide the link between objectives and implementation. One is to assume that there would be no resistance to commands at any point in the administrative system — perfect obedience. Alternatively, one could allow some recalcitrance to exist in the system and still achieve perfect implementation by assuming perfect administative control. Rule assumes that every action of every individual could be scrutinized and recorded, and that any disobedience would be punished or forestalled.

(4) Even if we make the first of the two possible assumptions for the third condition of perfect administration, a fourth condition would be necessary. Even if there were perfect obedience in the system, it would still not be sufficient to have one's objectives clear and one's commands quickly obeyed if these commands were in some way misdirected, and so a version of Rule's assumption about perfect information and communication would still have to apply. There would need to be perfect co-ordination between administrative units, perfect information concerning the situation in hand and the capacity to specify tasks or the content of one's orders unambiguously.

(5) Finally, all of these preceding conditions would not be sufficient unless adequate time was available for administrative resources to be brought to bear. Rule does not include this condition explicitly in his conditions for a total surveillance society, though it is certainly implicit. Our fifth condition, then, would be the absence of time pressure.

Clearly, no actual administrative system is likely to fulfil all — or any — of these five conditions. But a 'perfect' model of this type can be useful in two ways. First, as a *reductio ad absurdum* argument, which enables us to gain an idea of the limitations of most common-or-garden administrative schemes. Second, to use as a measure to set alongside particular administrative cases as a means of comparing them. The conditions may point to different types of administrative limits, which we can examine in turn.

Types of Limits

By relaxing the conditions of perfect administration, we can identify three broad types of limit, each of which has sub-types. These types are:

(1) 'External' or strictly extra-administrative limits on policy implementation.

(2) A class of more strictly administrative limits which are the corollaries of the five 'internal' conditions of perfect administration which have just been stated.

(3) A hybrid type, which we will call 'quasi-administrative' limits. This refers to cases where genuine administrative difficulties arise, but which have been more or

less deliberately created by political strategies or by lack of resources. This should not be confused with the distinction between absolute and relative limits.

In this chapter, we will discuss 'external' and 'quasi-administrative' limits, and we will consider more strictly administrative limits in the next chapter.

External Limits on Policy Implementation

As was briefly mentioned earlier, there are some cases where the failure to implement policies has nothing to so with 'administration', but lies in the absence of the 'external' conditions of perfect administration. It will be recalled that these conditions are unlimited material resources for tackling the problem, unambiguous overall objectives and perfect political acceptability of the policies pursued. Let us look first at 'resource' limits. These apply to failures in policy implementation which are not caused by disagreement, resistance or technical difficulties of administration, but rather by a shortage (relative or absolute) of materials or of money. For example, you cannot tax people to a level below subsistence for purely economic reasons, quite apart from any administrative difficulties which might be involved.

The other broad external limit to policy implementation is 'political'. Again, this is familiar: some failures in policy implementation are caused neither by shortages of resources nor by technical difficulties, but rather because the policies involved are politically too expensive for a given ruling group to judge itself able to afford the price. We will explore such cases shortly; but, as with all attempts to categorize, there is an interesting group of cases on the borderline. The intermediate cases here are those which are neither clearly 'resource' nor 'political' limits in an obvious sense, but which are created by odd kinds of 'consumer behaviour'. These are cases in which the more is supplied, the more is demanded, and vice versa. In circumstances such as these, policy implementation can be ineffective without any strictly 'administrative' failure.

The cases of road building and public transport in the 1960s illustrate opposite types of the same problem. In public transport, declining use of public transport facilities resulted in cutbacks and worsening standards, in turn occasioning a further decline in demand, and so on.[16] Road building was the converse of the public transport experience. The attempts to relieve traffic congestion by improving roads clearly played a part in encouraging more people to buy vehicles, travel by road and to live further away from city centres (with the resulting spatial distribution of people round cities making public transport much less viable than in areas of concentrated population). In the extreme case, such reponses to road improvement may work themselves through in such a way that the congestion problem simply recurs later on a different scale, as has been known to happen in some cases.[17]

Very similar responses are apt to attend increases in the supply of mental and geriatric hospitals; the more is supplied, the more is demanded, meaning that extra hospital capacity always tends to 'silt up'. Examples such as these illustrate problems which are clearly not 'administrative' in a strict sense, yet are difficult to classify as between 'resource' limits and political limits. Perhaps the only truly administrative failing in such cases is to be unaware of the social forces whose operation defeats attempts at solutions.

Political Limits

As we have already discussed, political limits refer to those cases where policy implementation fails as a result of the application of political power rather than by lack of resources or by unadministerability. Such limits are familiar and just as important as 'resource' limits, though they may be harder to locate. For example, most taxes would be likely to create civil commotion or political upheaval long before the actual point of economic destitution was reached. Also, some social groups are politically too powerful to accept taxation at all. The history of the French *bouilleurs de cru* (local distillers who were exempt from the alcohol tax) is a famous case of this. The influence of these distillers, especially in Normandy, Lorraine, Burgundy, the Loire and Couronne, was sufficient to defeat attempts to include them in the alcohol tax for over 100 years, beginning in the 1830s.[18]

The limits of what is politically acceptable to dominant groups typically 'distort' policy programmes in a number of familiar ways. For example, administratively separate systems often have to be sewn up into 'packages', so as to placate multiple interests at once. This means that 'tied aid' or 'administered benefits' tend to be favoured as instruments of welfare policy over simple 'negative taxes' or straight boosts to purchasing power, although the latter are typically favoured by economists because they maximize freedom of choice. The reason is that by subsidizing specific goods or services for the relief of poverty, rather than giving the poor money to do what they like with, one can benefit both the poor and the producers of the goods or services in question.[19] The same applies to other fields of policy. Many building and construction cases come into this category, and one well-known example is nineteenth-century city sanitation: the construction of London's giant sewers surprised even social reformers such as Charles Dickens, who had proclaimed his 'infinitesimal' faith in government over the issue.[20] Similarly, it should not be surprising that schemes for subsidizing the arts tend not to give aid directly to creative artists (where there is no element of 'double benefit'), but to the performing arts, construction of buildings and so on.

Another familiar 'distortion' arising from the limits of political acceptability is that schemes which benefit many territorial areas are typically preferred to schemes benefiting more concentrated areas. The latter, again, are typically favoured by economists, following the principle of concentrating investments at the point of the highest expected return. But the economic principle is typically unpopular in those areas which are not selected for benefits, and the political logic of spreading benefits widely (*sapoudrage*, as the French call it)[21] often results in the dilution of aid schemes which were originally designed to be selective. This is what has happened to the United States' 'Model Cities' programme and similarly to various 'growth point' regional development strategies in Britain, France and Italy.

Again, there are some interesting cases which are difficult to classify as clearly 'administrative' or clearly 'political', but which fall somewhere on the borderline. First, there is the use of 'administrative impossibility' as a rhetorical device. Using the technical language of administration or of management as a form of rhetoric to conceal choices may be a useful political tactic, especially where (as in Britain and the United States) there is a well-established idea that good government is government without politics. For this reason, 'administration' is often used as a political back alley, a convenient alternative to open policy decisions. For example, it may be more convenient to strike down awkward agencies or officials by cutting their travel allowances and the like, rather than by outright dismissal. Similarly, in colonial times the administrative difficulty of holding elections was sometimes used as an argument for slowing down the pace of decolonization.[22]

'Administrative difficulty' can thus be a political smoke-screen, a rhetorical rather than an 'objective' limit. Another type of possible limit is very closely related. This is that 'administrative' limits may also in a sense be constituted by the influence of high officials in political decisions, the ability of such officials to make their counsels prevail in discussions of policy. The idea of bureaucracy over-riding democracy is taken very seriously by some writers, such as Max Weber, and there are one or two well-known cases in British politics. Army loyalty to the government has been doubtful from time to time, as during the American War of Independence and in the Ulster crisis of 1914.[23] The same has happended from time to time with the civilian bureaucracy, and the idea of 'mandarins', 'evil geniuses' and *eminences grises*, referring to the power of permanent officials in political deliberations, is a recurring theme in British politics. The issue has recently been given prominence by the 'Crossman thesis', based on R. H. S. Crossman's experience in the Labour Government of 1964—1970, that Ministers are easily over-ridden by the 'Departmental view' of senior civil servants.[24] As Montagu Norman, Governor of the Bank of England in the 1930s, arrogantly put it, quoting an Arab proverb, 'The dogs may bark, but the caravan passes on'.[25] One famous case of this type of administrative limit is Lloyd George's 'People's Budget' of 1909, which was held up for months because the Parliamentary draftsmen asserted that the policies involved were impossible to write into law.

Other examples can be taken from lower down the hierarchy. Wamsley and Zald question whether United States National Guard officers could be effectively ordered to take their units into riots without loaded weapons.[26] A British case is the refusal by Surveyors (now called Inspectors) of Taxes to administer the super-tax of 1909. This refusal necessitated the establishment of a separate Surtax Office at Thames Ditton, which it took over 60 years to integrate into the normal tax machinery. This arrangement was publicly defended on the ground that surtax payers would thus gain greater confidentiality over their financial affairs than if the tax was administered by the local tax inspectors. This assertion was nonsense, but the myth persisted.

A less dramatic variant of the same sort of limit is where administrators, without showing open defiance or political bias, nevertheless knock the corners off policies in order to get such policies through the front door, so to speak. This limit applies at the level of implementation rather than at the level of policy deliberation. It thus involves a rather different kind of bureaucratic and technocratic manoeuvre, and is open to a lower level of officials. One example, which is discussed later in the book, is the adaptation by administrative agencies to programme-planning-budgeting and to other quantitative controls on budgeting and project approval, but of course the process whereby the eventual result of some scheme 'on the ground' bears little relation to the great thoughts of the man at the top is so familiar as hardly to need illustration.

Administrative Limits

The quasi-political limits which have just been discussed are those influences of 'administration' in policy outcomes which political scientists most easily recognize. Does this leave anything which could be termed a more 'objective' administrative limit, apart from the personal dynamics of high policy-making and the influence of 'the administration' in the political arena? Referring to the metaphor which was used in the last paragraph, might there be cases in which you cannot *in fact* get the grand piano through the front door without knocking the house down? Such questions have not received much attention in the past, and the conventional public administration literature contains relatively little analysis of implementation problems, although there is a good deal of undigested case material available on some topics. Indeed, S. K. Bailey has asserted that

> 'public administration scholars are too preoccupied with the highest strata of government and with administrators who are policy-makers more than they are administrators.'

We will be considering limits of administration in a strict sense by stripping down the internal conditions of 'perfect administration' in the next chapter. In order to distinguish *administrative* limits from other limits on policy implementation, we must find cases where the conditions both of political acceptability and of broad resource availability are met, but where execution still presents problems. For a simple illustration, consider the possibility of a tax on diamonds or other precious stones. It is unlikely that such a tax would be hampered by political acceptability or by resource availability. Diamonds and similar stones have considerable value in most times and places, and there would be no obvious political difficulty about levying a tax upon them. But how could such a tax be enforced? Diamonds are easy to conceal. They are not registered or recorded in any systematic way; and they are easily alterable, making positive identification difficult. Nor is there anything comparable to a stock exchange for transactions in diamonds, where prices can be ascertained and used as a basis for tax; many diamond markets have traditionally operated wholly on the basis of word of mouth transactions.

Almost all taxes on personal property suffer from administrative problems of this kind to some extent. It is difficult to prevent the concealment or destruction of property, to ascertain its value or even to make productive use of it in the same way as its former possessors. These problems do not apply only where administrative processes are governed by constraints of legality and fairness, but also apply where arbitrary confiscation is taking place.[28] For example, the attempt by the Allies to confiscate the industrial wealth of the German Ruhr district after World War II was largely unsuccessful. Inevitably, the confiscation effort was sabotaged by the local population and was carried out with catastrophic waste and inefficiency; much productive machinery was in practice allowed to rot. and good material was used for scrap.[29] Moreover, the physical equipment of the Ruhr proved to be fairly useless compared to the know-how which had produced it, and which so quickly reconstructed it in the post-war years.

Such administrative difficulties very often prove to be the sticking point in taxation policy, and that is one reason why examples taken from taxation will appear frequently in this book. Campbell tells us, in the context of British administration

> 'Ministers are known to have complained that reforms dear to their hearts have, when put to the (revenue) departments, floated back with the polite observation that the execution of some programme would involve doubling the staff . . .'[30]

This is a theme which has recurred through at least 100 years of British tax history. For example, Gladstone refused to introduce into the income tax system the differentiation of tax rates between 'earned' and 'unearned' income (as suggested by John Stuart Mill), not because he thought that it was undesirable, but because of 'administrative difficulties'. Similarly, when Sir William Harcourt introduced a graduated scheme of death duties in 1894, he said that it was merely 'administrative difficulties' which prevented the application of the same principles to the income tax. Indeed, it was Austen Chamberlain, who had earlier declared a belief in proportional rather than progressive taxation, who in fact introduced differentiation and graduation into the British income tax machinery.[31]

In the poorer countries of today, the same administrative limits as those which faced Gladstone and Harcourt, typically prevent the imposition of effective income and profits taxes. Surrey remarks that such taxes require much more precision on the part of tax administrators than indirect taxes, and as a result

> '. . . the glib "tax reform" analysis of the economist is often difficult or impossible actually to implement.'[32]

This is not to say that administrative limits to taxation are restricted to underdeveloped countries, though they are certainly more obvious the poorer the society involved. For example, the taxation of migrant workers and cash traders like taxi-drivers presents a problem everywhere. Two cases exploring administrative problems in tax collection in Britain are given later in the book.

Quasi-administrative Limits

The final type of limit on policy implementation to be considered in this chapter is that of quasi-administrative limits, as we termed them earlier. The term refers to cases where administrative limits are created by deliberate political decisions or by avoidable shortages of material resources. This is another category which is bound to be fuzzy round the edges. As we will see in the case studies later on, it is difficult in many cases to sharply distinguish those types of administrative failure which are 'internally' caused from those which are 'externally' caused, because administration can never be fully divorced from its social context. In an extreme sense, all administrative limits are contingent on outside conditions, in that a perfect society without scarcity of resources would hardly need any administration. But at a more prosaic level it is worth distinguishing genuinely administrative problems, such as the tax on precious stones which was discussed in the last section, from cases where administration has been deliberately crippled in order to make a policy more acceptable. Indeed, we are bound to make such distinctions, if only for operational purposes: trying to cope with externally created problems by tinkering with administrative structures or procedures is likely to be ineffective or even counter-productive.

There are several possible types of quasi-administrative limits. The most typical case is probably where multiple or ambiguous political objectives prevent administrative success, making it impossible to remove one obstacle without running into another. The same thing can happen when objectives change, meaning that success in terms of last year's criteria turns out to be a failure in terms of this year's criteria. Similarly, there is the case of unacknowledgeable objectives: the publicly stated objectives turn out not to be the real objectives. A case of this is 'symbolism' or 'tokenism',[33] that is, the adoption of measures which merely give the impression of dealing with some problem, but are not intended to be seriously implemented. Legislation prohibiting collusive 'rings' of buyers at auctions (impossible to enforce) or the imposition of capital gains taxes on bearer bonds (the ownership of which is untraceable, making effective taxation impossible) are illustrations of this kind of tokenism. Such measures achieve nothing, in the sense that they cannot be effectively administered, but they may have political usefulness.

Can we include as quasi-administrative limits cases where objectives themselves are so grandiose or silly that they are bound to be impossible to implement? One thinks of cases such as Prohibition in the United States and similar attempts by other regimes to foist changes in private behaviour on to an unwilling population. But to include such cases as quasi-administrative limits would be to destroy the logic of distinguishing between quasi-administrative limits and administrative limits proper. It is dissimulation, change or ambiguity in objectives which can give a slightly misleading impression of administrative failure; but if objectives are clear and sincere, whatever they are, failure to implement them must be counted as an administrative failure.

Quasi-administrative limits can be seen in terms of a clash between logics of action, to borrow a phrase from Lucien Karpik.[34] The logic of administrative action is effective control over a given population for given purposes. But there is also the political logic of mobilizing support, and administrative logic may clash with political logic or with overall economic constraints. For example, taxes on exports are relatively easy to administer, because policing is restricted to relatively few sea-ports,[35] but such taxes are often politically unpopular because they do not sufficiently discriminate ability to pay. Moreover, export taxes are often thought to be economically disadvantageous by those who believe in the 'foreign trade multiplier' theory of economic growth. In cases where administrative logic is subordinate to some other type of logic, we can speak of quasi-administration limits.

Of course, there is no necessary or *a priori* reason why these different logics should clash. In some cases they run the same way. For example, the introduction of the British Corporation Tax in 1965 both served as a useful political measure for the new Labour government (which defended the new tax as a means for encouraging investment in industry); and at the same time the tax was an important administrative expedient to prevent 'dividend stripping', a then growing method of tax avoidance which it was impossible to prevent under the old system of company taxation.[36]

Lenkowsky's account of the emergence of proposals for a 'negative income tax' by the British Conservative government in 1971,[37] reveals a similar 'coupling' of political and administrative logic. The Conservatives presented the measure as a major new step in poor relief, but it also coincided with attempts to simplify the PAYE ('pay as you earn') income tax system. PAYE income tax is deducted by employers from wage payments on a monthly or weekly basis, but it is a cumulative tax, and therefore there has to be a balancing calculation at the end of the year, when a taxpayer's total income is known. But, given a commitment to a progressive system of taxation, it would not be possible simply to remove the cumulative element of the tax without creating serious inequities, for example between people with steady earnings and those whose earnings fluctuate throughout the year. As a result, the idea evolved of using the tax machinery for paying *out* as well as for paying *in*, an expedient which would remove the cumulative element from the tax but which would still cope with the problem of fluctuating earnings. From that it is but a short step to a negative income tax. Perhaps it is this kind of process which Rudolph Klein has in mind when he quotes Edelman's remark that 'decision-making at the higher levels is not so much literal policy-making as dramaturgy'.[38]

Such examples of 'coupling' of political and administrative logics are relatively rare, but we will see several examples of quasi-administrative limits in the case studies which are presented later in the book. In many cases 'administration' is blamed for the failure of a policy, it turns out that the implications of proper policing are too unpleasant or too expensive to be accepted, not that the task is inherently impossible. J. B. Rule gives a good case of this when he observes that many cases where delinquents of one kind or another are able to give the authorities the slip by changing their names, addresses or locations, could be prevented by tattooing the whole population.[39] But would such a badge of slavery be accepted by the public at large?

Summary and Conclusion

The simple question about the limits of administration with which we began this chapter has turned out to be full of ambiguities and complexities. Perfect policy implementation, we argued, requires both extra-administrative conditions and conditions of 'administerability'. In this chapter we have looked at the extra-administrative conditions of perfect administration, namely unlimited resources, political acceptability and unambiguous objectives. The relaxation of these two conditions gave us two types of limits on policy implementation. The first is a class of strictly extra-administrative constraints, although these include difficult border-line cases, such as the influence of high administrators in policy-making and the use of 'administrative impossibility' as a political argument. The second type of limit is what we called quasi-administrative limits, to refer to situations where policy implementation is hampered by administrative difficulties, but such difficulties are created by scarce resources or by ambiguous objectives, not because the task in question is inherently impossible. In the next chapter we will move on to explore more strictly administrative limits to policy outcomes by dismantling the 'internal' conditions of our model of perfect administration.

Notes

1. Mitford, J., *Cons and Rebels*, Allen and Unwin, London, 1974.
2. cf. Norman P. and J. English, '100 years of slum clearance in England and Wales,' Discussion Paper Number One, Discussion Papers in Social Research, Glasgow, 1974.
3. Forrester, J. W., *Urban Dynamics*, M.I.T., London, 1969.
4. *Third Report from the Committee of Public Accounts*, HC 447, 1971—1972, pp. XXVI—XXVII.
5. Wilensky, H., *Organizational Intelligence*, Basic Books, London, 1967.
6. Wolf, E. R., *Peasant Wars of the Twentieth Century*, Faber and Faber, London, 1971.
7. Richardson, K., has collected some of these stories in *Do It The Hard Way*, Weidenfeld and Nicholson, London, 1972.
8. Parkinson, C. N., *Parkinson's Law*, Penguin, Harmondsworth, 1965.
9. Hall, R., and L. J. Peter, *The Peter Principle*, Morrow, New York, 1969.
10. Paterson, E. N., *The Limits of Hitler's Power*, Princeton University Press, New Jersey, 1969.
11. Dunsire, A., *Administration: the Word and the Science*, Martin Robertson, London, 1973.
12. cf. Gross, B., *Action Under Planning*, McGraw-Hill, New York, 1967.
13. Malthus, T. *An Essay on the Principle of Population*, Penguin edition (Penguin Books, Harmondsworth, 1970) p. 128 ff and p. 171, cf. D'Arcy Wentworth Thompson, *On Growth and Form*, abridged ed. by J. T. Bonner, Cambridge University Press, Cambridge, 1966, p. 201.
14. For example, Beer, S., *Brain of the Firm*, Penguin Press, Allen Lane, London, 1972; A. Dunsire, seminar paper, Strathclyde University, 8 November 1974, and *The Execution Process*, Martin Robertson (forthcoming), London.
15. Rule, J. B., *Private Lives and Public Surveillance*, Allen Lane, London, 1973.
16. Hirschman, A. O., *Exit Voice and Loyalty*, Harvard University Press, Cambridge, Mass., 1970.
17. For a discussion of the problem of 'traffic generation' by road building, see Thompson, J. M., *Motorways in London*, C. Duckworth and Co., London 1969, pp. 33—36 and also Fig. 4.
18. Ardant, G., *Theorie Sociologique de l'Impôt*, S.E.V.P.E.N. Paris, 1965.
19. cf. Olson, M., for a 'by-product theory' of the production of collective goods in *The Logic of Collective Action*, Schocken Books, New York, 1968, and the more recent reconciliation of income redistribution (provided it is 'tied aid') with the principle of Pareto-optimality by H. H. Hochman and J. R. Rodgers, 'Pareto-optimal redistribution', *American Economic Review*, LIX 1969.
20. Tomlin, E. W. F., *Charles Dickens 1812—1870*, Weidenfeld and Nicholson, London, 1969.
21. Boyd, R., Ph.D. Thesis, University of Glasgow, in preparation.
22. cf. Sanger, C., and J. Nottingham 'The Kenya General Election of 1963', *Journal of Modern African Studies*, Vol. 2, 1972.
23. Chorley, K. C., *Armies and the Art of Revolution*, Faber and Faber, London, 1943.
24. Crossman, R. H. S., *Diaries of a Cabinet Minister*, Jonathan Cape, (forthcoming), London.
25. Boyle, A., *Montagu Norman*, Cassell, London, 1967.
26. Wamsley, G. L., and M. N. Zald, *The Political Economy of Public Organizations*, D. C. Heath, Toronto, 1973.
27. In Charlesworth, J. C. (Ed.), *Theory and Practice of Public Administration*, American Academy of Political and Social Science, Philadelphia, 1963, p. 133.
28. cf. Marx, Karl, *The German Ideology*, International Publishers, New York, 1947; E. Burke, *Reflections on the Revolution in France*, Holt Rinehart and Winston, New York, 1959.
29. Batty, P., *The House of Krupp*, Secker and Warburg, London, 1969.
30. Campbell, G. A., *The Civil Service in Britain*, Duckworth, London, 1965, p. 104.
31. Dowell, S., *A History of Taxation and Taxes in England from Earliest Times to the Present Day*, Longmans, London, 1889, 4 vols.
32. In Bird, R., and O. Oldman (Eds.), *Readings in Taxation in Developing Countries*, Johns Hopkins Press, Baltimore, 1964.
33. cf. Groth, A., *Comparative Politics: A Distributive Approach*, Macmillan, London, 1971.

16

34. Karpik, L., 'Les politiques et les logiques d'action de la grande enterprise industrielle', *Sociologie du Travail*, 1, 1972, pp. 82–105.
35. For an 'administrative' theory of tax structure development, see H. H. Hinrichs, *A General Theory of Tax Structure Development*, Harvard Law School, Chicago, 1966.
36. Stanley, O., *A Guide to Taxation*, Methuen, London, 1967.
37. Lenkowsky, L., 'The politics of motherhood: the cost of policy change in the U.S. and Britain' paper presented at Conference on the Dynamics of Public Policy, Windsor, England, May 6–10, 1974.
38. Edelman, M., *The Symbolic Use of Politics*, University of Illinois Press, 1964, p. 78; quoted in R. Klein, 'Policy-making in the national health service', *Political Studies*, Vol. 22, 1974.
39. Rule, J. B., *op. cit.*

Chapter 2

Types of Administrative Limits

'Some proposals which are unobjectionable in principle have in fact had
to be rejected on purely administrative grounds.' *Third Special Report
of the Estimates Committee*, HC 18, 1961–1962 (Observations by the
Board of Inland Revenue on the Seventh Report from the Estimates
Committee, HC 245, 1960–1961), p. 3.

In the last chapter we looked at the external conditions of perfect administration,
and extra-administrative limits on policy implementation. In this chapter we will
try to classify some more strictly administrative limits by dismantling the five
conditions of perfect administration which were set out in Chapter 1. We will also
introduce some of the key mechanisms bringing about these limits in order to set
the scene for later chapters which pursue individual parts of the analysis in greater
detail.

Co-ordination and Multi-organizational Sub-optimization

The first condition of perfect administration was that administrative authority
should be unitary. The administrative system must be like an army, under a single
command, with every part relating to every other part (of course, real armies are
not at all like this). When we relax this condition, allowing authority to be divided
or multiple, the first set of administrative difficulties or limits appears. This is the
familiar problem of conflict and imperfect co-ordination arising from the division
of organizations into functional units, or into territorial units, or both. The basic
problem can be summed up in the phrase 'multi-organizational sub-optimization'.[1]
The hideousness of this phrase seems inevitable: it is not a simple idea. It refers to
situations where different parts of inter-connected systems are separately administered in such a way as to render the total administrative effect ineffective or
counter-productive.

The problem can occur on a variety of levels. To begin with a small-scale
example, in some Glasgow hospitals in the early 1970s, the telephone number for
fire was 222 and for the cardiac arrest team it was 333. In the other hospitals in the
city, fire was 333 and cardiac arrest was 222. In the context of mobile doctors and
nurses (for example, on a training circuit which involved working in several
hospitals) and of reflex behaviour in moments of crisis, the consequence was that in
some cases of cardiac arrest, the fire alarms were sounded instead of summoning the
cardiac arrest team, and vice versa in the case of fire.

To move to a larger scale of problems, it is well known that the general problem
of urban deprivation involves a number of separately administered but highly

inter-related elements. Schools, housing, transport, health care and the administration of justice are perhaps only the most obvious cases. Improving any one of these inter-connected yet separately administered elements on its own may be ineffective. For example, bad housing may negate the effects of improvements in education and of attempts to relieve the congestion of mental hospitals by re-integrating mental patients in the community. Similarly, improving housing without tackling social, psychological or cultural deprivation may be ineffective. Such factors are partly responsible for the 'counter-intuitive' effects in urban welfare policy which were discussed in the last chapter; and similar examples could be drawn from counter-insurgency administration, which draws in the police, military and civil authorities.[2]

There are two major ways in which 'multi-organizational sub-optimization' can come about. The first is the case of simple lack of co-ordination. A simple example is the infections caused by maids dusting or sweeping hospital wards while open wounds are being dressed by nurses (different union, different chain of command). Another case is the apparent chaos in road excavations by various utility contractors; it was reported some time ago that Main Road, Harwich, was dug up over 700 times in the 18 months ending January 1973.[3] Overlap between grant-giving agencies is a similar case, more common in the United States than in Britain. But this is not unknown in Britain, and one famous case is the pre-World War II Rosyth water supply scheme, which was paid for twice by grants from two different government departments — an error which did not come to light until 15 years afterwards.[4] A final illustration in this category is the system of British military stores administration in the early 1960s: cases might arise, for example, where the army had a surplus of Land-Rovers in Aden and a shortage in Cyprus, and the RAF had a surplus in Cyprus and a shortage in Aden, with each service consequently shipping identical vehicles in exactly opposite directions.[5]

The second major way in which the multi-organizational problem can come about is through conflicting objectives. Clearly, this is often a reflection of 'external' policy confusions and dilemmas. Familiar examples of this are conflicts between anti-trust agencies and agencies set up to promote industrial mergers; or between organizations set up to promote industrial development in peripheral areas (fishmeal factories, mining and so on) and organizations set up to defend scenic beauty. Another illustration is the system for disposing of surplus military stores in Britain after World War II. The Disposals Directorate in the Ministry of Supply pursued a policy of 'delayed release' of surplus material in order to avoid flooding the markets for such goods; but at the same time the Board of Trade pursued a policy of very rapid de-requisitioning of factory space, which meant that there was nowhere to store the surplus material. As a result, millions of pounds-worth of stores were left unguarded and rotting in the wind and rain.[6]

But not all cases of conflicting administrative activities are based on incompatible external demands. Writers such as Selznick[7] and Seidman[8] have stressed the fragmenting effects of different professions within administrative units, and much inter-organizational conflict can only be explained in terms of motives of 'internal' aggrandizement, 'Cost shuffling', as Keeling has pointed out,[9] is a more subtle version of this process, in which administrative units in related fields 'export' their problems to other units. An example from private business is the allocation of common overheads between administrative divisions (transport, stores, geographical divisions and so on) which may well affect the book-keeping 'profits' made by each division and thus the careers of their managers. Another case is the situation where there are trade-offs between maintenance costs and construction costs, and between construction costs and staffing costs, where staffing, maintenance and construction are handled by separate administrative units. For example, 'green field' sites may save construction costs, but require the importation of a labour force.

A slightly different case of the same general problem is the two-court system of administrative law countries, where disputes between private parties and disputes between a private party and a state administrative body, are handled by separate sets of courts. In theory, the distinction between the spheres of jurisdiction of the two types of court is clear enough. But in practice, there are innumerable borderline cases which tend to be exported and re-exported from one court sector to another, in those cases where the two types of court in turn reject jurisdiction or turn up issues which have to be referred to the other court system for resolution (50 years is not unknown in France).[10]

It is the existence of this sort of administrative structure which makes possible the 'pass-the-buck' techniques which are popularly, if unfairly, seen as a basic feature of bureaucratic behaviour. Perhaps the classic example of this process is the old 'casual ward' or 'spike' system in England, in which each spike exported its homeless occupants to spikes in other areas after a single night's lodging and thus created the 'tramp'. This problem has by no means disappeared even today. The old-style tramp appears to have virtually disappeared, but Supplementary Benefits treatment of itinerants to some extent perpetuates the problem and the socially destitute are still uneasily passed between the relevant organizations in different areas. To take one case, Glasgow Corporation some time ago refused to improve its facilities for homeless men for fear of attracting the homeless from other areas. Even within any given area, the same process operates, with the destitute being passed between general hospitals, psychiatric hospitals, local authority hostels and voluntary organizations, each of whose 'imports' may very well be another's 'export'.

This is an extreme case of the problem, and in this sort of situation attempts to increase 'efficiency' by one or all of the actor organizations in the system can have paradoxical and sub-optimal results (particularly in connection with an increasing tendency to manage by 'output' indices in public administration). Alec Nove, an economist, considers such administrative problems to be widespread in planned economies of the Soviet type, and detects the same characteristics in the management of British public enterprise, which by treating each organization as a separate unit, invites illogical export of problems between related sectors.[11] Exactly the same kinds of problem arose with the city welfare programmes mounted in the United States after the urban riots of the 1960s: cities which offered welfare facilities significantly better than those of their neighbours found that they were importing everyone else's social problems through the process of migration.

To some extent, multi-organizational sub-optimization is inherent in any division of labour system, but as administrative operations ramify in scale and scope, so the probability of 'bureaucracy tripping over its own feet' in this way will increase.[12] Secrecy, too, will of course exacerbate the problem. For example, Wilensky reminds us that in the 1960s FBI undercover agents were so numerous in the

United States Communist Party that they came close to dominating its membership and unwittingly began to inform on one another.[13] 'Cloak and dagger' operations of this kind seem to be particularly prone to the disease.

Many authors have emphasized the administrative difficulties which arise from multi-organizations. A recent and distinguished analysis of the co-ordination problem is offered by Pressman and Wildavsky in their theory of implementation.[14] Pressman and Wildavsky lay stress on the 'technical' difficulties of implementing an employment programme for blacks in Oakland, USA, which was begun with a flourish of publicity in 1966, but by 1969 had provided only 20 new jobs for blacks. The external conditions of perfect administration were met in this case, because the programme was generously funded and enjoyed strong political support. The difficulties which arose in implementing the programme were seen in terms of steering the programme through a variety of decision paths and clearance points, and Pressman and Wildavsky use this interpretation as the basis of a general theory of policy implementation. Owing to the fact that probabilities combine multiplicatively and thus become smaller in combination where they are less than unity, Pressman and Wildavsky produce a model whereby programmes of comparatively small complexity will be overwhelmingly likely to be blocked, even assuming a very high propensity to agree at all the necessary 'clearance points'.

This sort of analysis might be labelled as a 'horse-shoe-nail' model, referring to the old nursery rhyme where the kingdom is lost for want of a horse-shoe-nail; and it can be generalized to problems other than that of clearing a programme in a multi-organizational context. Administration is so specific an activity that grand programmes are particularly vulnerable to the banana skin or to the small piece of grit which immobilizes the whole machine. Everyone has their own example of this problem. One case is the difficulties which arose after the nationalization of the railway companies in Britain in 1947. One of the arguments which was advanced for nationalization was that greater economy and efficiency could be achieved by centralizing the railway network. But many of the assumed advantages of centralization could not in fact be quickly achieved, because it turned out that some railway companies had used right-hand-drive, and others left-hand-drive locomotives, and that these locomotives were not interchangeable because they required different signalling equipment.

Stories of planning aberrations in socialist countries are often of a very similar kind. One, perhaps apocryphal, concerns the first Cuban five-year plan, which was a wildly unrealistic affair devised by Czech experts. Since Czechoslovakia is landlocked, the experts forgot to set aside money for harbour facilities, with the result that large quantities of goods which had been shipped from the USSR and China could not be stored. Similarly, 1,000 cane-cutting machines which were sent to Cuba from the USSR in order to mechanize the sugar harvest turned out to be completely useless because nobody had realized that Cuban soil is not like that of the Ukraine.[15]

A final variant of the horse-shoe-nail problem is the case where the absence or scarcity of key workers defeats the effectiveness of some programme. Karl Marx called this the 'Iron Law of Proportionality', referring to the fact that the marginally scarcest resource is the key one in labour relationships. The same applies to the minimum work-load thresholds for skilled workers. That is, there is a minimum area or size of organization which is needed to keep a given number of workers with some particular skill fully occupied, since it is usually not possible to have fractions of workers in an organization. Dunsire identifies such work-load thresholds as a key determinant of administrative structures.[16] Where no time pressures are involved (as in the model of perfect administration), scarcity of key workers can be resolved over time by training, recruitment and so forth, but work-load threshold limits would arise independently of time pressures.

Problems of Administrative Control

The second condition of perfect administration is uniformity of norms or rules in the system. Clearly, it is administratively impossible effectively to pursue incompatible objectives at the same time: we have discussed the problem of multiple objectives as quasi-administrative limits, and such limits will not be further discussed here. But it should be noted that multiple objectives may be rooted in the administrative system rather than in deliberate outside political direction, as we saw in the last section in discussing multi-organizations.

The third condition of perfect administration is either perfect obedience or perfect control. Relaxing this condition, a third category of administrative difficulties or limits arises where administration is taking place in the context of *recalcitrance*. A hostile environment is, of course, the typical context of administrative processes, as many writers have observed. One writer tells us that in French administrative thought the 'administered' are 'instinctively' considered as adversaries,[17] and even Walter Bagehot, a classical liberal, observed that the 'natural impulse' of the governed 'is to resist authority'.[18]

'Resistance' in this context need not mean open or placarded disobedience. *Sub rosa* disobedience is just as important. Indeed, in a manner similar to that which was discussed for 'quasi-administrative limits, preventing *sub rosa* disobedience may increase open disobedience, and vice versa. For example, the French 'Poujadist' revolt of 1955 was sparked off by more efficient tax administration which made tax evasion harder than before.[19] Reciprocally, where no means of open resistance are available, hostility must find indirect channels, such as sabotage, slowdowns and work stoppages.[20]

Whether resistance is open or concealed, recalcitrance is a basic source of administrative difficulties, and some writers, such as Selznick, accord it a central place in writing about administration. A central feature of Selznick's theory is an 'environment of constraint commitment and tension'.[21] As we noted earlier in discussing perfect administration, if there were no resistance of any kind to authority, very little 'administration' would be needed. There might be problems of social decision and of co-ordination, but not of control. Conversely, as de Jouvenel has remarked, where authority has no agents, the formal decision-maker can command only what the subjects will be willing to carry out.[22]

Clearly, recalcitrance is something which varies in intensity from one situation to another. The extent to which resistance can be expressed in alternative or complementary channels, will also vary from one situation to another. For example, schoolchildren may express their hostility to the authorities by 'strikes', 'lesson refusal' (that is, attending school but not lessons), open defiance of teachers during lessons or secretive non-compliance. In cases like this, to suppress one channel of resistance may simply result in the problem breaking out in another form. Moreover, as we have seen, the shifting of a problem from one form of expression to another very often results in the problem crossing administrative boundary lines, with responsibility passing from one agency's or official's desk to another's. Clamping down on 'lesson refusal' at school level may increase the truancy control problem for the local education authority, and vice versa.

Apart from problems like this, a hostile environment can produce unexpected responses to administrative activities. One such response can be called the 'negative demonstration effect', borrowing a familiar term from economics. This refers to the case where the activities of the authorities directly trigger off antagonistic or perverse responses. Anyone with experience of managing children will be well aware that to forbid something is often to increase its attractiveness, and reactions of this kind are common enough in administration. But negative responses to administrative actions can also come about by quite 'rational' behaviour. For example, exhortations by the authorities for people to economize on some scarce resource may lead to panic buying of that resource in fears of chronic shortages or rationing. Such behaviour, or course, tends to lead precisely to such shortages, and so reinforces the propensity to do likewise on another occasion. Similarly, as Laurie has pointed out in relation to secret defence installations, it is a commonly-observed paradox that the best place to hide something is the most visible place; attempts to conceal it by warning notices and security devices immediately invites curiosity which may lead to detection.[23]

The negative demonstration effect is in fact a very widespread process, exasperating to administrators. It is very obvious in fields such as policing and crowd control: an over-clumsy response to a street scuffle, for example by sending in large numbers of police or troops in full riot kit, is a well-known formula for turning such a scuffle into a full-scale riot. There are also cases, possibly increasing in number, where people commit crimes in order to outwit the police or the authorities rather than for purely material purposes, the existence of the police being the motivation for crime.

The irony of the 'negative demonstration effect' is that social systems which respond to the authorities in this way would be better managed if they were not 'managed' at all, or at least not visibly managed. 'Provocation' of trade unions in industry by management often comes into this category, and the setting of 'norms' in incomes policies is thought to be a larger-scale case of the same process. Far from attracting agreement, the pay norm is often seen as a provocation, a challenge for trade unions to pit their strength against: success is then defined for unions in terms of the extent to which the official norm has been broken.[24] For this reason, the Dutch government abandoned published pay 'guideposts' in 1967, claiming that such guideposts had served as minimum targets rather than as maxima in practice; and the 'covert' guideposts of the British Conservative government between 1970 and 1972, and of the succeeding Labour government in 1974—1975, may have had a similar rationale. Indeed, the negative demonstration effect can be deliberately exploited for some purposes, as at those pop concerts where the management use the public address system constantly to urge the fans to remain in their seats. Such exhortations may be calculated to induce fans *not* to remain in their seats, thus helping to create an atmosphere of hysteria which in turn can help to strengthen a performer's image as the recipient of uncontrollable adulation.[25]

Control Limits

If the condition of perfect obedience is not satisfied, the perfect administration model requires perfect control. We will be exploring this condition more fully later in the book, but it is easily relaxed, because control resources are usually finite both in range and in effectiveness. Some typical control problems are illustrated in the case study of contracting and procurement in the next chapter. But here we must hark back briefly to the distinction between absolute and relative limits which was made at the beginning of the book. Few situations are *absolutely* resistant to administrative control, in the sense that they would remain 'un-administerable', no matter what level of administrative resources was deployed. Typically, when we speak of limits to administrative control, we are thinking of economic-type limits. In economic theory, 'limits' arise not when one runs out of resources in an absolute sense (such as fighting to the last man), but when the balance of advantage between alternative courses of action changes.

The principle of *de minimis non curat fiscus* is perhaps the most familiar case of economic-type limits to control, and it is a recognized feature of administration in many fields. Instead of pursuing fiscal offenders 'to the uttermost farthing', minor or impoverished offenders are not pursued because the revenue involved is too small to justify the effort of obtaining it. This is very common in tax administration, as we will see, but there are many other cases where it is not worth while to pursue administrative control to the point of 100 per cent compliance.

The economic-type limit is the simplest type of control limit, but there is an additional complication. Not only can we assume that the controls which the authorities have to deploy are limited, and that they will yield higher returns in some situations than in others. We can also assume that these controls have to be deployed at a minimum of two levels: the level of the administrative apparatus itself and the level of the 'administered' population.[26] To some extent, the first level of control is necessary for the other level to operate. For example, no government can effectively control its population if its army is mutinous and its officials rebellious.[27] A variant of the problem is given in the next chapter: cost control of prime contractors by governments often depends on effective cost control of sub-contractors. But there may also be contradictions between these two levels of control, in that the controls which are deployed on one level may prejudice the controls which can be applied at the other level.

For example, police officers who are given no opportunity to 'get their hands dirty' will be unable to obtain intelligence from the criminal 'underworld'; but allowing police officers to pursue secret intelligence activities on their own inevitably introduces opportunities for corruption. The same sort of problem applies with spies and secret agents, and Eisenstadt noted a similar control dilemma in his study of the great bureaucratic empires of history. Strong control over state officials by the rulers of such empires often weakened the control of the bureaucracy over the populace at large by reducing overall efficiency and initiative and giving rise to over-formalistic attitudes and activities.[28]

To analyse the problem more systematically, there are three main points at which control must be exercised in administrative systems. First, there is a 'vertical' or hierarchic channel of control between the higher and lower officials in a hierarchy. Second, there is the control exercised over the 'administered' as a group by the officials as another group. Third, there is 'horizontal' control among different administrative agencies, sub-units or officials. These types of control are typically inter-related in practice, as we will discuss in Chapter 7. For example, the 'administered' may be used as levers of control over officials through appeal systems. But for the moment we are trying to keep things simple.

Incompatibilities between levels or types of control can occur where an increase of control or a reduction of conflict at one of the three control points weakens control or increases conflict at another point. In the school case which we gave above, each of the two administrative agencies involved (the school and the educational authority) could minimize its conflict with schoolchildren by exporting the problem to the other agency. In fact, the more 'client-oriented' an agency is, the more likely it is to run into conflict with other agencies. Similarly, the more 'client-oriented' field officials are, the more likely they are to conflict with 'head office'. The extreme case of such conflict is that of publicly employed community workers who become 'tribunes of the people', mobilizing and articulating opposition to 'the bureaucracy' over local town planning decision and the like.

In fact, many writers have observed potential conflicts between effective control over an administrative apparatus by the top directorate and effective administrative control over the population at large. Hume noticed this, and Max Weber called it 'The Paradox of Sultanism'.[29] The more a ruler governs through naked force exercised by an army of thugs, the more he is at the mercy of those thugs; the more absolutist the control system, the more vulnerable it is to attack, since there is but a 'single neck to be severed' in order to effect a successful *coup d'etat*.[30] This is one reason why police or military government is typically unstable. Put as starkly as this, the problem is clear, but it should not be dismissed as a quaint or archaic problem. In the more modern context of corporate management, Lundberg sees the same dilemma

'The stockholder wants his executive to be a fierce hunting tiger vis-a-vis the world in general, but a tame tiger towards his master.'[31]

Categorization Problems

Closely related to the condition of perfect control is the fourth condition of perfect administration, that is, perfect information concerning the situation in hand and the capacity to specify tasks or the contents of one's orders unambiguously. This may seem an odd condition, but we will see in the discussion of contract administration in the next chapter how important the condition is in cases where control systems are based upon concepts such as 'profit' or 'cost', and we will explore the limits of language and categorization more fully in Chapter 4. Problems of ambiguity in language are (in principle at least) fairly easily remediable in face-to-face situations outside a legal context, or where someone's 'word is law'. But where (as is typically the case in large-scale modern public administration) control is based on written documents within a legal context, things are very different. Our tax case studies will bring this problem out sharply.

Problems of Limited Time

The final condition of perfect administration is the absence of time-pressure. But problems start to arise as soon as the administrator begins to operate in finite time. Within the broad sphere of 'time problems', the most familiar process is that of time-lags. This problem was noticed to some extent by the 'classic' theorists of administrative malfunctioning, such as Merton[32] and Crozier.[33] But Merton associated it with a rigid and blinkered 'bureaucratic personality', an assumption which is both very suspect and unnecessarily complicated as an explanation of maladaptation.[34] All that needs to be assumed is that the world outside does not remain still while the administrator acts.

We will see several cases of unexpected developments in time upsetting policy implementation in the next chapter, and, like categorization, the problem will be more fully explored in Part 2. In public administration, time-lags are virtually built-in, both through the public complaints and consultation machinery, and through archaic legal frameworks.[35] For example, the speed at which new industrial processes are introduced tends to be much greater than the speed with which the factory safety legislation is amended, meaning that strict legal control over safety provisions is impossible to operate in many cases. The same applies with administrative structures. To take the case of taxation, as late as 1964 General Commissioners of Taxes in Britain had to be persuaded to make and allow assessments which they never saw and were formally appointed by a body which no longer existed (the Land Tax Commissioners); assessors and collectors who no longer assessed or collected had to be appointed and sworn in, and so on.

Not only does the world fail to stay still. In some cases it takes conscious evasive action. A straight quotation from Hammond's history of American banks may serve as an example

'The device of moving treasure ahead of the investigators and thereby making a dollar of bank reserves do the work of a dozen belongs among the most venerable of monetary manipulations. Thucydides (VI, xliv) records a like performance in Sicily in 415 BC.'[36]

The time-lag process means that 'preparing to fight yesterday's wars' is a fairly general administrative problem. In a situation of linear change, such delayed responses are likely to be ineffective. In a situation of cyclical change, such as typically arises in macro-economic administration, delayed responses are likely to be counter-productive, and this is also likely to be true of any other situation in which the real time sequence is critical A variant of the process belongs to the story of contract administration in the next chapter: this is the 'great leap forward syndrome' which has been observed in aerospace and weapon system procurement.[37] In this case, attempts to leap-frog several stages ahead at once in order to make up for past delays and failures result in efforts to cut corners which have a higher probability of error and thus may push the schedule even further back.

Time-lags would be much less important as a limit on administration in a frictionless context or if the world to be administered had no will of its own, changing autonomously, or in some automatic, predictable sequence like a traffic light. But the administered world is typically not like this. It is a resistant medium which is learning too, and strategic behaviour by an 'enemy' is responsible for many of the administrative problems which we will be discussing in later chapters. Applied to time, the point is that it is *relative* lag which is of key importance where there is a 'learning enemy'. An extreme case is the response by the Cayman Islands, an up-and-coming tax haven, to anti-tax avoidance legislation passed by the UK in 1968/1969.[38] The Cayman Islands responded to the challenge by passing legislation to circumvent the UK legislation (in effect, creating a state of legal non-ownership in which property remained in the former owner's hands) and in return the British Treasury had to produce anti-anti-anti-avoidance legislation. Clearly this is an extreme case, but as the speed of communication and feedback in society increases, so the length of lag at which administrative actions become ineffective is likely to fall.

Problems of Reorganization

'Leads' and 'lags' are not the only problems associated with administrative activity in time. There are other problems, which will be discussed further in Chapter 5. As a brief introduction to some of these problems, we can take the case of administrative reorganization. Reorganization is normally intended to improve administrative performance.

Failure to improve administrative performance by reorganization does not arise from any single reason. Clearly one source of ineffective reorganization is 'external', and must be counted as a quasi-administrative limit. This would apply to cases where basically 'external' problems are tackled by internal re-structuring (for purposes such as 'buying time' or evading policy choices), or to those changes which are imposed for broad policy reasons without serious reference to internal administrative functioning. In such cases, reorganization may simply be a form of 'tokenism', as discussed in the last chapter. This can either be in the form of a straightforward name-change (Seidman points out that the United States foreign agency was re-named eight times between 1948 and 1970)[39] or of other forms of symbolic responses to change. For example, among other responses, British Rail and the Canadian Post Office have responded to criticisms of delay and inefficiency by adopting 'go-faster' stripes as their *motifs*. In similar vein, Samuel Brittan remarks, in the context of British economic policy

'Politicians can never free themselves from the hope that better information or improved administrative machinery can prevent the policy dilemmas which they so much dislike, from emerging.'[40]

The same process has been observed in many other contexts, such as Nepalese economic planning.[41]

But even serious, internally-oriented reorganizations may fail to improve administrative performance. One familiar type is the ineffective reorganization, which makes changes in titles, insignia, corporate livery, even perhaps top management, but changes nothing of substance and may indeed be a symptom of the inability to achieve 'deep change'. This type of reorganization is an attack on symptoms rather than causes, a process which Thomas Malthus likened to trying to change the weather by tampering with the quicksilver in the barometer.

Organizations seem to be typically harder to change at the bottom than at the top, as reflected both by industrial experience of reorganization and by change in state administration. For example, county administration in China and village administration in India survived almost unchanged through centuries of changing imperial rulers, and it seems that in the USSR the field administrative structure may have changed less than the repeated 'reorganizations' might suggest.[42]

Reorganization may even be counter-productive. This is because reorganization *itself* involves costs. The merits of alternative patterns of organization (such as the old question as to whether function X should go in office A or office B — a theme which we will be looking at in Chapter 4) are usually discussed outside their 'real time' context. It is as if one could discuss the 'best' arrangement of pedals on motor vehicles without allowing for the cost of changing from the present arrangements to a different system. In general, the shorter the time-period involved, the more likely it is that the difference in the cost of organizational pattern A and pattern B will be outweighed by the cost of *changing* from A to B or vice versa. In the extreme case, reorganization and ineffectiveness can become causally related: ineffectiveness causes demands for reorganization, but reorganizational costs reduce effectiveness in the short term, which leads to demands for yet more reorganization, and so on. Grusky's study of leadership change in American baseball teams revealed that teams with the poorest records had the highest rates of succession, implying that a vicious circle can develop between bad performance and reorganization.[43]

This problem, at least in the opinion of one official committee, has been among the ills of post-war British aerospace procurement, which suffered major reorganizations approximately every five years between 1939 and 1971. The Rayner report went so far as to quote a passage which it attributed to Petronius

'We trained hard, but it seemed that every time we were beginning to form up into teams we would be reorganized ... we tend to meet any new situation by reorganizing and a wonderful method it can be for creating the illusion of progress while creating confusion, inefficiency and demoralization.'[44]

As we have seen, Samuel Brittan is equally sarcastic about the 'reorganization complex' as a substitute for making choices in economic policy, and complaints similar to those expressed by the Rayner report have been made about the persistent changes in British economic management agencies. To take one case, at the time of the break up of the Department of Trade and Industry in 1973, staff regulations were still being prepared to replace those used in the Board of Trade, Ministry of Technology, Ministry of Power, Ministry of Aviation and the Central Office of Information, most of which had disappeared at least three years earlier.[45] The same syndrome is well known in nursing administration in the National Health Service.

Summary and Conclusion

In this chapter we have dismantled the internal conditions for perfect administration and explored the types of administrative limits which appeared. We saw that Pressmann and Wildavsky's analysis of programme clearance, illuminating though it is, cannot serve as a truly general theory of policy implementation difficulties, even when it is broadened to include the difficulties which we christened 'horse-shoe-nail' problems. The Pressman and Wildavsky approach neglects the other three limits which we identified, namely general problems of control, problems associated with time-pressures and problems associated with ambiguity in language and categorization. All of these three limits are worsened by a hostile environment, though even in a situation of perfect obedience, time and categorization would still present problems.

The administrative limits which we have identified in this chapter are of central importance, and the following chapters will be largely devoted to exploring them further. Problems of time and of categorization are considered in the next Part and the more general problem of limits to administrative control in Part 3. But, before analysing these problems more closely in Parts 2 and 3, we will look at the administrative difficulties which arise in the field of contracting and procurement, in relation to the analysis which has been developed in the past two chapters. The reader will wish to ask how far the problems of policy implementation which arise in this case are in reality extra-administrative problems arising from the non-fulfilment of the external conditions of perfect administration. To the extent that there are administrative difficulties, how far are these quasi-administrative limits — in other words, has the job been deliberately made impossible? Finally, what *kind* of administrative problems, if any, are they: which of the conditions of 'perfect administration' are broken, and which most seriously?

Notes

1. Stringer, J., 'Operational research for multi-organizations', *Operational Research Quarterly*, Vol. 18, 1967.
2. cf. Kitson, F., *Low Intensity Operations*, Faber and Faber, London, 1972.
3. *Drive*, May 1974, pp. 114—115.
4. *2nd Report of the Public Accounts Committee*, HC 55, 148, 1936—1937 pp. XIV—XV, para 14.
5. *10th Report from the Estimates Committee*, HC 282 1962—1963 (Military Expenditure Overseas).
6. cf. *1st Report of the Estimates Committee*, HC 96, 1946—1947.
7. Selznick, P., *TVA and the Grass Roots*, University of California Press, Berkeley, 1949.
8. Seidman, H., *Politics Position and Power*, Oxford University Press, New York, 1970.
9. Keeling, C. D. E., *Management in Government*, Allen and Unwin, London, 1972.
10. Schwartz, B., *French Administrative Law and the Common Law World*, New York University Press, New York, 1954.
11. Nove, A., *Efficiency Criteria for the Nationalized Industries*, Allen and Unwin, London, 1973.
12. Metcalfe, L., 'Systems models, economic models and the causal texture of organizational environments', *Human Relations*, Vol. 27, 1974, pp. 639—663.
13. Wilensky, H., *Organizational Intelligence*, New York Basic Books, New York, 1967, p. 135.
14. Pressman, J., and A. Wildavsky, *Implementation*, University of California Press, Berkeley, 1973.
15. Karol, K., *Guerillas in Power*, Hill and Wang, New York, 1970.
16. Dunsire, A., *Administration, The Word and the Science*, Martin Robertson, London, 1973.
17. Legendre, P., *Histoire de l'Administration de 1750 a Nos Jours*, Presses Universitaires de France, Vendôme, 1968.
18. Quoted in Dunhill, F., *The Civil Service: Some Human Aspects*, Allen and Unwin, London, 1956.
19. Avril, P., *Politics in France*, tr. John Ross, Penguin Books, Harmondsworth, 1969, p. 215.

20. Eldridge, J. E. T., 'Industrial conflict' in J. Child (Ed.) *Man and Organization*, Allen and Unwin, London, 1973, p. 179.
21. Selznick, P., *Leadership in Administration*, Evanston, Row, Peterson, 1957.
22. de Jouvenel, B., *The Pure Theory of Politics*, Cambridge University Press, Cambridge, 1963.
23. Laurie, P., *Beneath the City Streets*, Penguin Books, Harmondsworth, 1970.
24. cf. Ulman, L., and R. J. Flanagan, *Wage Restraints: A Study of Incomes Policies in Western Europe*, University of California Press, Berkeley, 1971; also M. Edelman and J. W. Fleming, *The Politics of Wage-Price Decisions*, American Foundation on Automation and Employment, New York, 1965.
25. Marsh, P., 'Bay city rumble', *New Society*, 12 June 1975, pp. 637—638.
26. cf. Hart, H. L. A., *The Concept of Law*, Oxford University Press, Oxford, 1961.
27. cf. Rule, J. B., *Private Lives and Public Surveillance*, Allen Lane, London, 1973.
28. Eisenstadt, S. N., *The Political Systems of Empires*, Free Press, New York, 1963, p. 279.
29. Bendix, R , *Max Weber*, Methuen, London, 1966, p. 344.
30. cf. Andrews, W., and U. Ra'anan, *Coup D'Etat*, Van Nostrand, New York, 1969.
31. Lundberg, F., *The Rich and the Super Rich*, Nelson, London, 1968, p. 239.
32. Merton, R. K., *Reader in Bureaucracy*, Free Press, New York, 1960 (2nd ed.).
33. Crozier, M., *The Bureaucratic Phenomenon*, Tavistock, London, 1965.
34. Cohn, M. L., 'Bureaucratic man', *American Sociological Review*, Vol. 36, 1971, pp. 461—474.
35. Baker, R. J. S., *Administrative Theory and Public Administration*, Hutchinson, London, 1972.
36. Hammond, B., *Banks and Politics from the Revolution to the Civil War*, Princeton University Press, New Jersey, 1957, p. 615.
37. Williams, G., P. Gregory and J. Simpson, *Crisis in Procurement: A Case Study of the TSR-2*, United Services Institution, London, 1969.
38. Stanley, O., *Taxology*, Weidenfeld and Nicholson, London, 1972.
39. Seidman, H., *Politics Position and Power*, Oxford University Press, New York, 1970, p. 26.
40. Brittan, S., *The Treasury under the Tories, 1951—1964*, Penguin Books, Harmondsworth, 1964.
41. Wildavsky, A., 'Why planning fails in Nepal', *Administrative Science Quarterly*, 17, 508—528 (1972).
42. Hough, J. F., *The Soviet Projects*, Harvard University Press, Cambridge, Mass., 1969; cf. E. N. Peterson, *The Limits of Hitler's Power*, Princeton University Press, New Jersey, 1969.
43. Grusky, O., 'Managerial succession and organizational effectiveness', *American Journal of Sociology*, 69, 21—31 (1963).
44. *Government Organization for Defence Procurement and Civil Aerospace* Cmnd. 4641 1971. I do not think, however, that this quotation in fact comes from Petronius, after a careful reading of the Satyrcon; and Sir Derek Rayner, author of the report, cannot authenticate the quotation.
45. *The Times*, 16 April, 1974, p. 2.

Chapter 3

Case Study Number One:
Contracting and Procurement

'A Boeotian crew! But nevertheless, they know on which side their
bread is buttered; and in general it goes hard with them but they butter
it on both sides.' A. Trollope, *The Three Clerks*, Oxford University
Press, London, 1952, p. 90.

Contracting is to some extent an alternative to direct administrative operations. It
has often been seen as a way of getting round the limits of conventional
administration. For example, in the United States since World War II there has been
increasing use of organizations not directly administered by government employees
in the execution of federal programmes. Such methods offered a means of
circumventing rigid 'civil service' pay codes and regulations, outflanking traditional
agencies and in many cases Congressional surveillance as well. By the 1960s, phrases
such as 'the grants economy' and 'the contract state' were being coined to refer to
the new style of unorthodox public administration;[1] and some observers even
discerned a 'new kind of public sector' in which many, perhaps most, of the
employees of the federal government were 'invisible'.[2]

Disillusionment with the idea of contracting as an administrative 'short cut'[3]
quickly set in after the failure of the US Poverty Programme of the 1960s. In fact,
as we will see, contracting escapes few, if any, of the limits of conventional
administration. The 'external' conditions of perfect administration rarely apply:
political direction is typically ambiguous and changeful and resources are far from
limitless. Such problems often overshadow the internal limits of administration
which we discussed in the last chapter: but in fact almost all of these limits can be
detected in contracting and procurement. In particular, limited ability to define and
discriminate unambiguously, a limited range of controls and limited effectiveness of
controls, time pressures and a rapidly changing environment, are problems which
pervade the whole field of contract administration.

The Development of the British Contracting System

The contracting system of eighteenth-century British government did not resemble
the modern 'military—industrial complex', which involves elaborate technical
projects in defence and defence-related fields. Naval construction and the
manufacture of guns and ammunition were largely done at the Royal Dockyards
and Ordnance Factories. The origins of the modern contracting system lie rather in

the nineteenth century, and the Crimean War seems to have been a major watershed. The war destroyed the ancient system of contracting with the colonel of each regiment for clothing and victualling his men (such contracts were tradition-ally a colonel's chief source of income). In 1854 army clothing and victualling was centralized into the War Office Army Contracts Department.[4] Once this central purchasing agency had been set up, the influence of nineteenth-century financial propriety was such that public competition was laid down as the normal method of making contracts. But, as so often in administration, this straightforward principle did not operate straightforwardly, and in fact open advertisement of the government's needs tended to drive prices up, obliging the authorities to replace open competition by 'approved lists' of contractors and by the use of brokers.[5] The cumbersome machinery of the centralized procurement system also caused delays because of the post-officing and cross-checking processes involved. These delays caused strains in the South African War (resulting in some temporary decentralization in 1904) but the system survived more or less intact until the First World War, when it broke down in the 1915 munitions crisis.

The other major development dating approximately from the Crimean War was an increasing reliance on private arms manufacture — the origin of the 'military—industrial complex'.[6] In the second half of the nineteenth century, technological developments such as the introduction of armour plating, heavy rifled guns and later the machine gun, presented governments with a dilemma. On the one hand, government could rely to a large extent on private arms manufacturers, allowing or encouraging arms suppliers to sell abroad during peacetime (with all the political headaches which are involved in arms exports). On the other hand, there could be a vast expansion of government arsenals, which would either have to make civilian goods during peacetime or to produce massive stockpiles of armaments, the bulk of which would have been obsolete at any given time.

The first course was obviously cheaper and the British government adopted it. As the 1936 Royal Commission on the Private Manufacture of Arms put it

' . . . successive governments over a long period of years have looked upon, and treated, the private armament firms of this country as an essential part of national defence.'[7]

The technological developments of World War I, such as chemical warfare, the combat tank, military aircraft and submarines, reinforced the process of reliance on private maufacturers. For example, it was difficult for the British government to respond to the introduction of mustard gas by the Germans in 1917, because most poison gases were produced by the dye industry and most dyestuffs used in British industry had been imported from Germany before 1914.[8] The British government accordingly fostered a semi-public company (British Dyes Ltd.) to produce dyestuffs and continued to support the dyestuffs industry after the war by grants-in-aid, loans and the prohibition of import except by licence.[9] Similar tactics were used in the explosives industry by the Ministry of Munitions, for example in the formation of Nobel Industries. British Dyestuffs and Nobel Industries were two of the four firms which formed Imperial Chemical Industries in 1926.

More straightforward problems of administrative control over contractors also arose in World War I, all of which seem familiar from the viewpoint of the present day. Among them were the problems of bargaining with 'rings' of contractors for items such as armour plate; accounting chaos; definitional ambiguities inherent in the notion of 'normal profit' in the attempt to suppress 'profiteering' and the difficulties of ascertaining costs and capital employed for cost-plus contracts, plus all the opportunities for fraud which a shortage of government accountants presents. For example, it was quite common for contractors to draw pay for 'dead' men on their books.[10]

The purchase of food and raw materials in bulk took government into relatively unknown territory and the administrative machinery depended heavily on advisory committees and self-governing trade associations, many of which were manipulated into existence by the government as a technique of indirect control. The process, which is described by Lloyd in a well-known and prescient book,[11] began with the supply of jute which was needed for sandbags in the trenches. Many similar arrangements followed, and as time went on administrators tended to control production processes nearer to the first source of supply, so as to limit profits at intermediate stages up to the final product.

Problems of contract administration did not entirely disappear after the war. Admiralty contracts for armour, Post Office contracts for telephone work, and especially aviation work,[12] presented particular problems in the inter-war years. An interesting example of the limits of private contracting, even of a non-competitive kind, from this era is the case of Power Jets Ltd., a company set up to develop turbine engines; since this company's work was covered by the Official Secrets Act, it could not release information about its activities sufficient to attract private capital, and accordingly the company had to be taken under direct government control in 1936.

The rearmament programme of the 1930s and the Second World War vastly increased the scale of such problems. Ashworth's history[13] indicates how government swallowed most of its pre-war inhibitions about awarding contracts without competition, lending money to contractors, providing them with plant and checking up on waste. In an attempt to reduce waste and profiteering, a series of overlapping controls were set up (Excess Profits Tax, generalized price controls, physical controls and contractual costings), but many of these controls relied largely on voluntary compliance in practice. The weapon of competition became increasingly difficult to apply as a means of controlling contractors, because there was no spare capacity in the economy. Instead, government had to use carrots rather than sticks, and increasingly resorted to fixed-price contracting, a system which allowed contractors to keep surpluses arising from efficient work, subject only to the depredations of the Excess Profits Tax.[14]

The Excess Profits Tax (like its World War I predecessor) was itself a highly shaky edifice, since to tax 'excess' profits you must somehow fix what is a 'normal' profit, and that triggers off a round of problems of a type which we will be examining in the next chapter. For example, if a standard figure is fixed for 'normal' profit, the problem immediately arises that customary mark-ups vary enormously from trade to trade, especially in retailing.[15] On the other hand, if 'excess' is fixed as the increase of profits over some historical base line, there will be all kinds of legitimate reasons why such a base period would be 'abnormal' for many firms. 'Base lines' are another class of administrative problems which we will encounter in Part 2.

Quite apart from the problems of relying on the Excess Profits Tax as a 'long stop', the policy of fixed-price contracts was very largely a *pis-aller*, in terms of the very small number of officials available to check up on contractors in wartime. But from about 1944 onwards, the Ministries of Supply and of Aircraft Production began to exercise their legal rights to test the prices of sub-contracts by post-costing projects and to seek rebates on the grounds that the prices which had been paid to the sub-contractors by the main contractors had been excessive (by late 1945, some £38 m had been collected in this way).[16]

As we will see, post-costing was a weapon which governments picked up again in the post-war period, and indeed there were wartime precedents for many of the other administrative controls over contracts which were later adopted. In the post-war period, government dependence on private industry for armaments has continued, though the balance has shifted from the secondary to the 'quaternary' industrial sector. Indeed, one major component of the pattern of increasing grant and contract expenditure has been increasing funding for science, especially in the 1960s. British government appropriations for research and development rose from about £12 m in 1953, when this item first appeared in the national income statistics, to about £130 m in 1970.[17] Another sector which rose sharply in financial importance over the post-war period and in fact overtook the older defence contracting sector, was a group of grant-funded welfare programmes. But in spite of these new developments, many of the older problems of contract administration remain, simply recurring more frequently, on a larger scale and in different contexts.

Problems of Categorization and Control

In contracting, limits of control in general and limits of discrimination and categorization are very closely linked. In theory, the control system is very simple, requiring no elaborate accounting controls: control is secured by price competition after formal advertizing for bids from 'all comers'. But in practice, this pure system rarely works effectively. It has the defect of advertizing government's needs, which may result either in collusion between suppliers or in speculators 'cornering the market' in the relevant goods or services, as has already been discussed. Pure price competition also takes no account of a firm's technical capacity or financial strength, and thus simple acceptance of the lowest tender may be to play into the hands of the incompetent, the irresponsible or the insolvent. Accordingly, competition is almost always restricted in some way.

Thus, as we have seen, the British government had almost abandoned 'at large' advertizing of contracts by the late nineteenth century and even acted through confidential brokers in some markets in order to conceal its activities, in the same way that central banks often operate anonymously in world currency markets through brokers. In the USA, the formal doctrine of advertizing still survives, but the rule is so peppered with exceptions in the Armed Services Procurement Act of 1947 that only about 20 per cent or less of defence procurement is now done through formal advertizing.[18] Indeed, competition is often drastically limited. In the USA, about half of the federal government's purchases are non-competitive in that not more than one supplier is involved in tendering; in Britain, non-competitive contracts amount to about one-third of the total of central government purchasing.[19]

Since governments cannot rely on market forces to ensure that they obtain a good bargain in many cases, there have to be systems for monitoring contractors' costs. Cost control by government inspectors is a standard feature of contracts which are let on a cost-plus-profit basis (in Britain about one-third of non-competitive contracts, mostly for research and development, are let on a cost-plus basis), but such control also applies to fixed-price contracts, for reasons which will appear later on. But several problems immediately arise in cost control. One is that cost control of prime contractors often turns out to depend on control of their multiple sub-contractors, who are typically much less amenable to central administrative supervision. Another typical problem of cost control is the allocation of accounting overheads between 'government' and 'private' projects by contractors.

The latter problem, a case of difficulty in discrimination, plays a large part in the perpetual rows about the prices charged by international companies selling drugs to the National Health Service (as in the 'Roche case', which is discussed later). For example, cases have arisen where the British government has bought proprietary drugs priced to include research and development costs when the government had already contributed to such costs in overheads connected with another contract. The problem can become particularly difficult in the case of multi-national corporations (notably in oil licensing and in drug purchasing) which are able to 'shunt' costs between different operating units at will.[20]

'Cost', in fact, turns out to be a relatively arbitrary accounting concept; and apart from the major problem of allocation of overheads, the treatment of depreciation, stocks, work-in-progress, private venture research and development, and marketing and selling expenses are some of the many other sources of confusion and argument. For example, the government might be unwilling to pay for advertizing on proprietary products on the grounds that it 'is not persuaded to buy' through advertizing, deciding on purchases by sober and rational search. But what if advertizing the product creates a larger market and thus reduces the unit cost of production below what it would have been without advertizing?

In grappling with such difficulties, considerations of equity may drive governments into what seems to be unnecessarily complicated computations. To take one case, the 'standard profit' on government contracts since the late 1930s has been computed on 'capital employed' rather than on the earlier and much less ambiguous basis of 'unit costs', because the 'unit cost' principle produced disproportionate profit on capital in expanding industries with increasing returns to scale. This is a problem which was brought to light by applying the 'unit cost principle' to the aircraft industry in the pre-World War II 'McLintock Agreements'.[21] But what is 'capital employed'? We are back to definitional problems of a type to be discussed in the next chapter. There have to be standard definitions of things such as 'capital' both for equity (the prevention of arbitrary decisions) and for the prevention of corruption and its diminutives among officials, but any such rule of thumb can be shown to produce anomalies. One senior civil servant has put the dilemma like this

'It is perfectly possible to say that in relation to any particular firm this or that is inconsistent, but what the government has to produce is an arrangement . . . which works without requiring an enormous analysis . . . which is totally beyond our accountants and their accountants . . .'[22]

Even without these problems, such monitoring operations are hampered by other problems which will become familiar in subsequent chapters: loss of skilled manpower from the public service to the private sector, and the shortage of specialist 'policemen'. In spite of the fact that between one-third and a half of British GNP passes through 'public' hands in some way and that nearly half of that sum is spent on grants and contracts, the British Exchequer and Audit Department numbers little over 500 people. Within the contracting departments themselves, control is typically hampered by acute shortages of accountants and technical cost officers, a problem which was sharply highlighted after the Ferranti and Bristol Siddeley contracting scandals of the 1960s.

The problem applies perhaps more dramatically in the United States. Thus the well-known 'Bell Report' of 1962 was the culmination of a build-up of anxieties about conflicts of interest in federal policy making and procurement (anxieties which had be heightened by earlier investigations and by President Eisenhower's farewell address warning of the dangers of 'military—industrial complex'). The Bell Report highlighted the decline of government-operated research and development facilities such as the Redstone Arsenal and the Jet Propulsion Laboratory; and also the serious extent to which the US federal government lacked the 'in-house' capacity necessary to supervize contracted-out operations, to the extent that supervision and even policy advice were contracted out. This often caused acute conflicts of interest in cases where advisory, research and development, and follow-on production contracts were linked.

Cost Over-runs

Perhaps the most familiar manifestation of ineffective control over contracts is the cost over-run. Cost over-runs are usually associated with contracts but they can also occur with grants, particularly welfare grants which represent open-ended commitments. A well-known case is the US government's payment system for costs incurred by eligible (aged) patients under the Medicare programme. The payment process was contracted out to third-party organizations which were to negotiate with the hospitals, and Blue Cross local organizations were used for 90 per cent of such payments. These Blue Cross organizations are in turn governed by boards consisting mainly of representatives of local hospitals, which means that the hospitals in effect negotiated with themselves.

Cost over-runs are also particularly common in development contracts, and many US military contracts in the 1950s involved costs in excess of original estimates of some 300—700 per cent.[23] The British experience was similar, if less dramatic,[24] with the exception of the Anglo—French Concorde airliner in the 1960s, which became a by-word for cost inflation, with cost over-runs of over 500 per cent. To a large extent, control of cost over-runs is limited by political forces rather than by strictly administrative limits. It is often politically difficult to cancel projects, particularly since government contracts tend to be channelled towards politically sensitive areas in the first place, as with the British regional contracts preference scheme and the Congressional location politics which frequently surround US contract awards.[25] Moreover, in the case of cost over-runs so serious that they put the future of a key contractor in jeopardy (such as

Lockheed with the C-5A aircraft and the Cheyenne helicopter in 1970 and Rolls-Royce with the RB-211 aero engine in 1971), the government is likely to be under strong pressure to underwrite them.

But there are more strictly administrative limits to control over cost over-runs. Even where governments have adequate policing capacity and where the issues are relatively clear, they have few effective cards to play against unsatisfactory performers. The basic problem is a theme which will recur in later chapters: the lack of sufficient middle-range threats which are neither so drastic that they can never be used nor so feeble as to be disregarded.

Both in Britain and in the USA, governments from the 1950s onwards have reacted to the problem of large over-runs with administrative expedients similar to those adopted in World War II. These were increasing use of fixed-price contracts and of contracts which combined elements of fixed-price and cost-plus contracts (known variously as incentive contracts, target prices or penalty clauses, and involving cost plus a sum varying according to 'results').[26] The adoption of fixed-price contracts was also thought to offer advantages in terms of administrative supervision. This was explicit in the Contractors' Weighted Average Share of Risk system,[27] introduced by the US Defence Department in 1967, in which contract administration and audit was relaxed in cases where contractors were undertaking largely (i.e. 65 per cent or over) fixed-price contracts.

But it became clear that 'fixed prices' were no panacea, and such procedural weapons of control can only operate within a fairly narrow range. First, it is not easy to persuade contractors to accept fixed-price contracts for long-range projects. Thus in the Anglo—French Concorde project and in the parallel SST programme in the USA (which was cancelled), the great bulk of the risks had to be borne by the government. Second, where (as in the case of Concorde) there is a guaranteed minimum profit, the incentive to reduce costs diminishes as costs approach the level at which the minimum profit operates and disappears completely once that level has been reached.[28] Third, the later in the life of a contract that a fixed or 'target' price is agreed, the lower the risk and the smaller the practical difference from a cost-plus type of contract. In many cases, such prices have been negotiated very late, or even subsequent to the completion of a project. Fourth, fixed-price contracts have drawbacks in the case of items not for sale in an open market and in which the government has no idea of contractors' actual costs. This is the logic of 'truth in negotiations' laws, which will be discussed shortly.[29]

Fifth, you can only have a fixed-price contract where work is clearly definable. Defining the task is a characteristic problem with ship and property repairs (cases in which the work required typically cannot be known in advance) and particularly with research grants and contracts. Penalty clauses, performance bonds, liquidated damages clauses and the whole intricate range of available 'incentives' are only useful in so far as there is some yardstick of performance; and specification is particularly important in an *inter-dependent* set of contracts because of the opportunities for mutual recrimination which they afford (that is, A claims that his failure has been occasioned by B's failure, and so forth).

Another important limit on the effectiveness of changed contract procedures in controlling cost over-runs is the difficulty of controlling government agencies themselves. It is often expedient for such agencies to concur with over-optimistic original estimates of project costs. Sir Robert Peel is said to have remarked that 'If you adopt the opinion of military men, we are never safe'. Military authorities tend to 'gold plate' their requirements (in the context of international technological leap-frogging and the continual raising of the stakes of military equipment) and the 'conspiracy of optimism' regarding costs or technical difficulties between the military, scientists and contractors is hard to break by changes in contract procedure alone.[30] The 'great leap forward syndrome', which we discussed in the last chapter, is a related problem. But this syndrome is also very difficult to correct by changes in procedure. One tactic adopted by the British Defence Procurement Executive in the early 1970s was to strike at the process by raising the 'feasibility assessment threshold' (that is, the point at which it is decided whether or not to go forward with a project) to about 15 per cent of total projected expenditure. But assessment thresholds are far from foolproof as a technique of control: they invite subordinates or contractors to try to trap their masters into supporting projects by concealing or minimizing evidence of failure until the project is so far advanced that revelation would damage superior as well as subordinate.

Post-costing and Renegotiation

Another attempt by both the British and US governments to control contracts more effectively has been the adoption of measures of 'post-costing', that is, retrospective examination of a contractor's accounts. These measures have been linked with 'truth in negotiations' laws and powers for renegotiation of contracts. Again, as we have seen, these measures follow wartime precedents. The US Renegotiation Board was set up in 1951 and the US Truth in Negotiations Act was passed in 1962; similar British measures followed in 1969.[31] British government contractors on fixed price contracts resisted the free inspection of their accounts by government procurement officials until matters were brought to a head in the 1960s by two major scandals referring to fixed-price contracts. In one case, that of Ferranti,[32] prices had been negotiated very late in the life of the contract; in the other case, that of Bristol Siddeley,[33] prices had been based on very out-of-date cost figures. In both cases, the contractors had misled government departments as to their production costs. After these revelations, Ferranti repaid £4.25 m on the Bloodhound missile contract and Bristol Siddeley repaid £3.9 m on aero engine overhaul contracts. A bargain was then struck between the Treasury and the Confederation of British Industry which provided for free access to contractors' accounts and premises by government officials up to the time that prices were fixed. In return, the standard profit rate on government contracts was raised from 7½ per cent — the rate used since 1941 — to 14 per cent. The same rights of access to accounts and premises applied (importantly) with the relationship between prime and sub-contractors, and this again followed US experience. But US experience with the 1962 'Truth in Negotiations' Act has not been very favourable; the Act is ambiguous and seems to have been widely evaded.[34]

Indeed, renegotiation and post-costing are weapons of control subject to limitations similar to those discussed in the previous section. They do not take efficiency into account, they are of a purely *post hoc* nature and are usually adopted by governments in a position of supervisory weakness rather than strength (as in the case of wartime contract administration). The amounts recovered by the US Renegotiation Board were relatively puny in relation to the total US contract effort (some $40 m in 1970, for example: in fact, the bulk of the excessive profits determined by the Board were in the period 1954–1958, in the early days of the control system). The comparable British institution, the Review Board for Government Contracts (a much smaller organization set up in 1969) meets in secret and shuns publicity, but its effectiveness is very doubtful.

Grants

In the field of grant administration, there has also been a search for middle-range threats as control procedures. In the USA 'audit exceptions' (a *post hoc* measure involving the refusal of funds for particular acts of expenditure rather than the blanket withholding of funds) are an example of this process. Martha Derthick describes the use of federal audit exceptions in Massachussetts in the late 1940s, when the salaries of elected board members engaged in administration were disallowed as part of a campaign to secure merit appointment systems in welfare administration.[35] The relative shift towards 'project grants' (in 1970, about half of all federal grants were project grants),[36] in which federal approval is a highly discretionary process, and away from grants obtainable 'as of right' according to clear-cut indices, may have reduced this problem to some extent, though it puts more pressure on the control process at the selection stage.

In Britain, too, the original system of 'as of right' grants for specific items has declined in importance. But this process began far earlier, in the early nineteenth century, when the British 'grant system' grew up (in the USA such a system did not develop until the 1920s and 1930s). The process has also gone much further, with a shift from specific grants to bloc grants rather than project grants, a system which was relatively far advanced as early as 1929. Henry Parris has described the shift away from 'all or nothing' grants, which offer little scope for middle-level controls, to more flexible types of financial weapons, such as the power to withhold *part* of a grant (as with the case of 'audit exceptions' in the USA) and the 'doubling up' of central and local expenditure,[37] which ensured that recipients of grants have some interest in economy of expenditure.

The similarities should perhaps not be exaggerated. US grant administration has always been a 'diplomatic' process to a large extent, because of the federal structure of government. But even in Britain, many of the simple nineteenth-century weapons of administrative control have lost their cutting edge with the virtual abandonment of specific grants to local authorities (almost 80 per cent of British local authority grants are now bloc grants compared to about 16 per cent in the early 1950s) and with the changing character of civil service inspectorates from 'law enforcers' to 'diplomats',[38] more concerned with persuasion and advice than with the application of financial or legal sanctions. These changes are due in part to the development of 'internal' processes of inspection and control and to professionalism within local authorities, but they mean that central government as such as few control instruments lying between draconian measures on the one hand, and simple advice and exhortation on the other.[39]

Rings of Contractors and Recurrent Contracts

To add to the problems of control which we have already discussed, an additional problem in contracting is that of dealing with 'rings' or with monopoly suppliers, involving a recurrent pattern of contracts. A well-known case of this is telecommunications. Lack of competition in Post Office buying of telephone equipment first began to draw criticism from the Public Accounts Committee in the 1920s, when a series of 'bulk supply agreements' began. These arrangements were originally made, so it is said, to standardize the British telephone system and to allow planning both by the Post Office and by the suppliers.[40] Under these agreements, which were periodically renewed, the Post Office negotiated prices with a cartel of telephone suppliers after an investigation of the costs of selected firms. The Post Office orders were also shared among the firms in the group (originally there were five firms involved, but the number later dropped to three), though under the agreements the Post Office could obtain a small proportion of telephone apparatus and exchanges from 'outsiders'.

The Public Accounts Committee protested for a long time against these arrangements, and the Post Office finally ended the formal process of buying through the 'ring' in 1969, when the last bulk supply agreement ended (the Post Office had unsuccessfully attempted to end the agreement in 1965). After 1969, established suppliers were to be guaranteed a diminishing proportion of annual orders (70 per cent at first, later falling to 50 per cent), the remaining orders being open to 'all comers'. Some new suppliers (such as Pye and Thorn) did enter the market in a modest way, but the ring very largely continued on a *de facto* basis, since there were virtually no firms outside the agreement who were capable of producing and installing a big telephone exchange. This was particularly true at that time, because the old electromechanical 'Strowger' and 'Crossbar' exchanges were being replaced with electromagnetic exchanges (known as the TXE-4 type), an intermediate type of exchange before the introduction of fully electronic systems.[41]

But monopoly relationships cut two ways. The ring depends on the Post Office as much as the Post Office depends on the ring. Thus, by insisting on the TXE-4 exchange rather than modifying the Crossbar exchange or going straight on to fully-electronic exchanges (an abortive attempt to do this in the early 1950s had presumably made the Post Office cautious), the Post Office had limited the ring's export potential. This is because the TXE-4 exchange was not thought to be easily saleable abroad, and thus GEC's and Plessey's prospects would be hampered by having to make a product for their only major home customer which could not be sold abroad.

Another example of the problems of effective control over rings of contractors is drug purchasing for the National Health Service. There are two components of this, direct central purchasing for hospitals and indirect purchase of prescription medicines via remuneration of retail chemists. Drug purchasing caused problems from the start of the NHS in the late 1940s, because the Ministry of Health had no reliable idea of the costs and profits of drug manufacturers, and no comprehensive investigation into this matter took place for over eight years.[42] Moreover, the difficulties of cost control were exaggerated by the open-endedness of the system of payment to chemists for drugs issued to customers under doctor's prescriptions. This means that the government pays for drugs, but doctors prescribe them, and thus the government has very little control over costs.

Since the early 1950s, the Ministry of Health has made efforts to curb extravagance in prescription by doctors by urging the use of standard drugs rather than the more expensive and heavily-advertized branded drugs wherever therapeutic effects are identical, but these efforts have been largely unsuccessful as a means of checking rising costs.[43] The control problem is by now a familiar one: there are few sanctions available to the Health Department between hard financial penalties in the form of withholding payment from doctors who are over-extravagant in prescribing (rarely used) and mere exhortation. In terms of exhortation, the Department engages in a significant 'counter promotion' effort to counter the sales literature and visits from company representatives with which doctors are bombarded, but such counter-promotion would have to be unusually effective to nullify the effect of approximately 3,000 drug company sales representatives in the UK market.

With the direct purchase of drugs for hospitals, the problems were almost as great, because of the difficulty of reckoning up costs and profits in relation to questions such as how far advertizing costs should be included in prices paid by the NHS; or, where companies are multi-national, what is the appropriate accounting unit for calculating costs and profits. The problems of devising standard formulae of general application are severe in this case, since the UK drug industry contains firms of very different sizes and many of the NHS suppliers (well over 50 per cent) are foreign-owned firms.[44] Moreover, it is an industry in which competition is through advertizing rather than through prices, and there is a high degree of monopoly on particular medicines subject to patents.

The largest item of cost in drug manufacture is development cost, and thus the longer the production run, the lower tends to be the unit cost of production. But manufacturers do not willingly reduce their prices as costs fall, particularly where the government is the consumer. The Ministry of Health began to investigate the finances of its suppliers in the early 1950s and discovered that proprietary drugs (patented brands) and basic drugs were in many cases over-priced, though this did not seem to apply to standard drugs. Proprietary medicines in particular showed profits of up to 60 per cent on selling prices, with return on capital as high as 100 per cent in some cases. Three firms made 'voluntary' price reductions after these discoveries, but the Ministry preferred not to deal with individual firms one by one, for fear of penalizing the low-cost efficient suppliers. Instead, the Ministry negotiated an industry-wide deal with the pharmaceutical trade association in 1957, which was known as the Voluntary Price Regulation Scheme. This scheme stipulated a range of criteria for determining maximum drug prices, including the prices at which the goods were sold abroad and the prices of similar or identical unbranded goods. New medicines were free of price control for three years after their introduction.

Modified Voluntary Price Regulation schemes were negotiated again in 1964 and 1967, but the effectiveness of these bargains was hampered by the authorities' continuing ignorance about the costs of producing proprietary medicines and the extent to which prices to the NHS were inflated by unnecessary advertizing expenditures (advertizing of drugs was reported to cost about £6½ m per year in the early 1960s and some £10 m in 1972). Moreover, there were definitional problems. In the first scheme, over 60 per cent of proprietary drugs had escaped price control under the export price criteria or under the three-year 'freedom period'; consequently in the 1960–1964 scheme the definition of 'new' drugs had to be tightened up in order to remove products owing nothing to fresh research from the price freedom period. More drastically, the Ministry of Health in 1961 invoked the powers of Government Departments to make or use any patented invention for 'the services of the Crown'. The American firm Pfizer had its monopoly in patents broken by these means aften an unsuccessful appeal to the House of Lords, and the Ministry effected some small savings as a result. But 'Crown user rights' appeared legally to apply only to the hospital services and not to the General Practitioner or Pharmaceutical Services of the NHS.

The ineffectiveness of the Voluntary Price Regulation schemes led in 1965 to the establishment of a committee of inquiry into the relationship of the pharmaceutical industry with the NHS and, following the Committee's report in 1967,[45] a Medicines Commission was set up to licence prescription medicines, to control advertizing and to classify medicines according to their essential therapeutic content.[46] But these arrangements had at least as much to do with safety as with cost control, and the failure to achieve effective cost control was a problem which once more came into the limelight with the Roche affair in 1973.

The Roche company, a Swiss-based concern, introduced a major new tranquillizer, Librium (chlordiazepoxide) into the UK in 1960, and followed it shortly afterwards by Valium (diazepam). These drugs revolutionized mental care and had an effect throughout the medical world, to the extent that by 1971 the British market for them was worth £8–£10 m per year and arguments about Roche's prices for these tranquillizers had been going on since 1964. The argument turned on the share of the research and development costs of Librium and Valium which could be attributed to the UK. Roche claimed that development costs were the reason for its high prices, but research was treated for accounting purposes a 'a central fixed cost' for the whole Roche group and moreover it was uncertain whether the payments by the Roche UK subsidiary for ingredients imported from associated companies abroad were at genuinely 'arms length' prices.[47]

In spite of these accounting perplexities, Roche refused to supply full information about its drug business to the British government and refused nine applications by other companies to manufacture Librium and Valium under licence. In 1971 the negotiations took a new turn when the Department of Health referred Roche to the Monopolies Commission (the British anti-trust agency) over drug prices and forced Roche to grant compulsory licences to two other firms. But in fact these two companies did not make much impact on the UK tranquillizer market because of Roche's hold over the market for hospital drugs and its influence with the wholesale chemists, who derive a substantial part of their income from margins on the top manufacturers' business.

The Monopolies Commission estimated Roche's return on capital to be more than 70 per cent and strongly condemned its prices.[48] After this, the British government ordered Roche to cut the price of tranquillizers supplied to the NHS by 40–70 per cent and to repay excess profits of some £11 m. Roche complied with this, but fought back vigorously against the goverment's attack. The Company appealed (unsuccessfully) to the House of Lords against the government's order and began court proceedings against the Department of Trade and Industry, besides making threats to revise its investment plans and to transfer manufacturing to other countries. The company even offered to pay the difference between its old prices and what the DTI thought reasonable into a blocked bank account pending court action, provided the government would allow Roche to continue charging its old prices meantime.

By this time the affair was no longer simply of domestic importance in Britain.

The outcome of the British struggle had implications for Roche's business in countries such as South Africa, Australia and the Common Market countries (the anti-trust department of the EEC Commission became interested in the case, as well as several individual EEC governments).[49] The affair began to have strong international implications, particularly when Roche began to attack British-based drug companies for making excessive profits in *their* export sales, and indeed in 1973 Beechams began to be investigated by the US Department of Justice for overcharging on antibiotics. In fact, the quarrel between Roche and the British government was settled by a compromise in 1975 when both drugs were approaching the end of their patent period.

Government-sponsored Rings

The Roche affair is of course an extreme case, but it highlights the complexity of price control and the limits of the available sanctions, particularly in a multi-national context. But governments often deliberately bring problems of dealing with monopolies and rings onto themselves, by encouraging concentrations of suppliers. The reasons for moving away from completely open competition towards 'approved lists' have already been discussed, and in some cases this extends to sponsorship of individual firms. Well-known historical examples are the personal friendship between Alfried Krupp and Bismarck, and the growth of Du Pont de Nemours, originally under Napoleon's patronage and later under the patronage of the US government.[50] More recent examples are the 'arsenalization' of the US aerospace industry by the air force in the 1940s (as described by P. M. Smith);[51] the use of contracts to effect mergers in the British aircraft industry in 1959; the concentration of the British computer industry, heavily dependent on government contracts, into a single firm in 1968 by means of government money;[52] and the use of selective, group and serial tendering in construction contracts, instead of step-by-step competitive tendering.[53]

In effect, the problem here is a variant of the level-of-control limits which we discussed in the last chapter. Most of these moves to encourage greater concentration of suppliers have been aimed to improve the efficiency or the competitiveness of British industry *vis-a-vis* overseas suppliers. The dilemma is that if the government encourages concentration by domestic firms, it may weaken its direct bargaining power in the form of the ability to 'shop elsewhere'; but on the other hand, if fragmentation among producers of equipment such as telephones, computers or power stations means that such producers cannot sell their goods abroad, government may in fact pay more, not less, for its purchases. This is because, unless the government opts for the strategically doubtful course of relying on overseas suppliers for such items, the whole of their development costs will have to be paid by the government (as sole UK user) in the absence of overseas sales. Though government's bargaining power may be greater if it opts for the second choice, the cash cost of the items obtained may be at least as great as if the government had opted for the first choice.

Even if the government opts for concentration, throwing away most of its sanctions, it may still end up with the worst of all worlds in that domestic suppliers may remain internationally uncompetitive even when concentrated and thus set off a 'dependency syndrome'. This applies to a variety of fields in which recurrent contracts to a small number of suppliers have built up relationships of reciprocal need between governments and individual firms, so that governments may be obliged to bail out firms in trouble and lose most of the theoretical advantages of contracting over direct administration.

Problems of Change and Adaptation

Most of the problems which we have identified up to now have related to limits of control in a general sense and limits of categorization and discrimination. But in the last chapter we also discussed problems of adaptation in time as an administrative limit, and this is something which will be explored further in Part 2. Problems of change and adaptation can readily be illustrated from the field of contracting and procurement, though in many cases the problems involved are not purely administrative.

First is the case of technological change, which is particularly marked in aerospace. The early World War II aeroplanes of the Spitfire—Lancaster type were fairly cheap to produce (for example, the Halifax prototype cost only £88,000) and the problems lay in organizing flow production rather than in design and development.[54] The stakes began to be raised with the introduction of jet fighters late in the war and with the German achievements in rocketry. The Korean War raised the stakes of military equipment still further and by the time that the sub-sonic V-bomber force, planned in 1946, came into service in 1956—1957, it was already obsolescent.[55] This was because, after Korea, supersonic speeds were clearly going to be necessary for interceptors and attackers; but the British aircraft industry produced a series of intermediate military aircraft, culminating in the supersonic TSR-2 strike bomber,[56] all of which were too slow and too late for their intended roles. The late development of swept-wing jets in Britain had created a cumulative handicap for British airframe technology, which began to lag further and further behind its French, American and Russian equivalents in the 1950s. Civil aerospace presented similar problems as lead-times lengthened and development costs rose.

Another type of change hampering contract administration is that imposed by changing strategic perceptions and financial circumstances, often occasioning sharp reversals of policy which throw the whole machine out of gear. For example, the outbreak of the Korean War in 1950 had not been anticipated by British strategists, and there was a serious lack of up-to-date fighter aircraft. The Royal Air Force was so ill-equipped that it was unable to take serious part in the Korean conflict, though Britain had the dubious distinction of having inspired the aero engines used by both the Russian and American fighters. In a panic attempt to get swept-wing squadrons to Korea to supplement the American F-86s, the British government hastily ordered Vickers (Supermarine) Swifts and Hawker Hunters in large quantities. Both aircraft were at an early design stage when they were ordered (neither had flown) and both ran into deep development trouble.[57] The Swift had a particularly unhappy history, and in 1955 the government order was cut from 492 to 170 after the abortive expenditure of some £40 m, because the aircraft, even when modified, was never fit for the job for which it was required. But by this time the Ministry of Supply could not claim breach of contract because it had accepted both the prototypes and a number of production aircraft, and in any case the specification was too vague and indefinite to be legally enforceable.

The more familiar story of the Blue Streak affair was similarly occasioned by U-turns in strategy. After World War II, British strategic thinkers had been relatively indifferent to ballistic missiles, but this changed in 1954 when Hawker Siddeley and De Havilland began development work on the Blue Streak project, an intermediate liquid-fuelled ballistic missile fired from an underground silo.[58] In 1957, after the abortive Suez expedition, the British government abruptly switched the defence emphasis away from conventional armed forces towards a J. F. Dulles-type policy of massive retaliation and 'the biggest bang for a buck', based on the Blue Streak missile.

Three years later, the project was cancelled after some £60 m expenditure. This was because to be effective as a defensive weapon, Blue Streak would have had to survive a first strike from an enemy only 1,200 miles away, and the cost of the number of missiles which would be needed in order to yield an acceptable probability of some silo doors remaining undamaged after the enemy's first attack clearly exceeded the politically feasible limit of British defence expenditure. As a result of Blue Streak's cancellation, the British government decided to buy the US Skybolt air-to-surface missile for the V-bomber fleet, but Skybolt in turn was cancelled by the US Defense Department in 1962, obliging the British government to change course once again and to base its second-generation deterrent on submarines instead, using US Polaris missiles.

In any case, the 'big bang' policy of 1957 began to be eroded as the threat of a nuclear war between major powers was paralleled and even overtaken by the threat of conventional and guerilla-type insurgent warfare between and within lesser military powers. This meant that the manned military aircraft, a concept formerly thought to be obsolete, was not dead after all, and development work thereafter began on several projects, including the ill-fated TSR-2. But the TSR-2 was in turn cancelled in 1965 after costs of £130 m had been incurred and instead the government bought US Phantoms and Hercules Transports, with a provision for 50 per cent of the work to be sub-contracted in the UK. In the case of the Phantom, the advantages of buying an aircraft 'off the shelf' were largely nullified by the decision to adapt it to take the Rolls-Royce Spey engine, which doubled the cost. In addition, in 1967, the government decided to buy 50 variable-geometry (swing-wing) US F-111 fighter-bombers at a cost of some $1 billion. But only a year later, this order was cancelled, in the wake of the 1967 devaluation of the pound and the British retreat from East of Suez.

Military stores were another victim of the changing strategic situation. The fiasco of the post-war disposals policy has already been mentioned in the last chapter; and throughout the 1950s and 1960s, especially for 'non-warlike' stores, large quantities of unused items easily available 'off the shelf' had to be sold as surplus (£14—£25 m worth per year in the early 1960s). There were also recurring cases of equipment deteriorating in store without ever having been used. This quantity of surplus goods was largely the legacy of the massive Korean rearmament programme and later of the run-down of the Territorial Army. Perhaps the most publicized case was that of army boots, of which there were well over a million surplus in 1958 and still 650,000 in 1967.[59] But the 1964—1965 Estimates Committee also noted

'81,000 woollen vests, 174,000 singlets, 159,000 long drawers and large quantities of shirts, pyjamas, blouses, bed jackets, gum boots, mittens, navy blue comforters (enough for 2/3 of the personnel of the existing Navy) and even fezzes and cummerbunds . . .'

in catalogues of surplus items.[60]

But it is not only strategic changes which bring about such problems. Unforseen economic change presents another type of adaptation problem. A case of this type is the fate of the bulk-buying schemes after World War II. In contrast to the rapid ending of bulk purchasing after 1918, the British government after World War II continued to buy in bulk imported food and raw materials, such as metal and cotton. Even in 1949 about 55 per cent of UK imports, amounting to £1,000 m or so, were purchased by the Board of Trade, Ministry of Supply, Ministry of Food and Ministry of Works.[61] Much of this took the form of long-term agreements with suppliers in soft currency areas (such as Canada, Argentina and the West Indies) in the context of post-war shortages of raw materials, which were expected to continue. In 1947 the British government had long-term contracts with 26 countries, mostly for basic foods and usually for the entire exportable surplus or a large proportion of it.

These schemes were primarily intended as an instrument of national planning and as a means of saving dollars (though elements of colonial development policy later crept in). But the expected did not happen, and in fact world raw material prices began to fall from their post-war levels. This meant that the long-term contracts at higher than current world prices were a severe handicap for an economy as dependent on manufactured exports as the British economy is, and British exporters claimed that their sales in world markets were severely hampered because they were obliged to buy their raw materials at more than world market prices. The system began to be abandoned in the late 1940s, and bulk purchasing had already been eroded to a considerable extent by the post-war Labour government when it left office; the return of the Conservative Party to power in 1951 merely accelerated the scrapping of the system.[62]

Another type of unforseen economic change is inflation of costs. This is particularly difficult in the case of construction projects, where the 'lead time' is 2–5 years or more. In the inflationary years after 1945, all government building contracts were let on some variant of the cost-plus system; after 1957 the Ministry of Public Building and Works switched to a policy of fixed-price tendering for some projects, but this formula could not be applied to projects which could not be properly costed in advance or which were more than two years in duration.[63] A more general strategy for grappling with runaway costs in construction in the post-war period was a shift to system building and prefabrication.[64] But this has built-in disadvantages as well: it narrows the field of tenderers, since it is more capital-intensive than orthodox building methods, and it also carries the disadvantage that the effects of mistakes can be very widespread, on the 'horse-shoe-nail' principle. One example of this was a vulnerability to 'progressive collapse' in the structures of about 40 identical blocks of high flats of the Neilson–Larsen type, which was discovered after the semi-collapse in 1968 of a tower block built by Taylor Woodrow at Ronan Point.

Construction is also a contracting area which is particularly vulnerable to a multi-organizational problem, in that conditions of profitability can be drastically affected by government agencies other than those in charge of contract management, and this adds to the difficulty of fixed-price tendering in this field. For example, the Treasury's imposition of a payroll tax (Selective Employment Tax) in 1966 upset all the costs on fixed-price contracts for other government agencies, and thus 90 per cent of the costs of SET had to be reimbursed for government contracts. Similar problems can occur with price rises by nationalized industries, changes in import duties and other legislative changes introduced during the life of a contract.

Two further kinds of change create administrative difficulties in the contracting process. One is change in the organizations to which contracts are awarded and the other is change in procurement agencies themselves. Not only is the 'contractor' sometimes a less tangible and stable entity than might at first appear; the same applies with the procurement agencies themselves. We referred to the saga of 'reorganization cycles' in post-war aerospace procurement in the discussion of reorganization problems in the last chapter. So far as the other problem is concerned, the saga of London Weekend Television in the late 1960s illustrates the effects of change in the organizations to which contracts are awarded.

London Weekend Television was one of two companies which secured the contracts for the lucrative London commercial TV market from the Independent Television Authority in 1967. It did so in large part because it promised to produce 'serious' and high quality TV programmes and assembled many respected individuals on its payroll, including Michael Peacock, who had held senior posts in the British Broadcasting Corporation. But Peacock was sacked by the London Weekend Television Board in September 1969 and several other senior executives resigned with him. The original promises made by LWT were heavily compromised, but even so losses built up and by 1971 the company was in financial difficulty. At this point Rupert Murdoch (owner of the *News of the World* and *Sun* newspapers) assumed control by buying up a large shareholding in LWT. Fears that LWT would adopt 'vulgar' or 'gutter press' standards were heightened when Murdoch sacked seven senior executives, including Peacock's successor, and proceeded to supervize the programme schedules himself. Eventually, after threats by the ITA to revoke LWT's contract unless Murdoch could find someone else to exert day-to-day managerial control of LWT, a new managing director was appointed.[65]

Similar problems have arisen with other TV companies through takeovers, for example with Thames TV in 1969. A problem similar to the LWT affair also occurred in 1964, when the British government sold the British Lion film company, formerly in public ownership, to a private consortium under Sir Michael Balcon, a well-respected figure in the British film industry. This consortium succeeded in obtaining the company by making promises of continued independence and a greater film production effort. But Sir Michael resigned from the chairmanship almost immediately after the new company had been formed, and many of the promises made by Sir Michael were not carried out. Indeed, the company was taken over by Barclay Securities in 1972 with the intention of using the site of Shepperton Studies for property development, whereas a specific term of the sale of British Lion in 1964 had been that these studios should not be sold for development; and after a long argument, part of the site had to be retained for film production.[66]

Conclusion

The case of contracting and procurement illustrates most of the administrative difficulties or limits which we discussed in the last chapter and which will be further explored in Parts 2 and 3. We have seen how difficult it is to pin down vital concepts like 'capital', 'cost' or 'profit' unambiguously, and even without these difficulties there are more general problems of control — only a limited range of sanctions is in practice available and many of these turn out to be limited in effectiveness. Moreover, strategic decisions, economic trends and contracting organizations themselves, often change rapidly and unexpectedly. There are multi-organization problems too, as we have seen in the case of construction. Another example of this is the interlock between specialized and centralized procurement agencies. If you adopt full specialization, you lose the advantages of a centralized buying system, and vice versa, so in practice the two principles are always combined, creating inevitable overlaps.[67] In both the UK and the USA there have long been co-ordinating committees to prevent the grosser types of competition between different military agencies. But there are inevitably inter-locking jurisdictions between 'science', 'defence' and other operating departments, and between agencies concerned with government property and other procurement agencies. These problems can be minimized, but there is no way of wholly eliminating them.

Most of the administrative limits which we identified in the last chapter, then, are revealed in this case. But many of these limits are 'quasi-administrative', in that many of the problems of accountability and control which have been discussed here are not primarily the result of defective administrative procedures, and therefore it should not be surprising if changes in procedure effect little 'improvement'. Many of the contracting problems which have been discussed are to a large extent the consequences of the basic dilemma of buying products which do not yet exist, from changing perceptions of strategic situations and from political decisions about support for particular firms or industries. An example of the last type is the British government's purchase of £10m worth of useless Comet I airliners and airframes in 1955 as a means of bailing out De Havilland after the Comet crashes in 1955 (some of these were incomplete airframes to be held in reserve against a hypothetical future requirement, others were existing aircraft bought for allegedly research purposes.[68] Political decisions of this kind cut across purely 'procurement' objectives and can sometimes produce what seem at first sight like administrative absurdities. A classic case is the continuing production of aero engines by British contractors after the Armistice in 1918, these engines then being taken to National Factories to be dismantled.[69] Employment considerations were behind this: both contractors and National Factories had to be kept occupied until after the 1918 election.

It is not the character of such political decisions per se which create administrative difficulties, but rather the absence of a stable set of objectives, whether of a 'value for money' or of a political kind, and the oscillation between contradictory objectives. Contracts are often used as auxiliary weapons for all kinds of government policies, but this tactic is rarely consistent or carried to its logical conclusion. The Labour government's ill-fated National Plan of 1965[70] suggested that contracts should be used to promote general industrial efficiency, and other government documents[71] followed in the same vein, but the policy, if indeed it was ever serious, came to nothing. The government declined to go so far as to set up a central agency to mobilize the purchasing power of the whole public sector,[72] and in any case the bulk of public sector purchasing is outside the direct control of central government.

Many contracting problems are thus quasi-administrative rather than purely administrative limits. But even without the large-scale difficulties, contracting is sharply limited in effectiveness as a method of administration. In some cases, as we will see in Part 3, there are good (or bad) reasons for operating through grants and contracts rather than direct administration of projects — for example, for un-acknowledgeable or illegal operations, for the performance of sensitive or unpopular tasks, for the deliberate pursuit of incompatible objectives and in administrative 'outflanking operations'.[73] But where such motives do not apply, the resort to grant and contract is often a doubtful tactic as a short cut to programme implementation. Indeed, Altensetter[74] (with reference to health) has discerned a 'paradox' in government-by-grant in that it involves more 'bureaucracy' (in the sense of clumsy 'paperwork' and checking-up procedures) than direct administration itself, and, as we have seen, similar problems arise in contract administration in many cases. Indeed, the seventeenth-century pattern of contracting out tax collection broke down at the point where tendering for the tax farms was being rigged by collusive syndicates, but these syndicates had established an ongoing tax-collecting bureaucracy which could simply be transferred to the direct control of government. The same thing applied to France after 1789.[75] Some people have argued that the present system will go the same way, owing to the highly cartelized nature of the contract sector, which means that, like seventeenth century tax farmers, contractors are far from being easily hireable and fireable entities, and that even in situations where their performance is clearly unsatisfactory, 'throwing the book at them' may be ineffective or even counter-productive. These are broad problems of control to which we will return in Part 3, after examining the more specific problems of categorization and adaptation in the next Part.

Notes

1. cf. Hood, C. C., 'Government by other means' in B. Chapman and A. Potter (Eds.), *W.J.M.M. Political Questions*, Manchester University Press, Manchester, 1975, pp. 147–160; H. L. Nieburg, *In the Name of Science*, Quadrangle Books, Chicago, 1966; K. Boulding, *Economics as a Science*, McGraw-Hill, New York, 1970.
2. Heyman, V. K., 'Government by contract', *Public Administration Review*, 1961, Vol. 21, p. 59.
3. Pressman, J., and A. Wildavsky, *Implementation*, University of California Press, Berkeley, 1973.
4. Lloyd, E. M. H., *Experiments in State Control*, Clarendon Press, Oxford, 1924.
5. HC. 362, 1856, HC. 93 1857 (Session 1), HC. 319, 328, 398, 418, 438, Session 1857–1858.
6. Scott, J. D., *Vickers, A History*, Weidenfeld and Nicholson, London, 1962.
7. *Report of the Royal Commission on the Private Manufacture of and Trading in Arms*, Cmd. 5292, 1936.
8. Prentiss, A. M., *Chemicals in War: A Treatise on Chemical Warfare*, McGraw-Hill, New York, 1937.
9. *State Assistance to the Dye Industry*, Cmd. 9194, 1918.
10. cf. Lloyd, E. M. F., *op. cit.*, Crowell, J. F., *Government War Contracts*, Oxford University Press, New York, 1920 (on the US experience).
11. Lloyd, E. M. H., *op. cit.*
12. *Second Report of the Public Accounts Committee*, HC 31,106 1927.
13. Ashworth, W., *Civil History of the Second World War — Contracts and Finance*, HMSO, London, 1953.

14. cf. *The Economist*, June 15th and 29th, 1946.
15. cf. *First Report of the Public Accounts Committee*, HC. 38-1, 1945—1946.
16. cf. *2nd Report of the Public Accounts Committee*, HC. 104 1945—1946.
17. *Annual Abstracts of Statistics*, HMSO, London, 1952—1972.
18. Page, D. F., *Negotiation and Management of Defense Contracts*, Wiley, New York, 1970.
19. Page, D. F., *op. cit., 1st, 2nd and 3rd Reports of the Public Accounts Committee*, HC. 66-1, 297, 1969—1970.
20. cf. Stephenson, H., *The Coming Clash*, Weidenfeld and Nicholson, London, 1972, p. 140.
21. cf. *Economist*, June 16, 1946; *Report of the Review Board for Government Contracts*, HMSO, London, 1970.
22. Melville, Sir R., see *Reports from the Committee of Public Accounts*, HC. 166-1, 297, 1969—1970. Mins. of Evidence Q. 2702.
23. Danhof, C., *Government Contracting and Technological Change*, The Brookings Institution, Washington, 1968, p. 267, fn. 82.
24. cf. for example *Second Report from the Public Accounts Committee*, HC. 51-1, 219-1, 256-1. 1959—1960.
25. cf. Seidman, H., *Politics Position and Power*, Oxford University Press, London, 1970.
26. cf. Turpin, C., *Government Contracts*, Penguin Books, Harmondsworth, 1972.
27. cf. Page, D. F., *op. cit.*, p. 507.
28. HC. 166-1, 265-1, 297, 1969—1970, p. xxxvi, para. 93 (c).
29. Edmonds, M., 'Government contracting and renegotiation', *Public Administration*, Vol. 50, Spring 1972, pp. 45—54.
30. cf. *Government Organization for Defence Procurement and Civil Aerospace*, Cmnd. 4641, 1971.
31. cf. Edmonds, M., *op. cit.*
32. Cmnd. 2428, and Cmnd. 2581.
33. HC. 129, 1966—1967.
34. cf. Page, D. F., *op. cit.*, pp. 110—111.
35. Derthick, M., *The Influence of Federal Grants*, Harvard University Press, Cambridge, 1970.
36. Reagan, M., *The New Federalism*, Oxford University Press, New York, 1972.
37. Parris, H., *Constitutional Bureaucracy*, Allen and Unwin, London, 1969.
38. Hartley, O., 'Inspectorates in British government', *Public Administration*, Vol. 50, Winter 1972.
39. Griffith, J. A. G., *Central Departments and Local Authorities*, Allen and Unwin, London, 1966.
40. *Third Report from the Public Accounts Committee*, HC. 265, 1954—1955 (GPO Bulk Supply Agreements).
41. *Third Report from the Public Accounts Committee,*, HC. 166-1, 1969—1970.
42. *Third Report from the Public Accounts Committee*, HC. 124, 1955—1956.
43. cf. *Second Report from the Public Accounts Committee*, HC. 51-1, 219-1, 256-1, 1959—1960; *Third Report from the Public Accounts Committee*, HC. 252 1960—1961.
44. cf. *Report of the Committee of Inquiry into the Relationship of The Pharmaceutical Industry with the National Health Service*, Cmnd. 3410, 1967.
45. *Ibid.*
46. cf. *First Report of the Medicines Commission*, HC. 468, 1971—1972.
47. *Monopolies Commission Report on Chlordiazepoxide and Diazepam*, HC. 197, 1972—1973.
48. *Ibid.*
49. cf. *The Economist*, 7 July 1973, p. 89.
50. Engelbrecht, H. C., and F. C. Hanighen, *Merchants of Death: A Study of the International Armaments Industry*, Routledge, London, 1934.
51. Smith, P. M., *The Air Force Plans for Peace 1941—45*, Johns Hopkins University Press, Baltimore, 1970.
52. *Fourth Report from the Select Committee on Science and Technology*, HC. 621-1, 1970—1971.
53. *Report on the Placing and Management of Contracts for Building and Civil Engineering Work*, HMSO, London, 1964; *Contracting in Civil Engineering since Banwell*, HMSO, London, 1967.

54. Worcester, R., *Roots of British Air Policy*, Hodder and Stoughton, London, 1966.
55. *Second Report from the Estimates Committee*, HC. 34, 1956–1957 (The Supply of Military Aircraft).
56. cf. Worswick, G. D. H., and P. H. Ady, *The British Economy in the 1950s*, Clarendon Press, Oxford, 1962.
57. cf. *Third Report from the Public Accounts Committee*, HC. 75-1, 93-1, 196-1, 243-1, 1957–1958.
58. cf. Worcester, R., *op. cit.*
59. *Third Report of the Public Accounts Committee*, HC. 192, 1967–1968.
60. *Eighth Report from the Estimates Committee*, HC. 359, 1964–1965 (Non Warlike Stories for the Services).
61. HC. Deb. Vol. 465 c. 1453.
62. cf. Worswick, G. D. H., and P. H. Ady, *op. cit.*, esp. Table I at p. 554.
63. cf. 53 above; also J. R. Colclough, *The Construction Industry of Great Britain*, Butterworths, London, 1965.
64. cf. *Eighth Report from the Estimates Committee*, HC. 284, 1960–1961 (School Building).
65. cf. Hague, D. C. (Ed.), *Public Policy and Private Interests: The Institutions of Compromise*, Macmillan, London, 1975; Chapter 7, 'The Arts, Sport and the Mass Media'.
66. *Ibid.*
67. cf. Cowell, F. R., 'Central purchasing', *Public Administration*, Vol. 10, 1932.
68. *Sixth Report from the Public Accounts Committee*, HC. 348, 1955–1956.
69. *First Report of the Select Committee on National Expenditure*, HC. 113, 142, 168, 238, 245, 1919, para. 29.
70. Cmnd. 2764, p. 9 and p. 51.
71. For example, *Public Purchasing and Industrial Efficiency*, Cmnd. 3291, 1967; *Report of Joint Review Body on Local Authority Purchasing*, HMSO, London, 1968.
72. cf. HC. Deb. Vol. 861.
73. cf. Hood, C. C., 'Government by other means', *op. cit.*, 'The rise and rise of the British quango', *New Society*, 16 August 1973, pp. 386–388.
74. Altensetter, C., 'Determinants of health services delivery in the USA and West Germany' paper presented to 9th IPSA Conference, Montreal, August 1973, p. 15.
75. cf. Matthews, G. T., *The Royal General Farms of Eighteenth Century France*, Columbia University Press, New York, 1956.

Part 2

Adaptation and Categorization

Chapter 4

Categorization and its Limits

'As in other sciences, so in politics, it is impossible that all things should be set down precisely in writing, for enactments are universal, but actions are concerned with particulars.' *Report of the Committee on the Codification of the Income Tax* (quoting Aristotle) Cmd. 5131, 1936, p. 17, para. 24.

In Chapter 1, the fourth 'internal' condition of perfect administration required perfect information concerning the situation in hand and the capacity to specify tasks or the content of one's orders unambiguously. This may seem to be an innocent enough condition, but in the case of contracting in the last chapter we saw some of the difficulties which can arise in practice over specification and definition. In this chapter we will analyse the problem a little further, bringing out some of its different dimensions. The problem of categorization is an ancient one, as the epigraph above indicates. It is a 'classical' problem of administration in every sense. To administer is to categorize. To categorize is to arrange things in some order, or according to some criterion, such that they divide into groups or classes. In this chapter, we will consider only the problems associated with categorization in 'space', assuming administration to be otherwise 'perfect'. In particular, we will assume away most of the problems relating to the time element.

There are two levels of categorization which will be considered separately. The first is the process of physical arrangement. The second is discrimination by the use of language. One can categorize in 'space' without explicitly using language, simply by arranging a given set of objects in some physical order. Flower or furniture arrangement is an example of this type of categorization. This can be contrasted with classifying flowers into species or genera, which is an example of the second type of categorization. Here no physical arrangement is necessarily involved: arrangement consists of 'labelling' items with words, codes or concepts. This type of arrangement is not limited to the dimensions of physical space: it can include any number of analytic dimensions, as we will see later.

Both types of categorization are relevant for administration, and the two types of categorization are typically related in practice, although they have been separated here. For example, in some types of formal garden using the 'Bentham and Hooker' system, the plants are physically laid out according to species and genera. But the first type of categorization is limited by the fact that you can only arrange what is physically present, and typically this can only be done in one order. On the other hand, and indeed as a result of these limitations, physical

categorization may present fewer problems of ambiguity than analytic categorization.

Physical Arrangement: Geographical

Let us begin with direct physical arrangement — the case where the items to be
ordered are 'given' and the available space is fixed and more or less known.
Everyone at some time faces the problem of how to arrange items of furniture
within a room or a house, and a similar type of problem is familiar in
administration. The most obvious form of the problem is the geographical one, that
is, how to divide up physical terrain for the purpose of administration. How and
where are the lines to be drawn on the map?

Problems of this type are pervasive in administration; so much so that John Gaus
recommends that administration should be studied, literally 'from the ground up'.[1]
Should Area A go in with Area B for purpose X? In public administration, there is a
long-standing debate about the perceived conflict between dividing up territory for
maximum ease of administration and dividing up territory according to the
boundaries of pre-existing 'communities'. The argument has been conducted in
these terms at least since the French Revolution and the creation of the French
départements in 1789.[2] Just as in many cases of furniture arrangement, one can only
achieve one desirable objective by sacrificing another, though various people have
tried to reconcile the two criteria. For example, H. G. Wells in 1903 suggested that
watersheds make the best areal boundaries, because both communities and
administrative services (such as drains, railways, water and roads) tend to be divided
by watersheds in many cases.[3] Ingenious as this is, several subsequent generations
of 'social geography' have not been able to solve the problem to everyone's
satisfaction.

Moreover, it is in many cases impossible to divide geographical space into rigidly
exclusive administrative areas *whatever* criterion one adopts. For example, there is
typically no single unit of administrative convenience, but rather multiple and
conflicting units. Different administrative tasks suggest different 'maps'. How are
these maps to be reconciled with one another? Nor is the 'community' criterion by
any means exempt from such problems. A geographical area may contain different
and wholly opposed 'communities' which are spatially distributed in such a way as
to render drawing a line on a map according to 'community' boundaries simply
impossible. Large-scale and dramatic cases of this which everyone knows are the
distribution of Protestants and Catholics in Northern Ireland and the distribution of
blacks and whites in the United States, and there are many historical examples as
well. One case, discussed by de Jouvenel,[4] is the problem of following 'community'
boundaries in the division of Upper Silesia between Germany and Poland after
World War I. Problems of this type have been so serious in European history that in
many cases populations have been forcibly reshuffled in order to fit ethnic
communities to lines on maps. Examples are the expulsion of ten million
German-speakers from the Sudetenland after World War II or the exchange of the
Turkish minority of Thrace for the Greeks of Western Asia Minor in 1923.[5] But
this is a paradoxical (and highly unpleasant) way of following the 'community'
principle.

Where geographical space cannot be easily divided into clear-cut and rigidly
exclusive administrative areas according to either of the two broad principles which

we have discussed, the result is likely to be a 'multi-organizational' pattern in any given area. The 'pathology' of this has already been discussed in Chapter 2 and the problem will be further explored in the following two sections.

Physical Arrangement: Functional

The problem of leaky divisions does not only apply to lines on maps in a geographical sense. It also applies to the general problem of dividing up policy functions among administrative units. Writers such as Downs[6] and Randall[7] refer to an organization's 'policy space' as its territory in a non-geographical sense. The metaphor of 'space' which is being used here is a mathematical one, referring to analytical dimensions, but the problem is still largely of the 'furniture arrangement' kind: how to divide 'policy' for the purpose of administration.

'Policy space' is, if anything, even more difficult to divide up into rigidly exclusive boxes than geographical space, because more dimensions are involved. As with geographical divisions, arguments about how best to divide up functions in administration, whether one should do it by purpose, process, area and so forth, go back to ancient times. To illustrate the problem, should 'defence forces' be divided into land, sea and air (the traditional divisions) or into some other classification, such as 'strategic retaliation forces'/'continental air and missile defence'/'airlifts and sealifts'/'civil defence'/etc.? Traditionally, it was taken for granted that there was 'one best way' to divide up functions.[8] For example, Aristotle took this approach. But nowadays, as we will explain in Chapter 8, the dominant approach by administrative theorists is to stress the extent to which administrative structures are dependent on specific circumstances. To take a simple case, the best shape for a kitchen depends, among other things, upon what you want to cook, which may vary from day to day and from person to person. There is no single optimum.

Obvious as this may seem, the variations in structure demanded by different circumstances are typically not recognized in arguments about the division of labour in administration, which are often conducted in terms of rigid dogma. Very often arguments of this type are basically political. To argue that it is 'administratively' absurd for problem X to be dealt with by n different organizations is a roundabout way of saying that problem X is more important than the problems which are the current prime focus of organization. It is true that there are some supposedly neutral 'principles' of division of work in classical administrative theory, but these principles are multiple and contradictory. The fact that the principles are contradictory does not necessarily mean that they are useless, only that they are limited. A parallel can be drawn with legal decision-making, where there is very often a choice between contradictory alternative legal 'principles' and it is a question of the point at which the 'balance' between opposing concepts shifts. A case in point is the 'principle' of bindingness of contracts and the 'principle' of state sovereignty, which are contradictory in the case of government contracting.[9]

Types of Multi-organizations

The difficulty of dividing policy space into exclusive units creates 'multi-organizations'[10] in functional or policy space in the same way as happens in geographical space. This gives us three possible types of multi-organizations. The simplest case is the geographical one, where administration is divided by area and a single piece of ground extends into a number of contiguous but separate administrative areas. For example, under the old Income Tax system in Britain, land extending into several Income Tax parishes would be taxed separately in each parish, thus involving the unlucky owner or tenant in negotiations with a number of different officials.

The second, intermediate, type of multi-organization is where functional and area agencies get tangled up. For example, the confusion caused by lack of co-ordination between ministries in Nazi Germany was so great that at one point the Economics Ministry created an 'East Department' at the same time that the East Ministry was creating an 'Economics Department'.[11] Similar sorts of problem have arisen with industrial retraining programmes in Britain, where it has turned out that redundant workers in industry A were being retrained for jobs in industry B, while in another part of the country redundant workers in industry B were being retrained for jobs in industry A. This is, of course, the basic theme of many 'funny stories' in administration; and other more mundane examples of overlapping zonal and functional classifications could be given.

The third type of multi-organization is that which arises within a field of purely functional divisions. One case of this is the medical field, where specialisms often overlap and indeed are bound to do so in cases where symptoms are ambiguous. For example, an infectious disease may present the same symptoms as a non-infectious disease, and this means that some patients are bound to be transferred from one medical unit to another as the diagnosis of their problem changes. In practice, this may mean painful and perhaps dangerous ambulance journeys through congested traffic for people who are (by definition) seriously ill. Such problems can be alleviated by aggregating and resiting hospitals, but the problem will never wholly disappear, because diagnosis cannot be an exact science and some hospitals will always be better than others for the treatment of specific medical problems.

As in the example which has just been discussed, the multi-organization problem is in many cases a dilemma. In a situation where there are multiple constraints, it is not easy to find an unambiguously 'best' solution. All that one can do is to find a solution which satisfies all the constraints. Economists have a formal technique for dealing with problems of this type, known as linear programming.[12] In the cases which we have been discussing, the problem is to decide the point at which the removal of an interface in one place will create an equivalent interface somewhere else. Of course, not all divisionalization problems are dilemmas: clearly there are many circumstances in which drawing the boundary in one way will create fewer interfaces than drawing it in another, without removing *every* case where responsibilities overlap. The limiting cases would be, first, the situation where there is one (and only one) arrangement which creates no interfaces. The other limiting case would be the situation where each alternative form of organization would involve exactly the same area of total overlap (or underlap) as every other alternative. The second case is a pure dilemma, comparable to some of the dilemmas of the community principle in area divisionalization which we discussed earlier.

Figure 1 presents a very simple example of a case where policy fields interlock in such a fashion that it is impossible to make any one of them a prime focus of organization without involving at least two administrative units in each of the other two, unless one accepted areas of underlap. It should be pointed out that to count

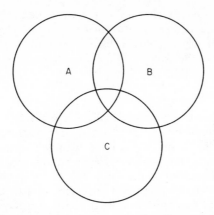

Figure 1. Interlocking policy fields. One cannot have a single agency handling any one of policy fields A, B or C without causing the responsibility for each of the other two policy fields to be divided between at least two agencies

problems like this as dilemmas depends upon two assumptions. The first assumption is that it is impossible to handle all policy problems by a single-all-purpose administrative agency. This is like approaching the furniture arrangement problem by knocking the internal walls of the house down. The second assumption is that the number of agencies which could be created is not unlimited. In other words, one cannot create a separate room for every piece of furniture. If we do not make this assumption, the problem disappears, because in principle, one could simply create a specialized agency for each area of overlap.

These assumptions are usually justified. The one-agency solution can only apply in limited fields; above a certain size of policy responsibility, the single agency would have to be internally departmentalized, and therefore the same problems would simply arise within the agency. So far as the multiple-agency solution is concerned, there are many reasons in practice which limit the proliferations of agencies and which limit the effectiveness of a system composed of a very large number of agencies. At some point, the loss of control over the whole administrative system, the co-ordination difficulties created and the incomprehensibility of the system to a single mind,13 would outweigh the effects of removing interfaces between agencies.

If these two assumptions are accepted, limits of categorization, in the sense of multiple areas of overlap or of underlap between policy problems, are likely to be a very general problem in administration. The same effect is produced if one assumes that alternative modes of categorization can be mutually incompatible in a *conceptual* sense. We will be exploring this idea a little further when we look at the second broad level of administrative categorization, discrimination by the use of language. Moreover, we have been considering the problem so far as the purely geometrical one of finding the pattern which creates the least overlap as compared to the overlaps which would be created by any of the alternative patterns. Obviously, in practice we do not consider merely the 'area of overlap' or underlap in a geometrical sense, even if such areas could be measured in fact. We also think in terms of the relative importance of different types of interfaces, a matter which is usually disputable and which tends to change over time. This introduces some 'non-technical' aspects of the problem, which we will now briefly consider.

'Non-technical' Influences

A variety of 'non-technical' elements complicate the purely technical problems of where to draw administrative boundary lines in a geometrical sense. An important one is the element of inertia and empire-building by administrators. This element is stressed by writers such as Downs who emphasize the importance of career interests as determinants of administrative processes. So far, the problems which we have identified would arise even if members of each administrative unit were assumed to be totally indifferent to how boundaries were drawn or redrawn. In fact, it is much more realistic to assume that administrators will seek to defend and to expand their territories, and dramatic examples of such attitudes by administrators are easy to find. We have already mentioned that the British Surtax Office fought off attempts to dismember it by the general tax inspectorate in 1918, 1925–1926, 1951 and 1960, only succumbing in 1973. An equally striking case is Sir Harold Butler's description of Sir Malcolm Develingue, who was

> 'prepared to die on the steps of the Home Office rather than yield one iota of its prerogatives (in this case, the Factory Acts) to any upstart Department. He defended the fort with such fiery pertinacity and inexhaustible ingenuity that he held it triumphantly.'[14]

This sort of territoriality is very widespread, and it narrows the area of tractability in the arrangement of administrative functions beyond its purely technical limits. Even in the world of research and education, supposedly a domain of pure reason, the division of interconnected knowledge into separate administrative boxes adds career ladder pressures to purely academic considerations as to how the boundary lines should be drawn. In fact, it is often remarked that scientific and artistic innovation typically consists of juxtaposing separated concepts or data, and that consequently the jealously guarded subject areas created by administrative divisionalization can impede innovation as well as developing it. Unless organizations of this type can be kept fluid, they can easily achieve the reverse of their avowed objectives, guarding existing disciplines and attitudes against heretical innovation or cross-fertilization.

Even if the forces of inertia and empire-building do not affect formal structures, they may affect informal practices. That is, informal arrangements may be substituted for formal barriers where formal barriers are removed, with the older structure preserved more or less intact. Experience of such informal practices may partly account for the fact that administrators tend to hold contradictory views about the effects of reorganization. On the one hand, there is the view which was discussed in Chapter 2, that reorganization of too rapid a frequency becomes disruptive. On the other hand there is the view, very strong in administrative folklore if not in textbooks, that basic operating units and social patterns tend to remain in spite of changes higher up. Historical examples in British government are the Poor Law side of the old British Local Government Board and the skeletons of the First World War ministries which were abolished after the war, such as the

Mines Department and the Directorate of National Service, to reappear in the next war and in the subsequent nationalization programme. This feature of administrative change is also brought out very clearly in Dunsire's account of the 'reorganization' of the Ministry of Transport and Civil Aviation in 1959.[15] The contradiction between these two views of the impact of reorganization on the administrative process is a question which deserves more careful research than it has received up to now.

Another 'non-technical' point which has to be considered is that an element of jurisdictional overlap is necessary for many types of administrative control systems to operate. We will be discussing administrative control in Part 3 and overlap is implicit in many of the systems which we will discuss. If there were no duplication at any point (at intra-, inter- or supra-organizational level), everyone would be doing work which no-one else could understand and therefore evaluate. This is the reason for the proliferation of political police forces in many countries, or the parallel hierarchies of party and state officials in the communist countries.

Finally, it may be that the broad problem of non-exclusive categorization and its corollary of multi-organizations is something which varies among the broad fields of administration. For example, in the Betting Tax case which we will consider in Chapter 10, administrative multi-organizations play only a rather peripheral part in the story. On the other hand, anything to do with land or with the 'environment' is typically a multi-organizational problem. At the time of writing, there is a British Ministry titled 'Department of the Environment'. But a true Department of the Environment would have to be a Ministry of Everything. As an American senator once sagely observed, 'The environment . . . is all around us'. More restricted policy fields may involve fewer agencies, but there are always awkward cases, even at a low level. For example, 'rodent control' in Britain has in the past created both central—local interfaces and interfaces between such central government departments as Agriculture, Health, Transport (ships and port sanitary districts) and Public Buildings and Works (Royal Parks, palaces and so on).[16]

Language and Categorization

So far we have been discussing the physical divisibility of administrative structures — lines on maps and physical divisions by geographical area of by 'functional' area, and so on. Such problems of arranging the administrative furniture belong to our first level of categorization — 'spatial' problems — and constitute one type of limit. But there is also the other aspect of the problem, that is, the use of semantic language or of words as a means for discriminating and categorizing.

Modern administration very largely proceeds by the use of words. The whole concept of 'rational—legal' administration (that is, administration under law and administration as a rule-governed activity) rests on the idea of literacy and of written rules, a point emphasized by Max Weber and by most subsequent writers on administration. The ability to write, whether clearly or with deliberate obscurity, has traditionally been hailed as the greatest of bureaucratic virtues. But the influence of semantic language on administrative processes has been very little explored in a systematic way. How far can words be used as a means of administrative control? Is the discriminatory span of words capable of categorizing functional or 'policy' space in an adequate way, particularly in situations where the environment is hostile?

'Lumpiness' and 'Slippage'

A full answer to the question which we have just posed would take us into deep philosophical water. Philosophers of language have puzzled for a long time over problems such as vagueness, context and metaphorical meaning.[17] At first sight, one might say that there is *no* limit to the discriminatory span of natural language. Chomsky asserted that there is no theoretical limit to the number of normal sentences which can be produced in a natural language, and this statement is by now generally familiar.[18] It is also said that the total possible combinations of the number of distinguishable sounds which the vocal apparatus can make is greater than the number of atoms in the universe.[19] But we do not in fact use anything like that amount. This is not accidental. Indeed, one of the defining characteristics of a language (any language) is that it is a finite set of categories, even if those categories are infinitely combinable. Nearly all languages are based on the formal recognition by the society of only 40 or so different sounds.[20]

One of the general problems in using language is therefore that of fitting an infinite experiential universe into a finite set of boxes — 'interpreting' it in terms of those categories. The problem is easiest to see when one is using an artificial language in terms of a very restricted set of categories, and it is also directly applicable to administration, because administrative 'languages' are in many cases artificial. The seven-point scale of the standard 'semantic-differential' test (with categories ranging, for example, from 'excellent' at the top end to 'very bad' at the bottom is a familiar case of an artificial language. The advantages of such a system are obvious; but none of the categories may *quite* express a particular person's feelings on some point, and there are comparable cases in administrative categorization. The problem is perhaps worst where there are only two categories — pass/fail, safe/unsafe, yes/no. Dunsire, exploring the role of language in administration from a slightly different angle, calls either/or choices 'switching choices'.[21]

The problem of categorization is not only encountered in using an artificially restricted set of symbols. There are limits to human capacity for absolute judgment or discrimination which can quite easily be demonstrated, for example, in judgments of pitch, tone or auditory loudness.[22] And things are difficult enough in everyday life. Even our most basic categories (sane—insane, male—female and so on) are more precarious than we would like. In semantics, as in other natural processes, boundaries are where things tend to happen.[23] Consider the problem of defining 'money', a problem which has some administrative significance. It is well known that in some times and places a wide variety of objects have been used as 'money'.[24] A. T. K. Grant remarks

> 'To attempt to draw a frontier between money and near-money is unrealistic; it is in movements across the area where the frontier would lie that significant developments are to be found.'[25]

In other words, 'money is what money does'.[26]

Clearly, it is difficult for an administrator to 'control the money supply' unless he knows what he means by 'money', and the problem arises in many other cases.

Moreover, as we will further explore in the next chapter, there is frequently a built-in dynamic to the ambiguity of language. To an artist or a scientist, it is a familiar experience to be operating on the frontier of the use of language and indeed to be deliberately seeking to dynamite conventional categorizations. William Empson's *Seven Types of Ambiguity*[27] is a classic study of this process as it operates in poetry, and many of his seven types could be identified in the administrative use of language.

It is thus difficult enough to pin meanings on words in everyday matters. Artists blur the distinction between 'art' and 'kitsch' by deliberately introducing elements of 'kitsch' into their work.[28] The upper class have to some extent undermined Professor Ross's famous 'U' and 'Non-U' categories of words and phrases by deliberately adopting 'Non-U' working-class words like 'telly' for TV. As J. L. Austin put it, in the context of philosophy

'The continual discovery of fresh types of nonsense . . . has done, on the whole, nothing but good.'[29]

The point is that our categories are not only finite, they are also relative. There seems to be a basic 'astigmatism' in the way we use words. Words are like stepping stones or the dots on a TV transmission. If one concentrates exclusively on any one of them, it becomes meaningless, just as (to change the simile) a pipe may leak when the pressure is turned up. In fact, linguistic philosophers seem to have concluded that words do not intrinsically mean anything. As Gidon Gottlieb puts it

'Vagueness . . . is always a question of degree; it can never be vanquished.'[30]

Similarly Winograd, exploring natural language from the standpoint of 'robotics', remarks on the contextual nature of interpretation and definitions

'There is no self-contained set of "primitives" from which everything else can be defined. Definitions are circular, with the meaning of each concept depending on the other concepts.'[31]

Context, it seems, is everything. 'Meanings' are the outcome of a complex, ongoing process of social learning. Words can be given exact definitions only in specific contexts and at specified points in time (in fact, they are a useful mirror of social processes).[32] Cresswell has brought out this point exhaustively by pointing out the potential ambiguities in phrases such as 'the love of God' or the use of words such as 'large' (for example, a 'small' elephant is a 'large' animal).[33] With sufficient context and a will to communicate, no problems arise; picked out on their own, such words and phrases are highly ambiguous. Thus as one becomes more proficient in the use of a language, one moves away from pat definitions of a simple lexicographic type (the 'phrase-book' model) towards 'contextual definitions'; that is, the definition of a word by giving a long list of quotations in which it appears, as is the case with the more 'advanced' type of lexicon.[34] One might say that words are symbols, not signs, and that meanings are therefore variables and not values.

Administrative Implications

All this discussion may seem esoteric, a far cry from the 'bread-and-butter' process of administration, but in fact there is an important connection. In administration, words are needed for action, specifically for control, as well as for 'appreciation'. A dispute among paleontologists as to whether dinosaurs should be classified as birds or reptiles is intrinsically interesting and is a process in which academic reputations may rise and fall, but little else is at stake; it does not really matter how long the dispute goes on, or indeed whether the question is ever finally resolved. It makes no difference to the dinosaurs, who have been extinct for over 100,000,000 years. But an administrative dispute such as whether a particular building is an 'industrial building' for the purpose of some policy measure is somewhat different. Such a dispute typically has to be clearly resolved, and in some finite time, because public money or legal status is involved; and moreover it matters quite concretely which category is eventually chosen. Administrators therefore have to proceed on the assumption that words mean something. Empson defines the administrative aspect of knowledge as the 'desire to put the thing known into a coherent structure'.[35]

It is interesting to speculate how far the administrative problems of operating in the context of a living, changing popular language are historically confined to the age of vernacular administrative languages. The classical administrative and liturgical languages – Latin, Sanscrit, Arabic, written Chinese – bore little relation to the language of common speech.[36] But this is not relevant for our present purpose. To examine more fully the difficulties of using language in administrative control, let us take first the 'lumpiness' problem, which is very well known in administration and which can arise in at least two ways. One is through a process which we have already discussed and which could be termed 'discrete banding'. The problem arises where attempts to divide a discrete population of cases into a smaller number of non-incremental 'bands' or groups for the purposes of simplicity, becomes arbitrary and creates absurdities at the margin.

Grouping of this kind can be seen in cases such as the taxation of income or of property, postal charges based on categories of weight, motor tax or fuel ration schemes based on engine capacity, or the division of a multitude of examination results into three or four degree 'classes', as in the British university system. All of these processes involve non-incremental 'banding' and inevitably benefit cases at one or other extreme of each 'band' at the expense of cases at the other end (depending on which way the charging or allocation process is running). The wider the bands, the greater the problem becomes. An example is the division of 'inshore' from 'deep sea' fishing vessels for the purpose of subsidization in Britain. 'Inshore' vessels (which receive subsidies different to those received by other vessels) are arbitrarily defined as vessels of less than 70 feet in length. But some boats longer than 70 feet fish 'inshore' and some shorter vessels fish in 'deep sea' waters. Similar anomalies can be picked out of most fields of administration. But to abandon arbitrary rules of thumb may be to turn every issue into a complicated philosophical debate.

The other aspect of the 'lumpiness' problem is logically similar but perhaps deserves to be mentioned separately. That is the question of 'cut-off' points. As we have already pointed out, it is very common in administration to exclude the smallest operations from the administrative net, on the *de minimis* principle. In Britain the *de minimis* principle is extended to measures such as price control schemes, industrial training levies, taxation and many types of regulation. Enterprises of less than a defined size are excluded. But any cut-off point is inevitably arbitrary, and it also opens up the danger that large operations will (purely formally) split themselves up into a number of small operations of less than the defined minimum size, in an attempt to escape control. This occurred to some extent with the American price control machinery in the early 1970s, and, as we will see in Chapter 6, the fear that the same thing would happen in land taxation has repeatedly led the British authorities to saddle themselves with an unpopular and unproductive burden of 'back garden' cases. We will also see in Chapter 10 that a variant of the problem occurred as a result of a political decision to tax only 'legal' bookmakers in the British betting tax of the 1920s.

'Slippage, too, is at least an equally difficult problem in administrative language. In perfect administration, orders could be specified unambiguously. But, as we saw in the previous section, language is highly ambiguous even in the ordinary process of social intercourse. We cope with this problem in ordinary conversation because of a will to communicate.[37] But in a recalcitrant system, where there is no will to communicate, ambiguities in language will be exploited to the full. This is aggravated by a fact mentioned earlier: to avoid arbitrariness, administrative 'acts' have to be based on a formal or artificial language, not on 'native wit and common sense'. This induces a condition comparable to paranoid schizophrenia in individuals; that is, incoming stimuli either fit into rigid preconceived categories or else do not exist.[38] There is no automatic process for adjusting the categories in the light of experience (or of 'common sense') as happens with 'normal' individuals.

In perfect administration, information transmission is perfect: that is, each unit receives and transmits data that requires minimal or no 'interpretation'. This minimizes discretion, litigation and argument.[39] But 'in war the simplest things become difficult'.[40] We think that we know what we mean by words such as 'region', 'army', 'speculator' and the like, but when we base administrative operations on such words, their inherent vagueness quickly becomes apparent. For example, after Napoleon's victory at Jena in 1806, the French limited the size of the Prussian 'army' to 42,000 men. The Prussians in large part circumvented this restriction by resorting to a system of three-year military service for each adult male. This meant that at no time did the Prussian (standing) 'army' exceed the limit; but the (reserve) 'army' was steadily expanded.[41]

The same problem recurs at less exalted levels of implementation. *Omnis definitio periculosa est*. In some cases, the problems are obvious. To take a comical one, some years ago the Zanzibari authorities banned the wearing of 'see-through' shirts by Zanzibari women. But how do you define 'see-through' unambiguously? Most shirts are 'see-through' in some sense. In France, similar problems have arisen in defining 'veterans', 'games of chance', 'dangerous buildings' and in drawing distinctions such as those between 'luxury' and 'ordinary' hotels, or between 'scientific articles' and 'polemics'.[42] Similarly, subtle distinctions such as that between 'earned' and 'unearned' income for taxation purposes, generate absurdities very easily. For example, occupational pensions count as 'earned' income, whereas old people who have provided their own 'pension fund' in the form of life savings are in some cases taxed as if this income were 'unearned'.

Even the most obvious-seeming classicicatory scheme may break down under pressure. Even the old Window-tax, according to Dowell, became difficult to administer in consequence of the disputes which arose regarding what was and what was not considered to a 'window'.[43] Similarly, a 'jacket' proved to be impossible to define for Purchase Tax purposes. 'Children's clothing' is another persistent bone in the official throat, since large 'children' and small 'adults' overlap in physical dimensions, particularly in the context of improving nutritional standards which mean that adolescents will tend to be taller than their parents. Other problems can occur with the vagaries of the human shape. For example, in 1973 the waist measurement of the then current 'Miss World' was that of the average young girl of 12.[44]

There are a host of comparable problems. For example, is a 'garage' grown from a privet hedge trained over a wooden frame a 'growth' or a 'construction'? Such a case arose with respect to planning permission in Hertfordshire in 1969.[44] Are umbrellas 'clothing'? Are sweets 'food'? Is 'turtle flesh' 'seafood' or 'reptile meat'? Not all such cases are as trivial as the examples given above may appear: in Nazi Germany, for a person of mixed blood to be defined as a 'Jew' or 'non-Jew' was literally a matter of life or death.[45] And all of these issues have potentially deep philosophical undertones. A full definition of food would have to take into account all the ways in which eccentric or extraordinary people may sustain themselves. Such a definition would also run into difficult border country between 'eating' and 'drinking' (we 'drink' soup but is it 'food'?) and between what is eatable and what is edible. Much of the world is edible. But it is not 'food'.

In 99 cases out of 100, no philosophical analysis is in fact required, because it does not really matter which of two or more overlapping categories an awkward case is put into. But in other cases, the undermining of some apparently innocent distinction may cause an administrative 'dam' to break. As we will see in Chapter 10, this happened in Britain in the early 1960s, when the precarious distinction between commercial gaming establishments and non-commercial 'clubs' broke down (as also happened in the case of cinema 'clubs' showing uncensored pornographic films) and a tidal wave of commercial bingo halls and gaming clubs swept across Britain. There are genuine fears that similar problems may apply to the difference between 'hard' and 'soft' drugs in relation to the debate about differentiating the legal position of the two types of drugs. The border country between 'drugs' and items like shoe polish and household glue is itself a very difficult area. For example, persistent glue sniffing gives a mild 'kick' and can damage the brain cells. The problem occurs in a different context with censorship and the prohibition of 'corrupting' material. As Brown has pointed out, nothing is totally innocent.[46]

Clearly in such cases, we are not facing merely 'honest perplexity', but also the ambiguities which are created with deliberate human ingenuity. The extreme form of such ingenuity is Empson's case of Shakespeare's puns, which make a single word or phrase have half-a-dozen possible meanings, dependent upon which context you take, to the point where the structure of language begins to be threatened. Nothing so elegant is usually to be found in the administrative process, but the same basic forces are at work. The result is that strain is thrown upon words in administration, and steadily more refined definitions have to be invented. Sir Ernest Gowers discussed this problem in his famous *Plain Words*,[47] showing how attempts to keep administrative language simple fail because people devise ways of becoming 'invisible' to the law or to the regulations, if not to 'common sense'. Indeed, there are situations in which simplification can be achieved by more complexity in the sense of inventing new categories. An example is the British 1971 Immigration Act, which was an attempt to reduce the confusion of earlier immigration laws by defining more precisely the concept of UK citizenship. The result was that the Act produced no less than six different degrees of 'foreign-ness' (that is, patrial Commonwealth citizens, non-patrial Commonwealth citizens with a UK grandparent, citizens of the Irish Republic, EEC nationals, non-patrial Commonwealth citizens without a UK grandparent and 'the rest').

'Officialese' and legal English are thus in large part the result of an effort to plug all the bolt-holes. It must be admitted that an official style of hollow pomposity is something which is often resorted to out of a desire to paper over cracks or to conceal inconsistencies. Nevertheless, as Sir Ernest Gowers pointed out, it is not merely gratuitous pomposity or love of obscurity which turns familiar words like 'crops' into ponderous legal/administrative phrases like 'unsevered vegetable growth', but the need for precision in the context of recalcitrance. The tax system is particularly rich in examples of this process. As Sir Joseph Stamp put it (in 1915)

'To expect a tax form which shall read like a pill advertisement on the railway, and yet close down on everyone, is asking for the moon'.[48]

Judges and lawyers often lament the increasing proliferation of detail rather than of broad 'principle' in statute laws. As Burdeau put it 'Les lois ne sont plus des principes, mais des solutions'.[49] But the motivation for such proliferating detail is precisely the desire to avoid obstacles to policy implementation in the form of adverse court decisions, such as we will see in the Land Tax case of Chapter 6 and in the Betting Tax case in Chapter 10. True, the tactic of proliferating detail is frequently counter-productive in this respect. But that is a slightly different argument.

The ingenuity involved in 'officialese' may be perverse, but it is still ingenuity. Very largely, what is involved is a process of complex 'stipulative definitions', that is 'deeming' things to be other things for legal or administrative purposes. Examples are the concept of property which is 'deemed' to pass at death even if it does not in fact do so, property which is not 'deemed' to be disposed (for example, as security for debt), income which is not 'deemed' to be income, as in the case of gambling winnings; and so on. Lord Justice Emslie has parodied this sort of ingenuity as follows

'In the Nuts (unground) (other than ground nuts) Order the expression nuts shall have reference to such nuts, other than ground nuts, as would but for this amending Order not qualify as nuts (unground) (other than ground nuts) by reason of their being nuts (unground).'[50]

One associates this kind of thing with the complexities of modern life, but there are also historical parallels. It is interesting to note from English history that even such early taxes as the Saladin Tithe of 1188, the poll-tax of 1377, even the old Dane-geld, were surprisingly complex in terms of the exemptions and abatements which they contained.[51] More recently the 1806 Income Tax Act ran to 300 yards of parchment,[52] and the 1952 Consolidated Income Tax Act was bigger than the Bible. The resemblance to a 'pill advertisement', it seems, is becoming steadily fainter.

Another set of definitional problems is provided by 'sets' of objects, particularly where the 'set' invites different treatment, or commands a different price, than its individual units. We will see an interesting case of this in the Betting Tax case, but a much better-known example is the treatment of families in taxation or in social administration. The authorities pursue cases of 'fictitious desertion' of spouses in order to check on social security fraud by allegedly single women, and similarly the authorities may have to take account of the family as a taxable unit in order to counter income-splitting, that is, the spreading of income or of wealth around all members of the family equally in order to minimize tax liability. It is difficult to underestimate the complexities which such tactics introduce into tax legislation.

Similar problems arise where administrative authorities cannot use operational definitions for other than linguistic reasons. This may come about either because the concepts which are being employed refer to motives or intentions (which usually cannot be proved) or for other reasons have to rely in practice on circumstantial evidence rather than on direct verification. Again, this applies to the concept of 'co-habitation with a man' which constitutes a bar to eligibility for social security benefits for unmarried or separated women in Britain.

The role of technology in the process of generating ambiguity is not very clear. Administrative distinctions may be undermined by the ambiguity inherent in language without obvious technological change. The famous psychologist Pavlov produced 'experimental neurosis' in dogs by making steadily more ambiguous the distinctions between those symbols which represented food and those which represented pain.[53] The same kind of thing can happen with administrative distinctions. For example, where tax preference is given to 'capital' as against 'income', the distinction between the two may break down, because, the shorter the period of retention, the more a capital profit approximates to income. Hence the invention of the hybrid concept of 'capital gains' as a subject for taxation. Moreover, technical innovation almost always threatens conceptual boundaries. For example, when Blériot landed in England after the first cross-Channel flight, he was treated as a 'yachtsman' by the British Customs officials.[54] Since then the development of flying boats and hovercraft have challenged the administrative distinction between aircraft and ships,[55] and, more recently, offshore oil rigs have presented a problem — are they 'islands' or 'ships'?

It is easy to become punch-drunk by so many niggling cases of lumpy, leaky and slippery categories. Can natural language ever be an adequate tool for controlling a hopelessly complex environment? But to some extent it is a tautology to say that we cannot categorize things because they are 'complex'. The 'simplest' things can be 'complex' unless we know how to handle them. In fact, the problems of 'lumpiness' and 'slippage' are caused by a special type of complexity, that of ambiguity and changefulness. Complexity of this type does not lie in the number of items involved, but rather in the range of variation of those items. Thus, as we have already mentioned, a system with many categories may in a sense be less complex than a system with fewer categories and a greater propensity to produce 'hard cases', such as 'switching choices'.

Other Problems

Apart from 'lumpiness' and 'slippage', there are two other related problems in the use of language and categorization. First, it takes time to change from one set of categories to another; and second, alternative categorizations may be mutually exclusive.

So far as the first problem is concerned, the impact of the 'time dimension' on administrative processes will be explored more closely in the next chapter, so the point appears here simply for the sake of completeness. At this stage, the discussion is concerned largely with the 'space' rather than the 'time' dimensions of perfect administration, insofar as the two can be separated. We are imagining ourselves in a timeless world, like the Mad Hatter's tea party in *Alice in Wonderland*,[56] where it is always six o'clock. There are all sorts of paradoxes in such an assumption, of course.

Second, there is the problem that alternative categorizations may be mutually exclusive. The stock psychological example of this problem is the 'Necker Cube', a tilted three-dimensional cube drawn on a flat surface in such a way that there are two incompatible ways of 'seeing' the cube.[57] There are other famous *Gestalt* figures, where you 'see' the figure either as one shape or as another, but you cannot see both at once. Categorization, too, can take mutually exclusive forms.

We have already discussed the problem of incompatible forms of ordering where categorization is a physical process taking place in geometrical space. But whereas mutually exclusive categorization is more or less inherent in physical categorization, it is not necessarily so in cases where categorization is an analytical or symbolic process. In some cases it may be possible to have multiple systems of categorization. For example, a collection of books can be classified by author, title, date and so forth, though the number of possible ways in which the books can be physically arranged at any one time is more limited. Similarly with modern data retrieval systems, customer accounts (for example) can be simultaneously classified by name, address, account number and so forth. Again, it is possible to have 'programme' and 'line-item' budgeting systems existing side by side for 'management' and 'fiscal' control, respectively, as happens in some British government departments.

But mutually exclusive categorizations for operational purposes are probably the more typical cases. In such cases, the problems of one scheme of categorization may only be solved at the cost of accepting the problems of a mutually exclusive alternative scheme, replacing one kind of anomaly by another. We saw this in discussing internal structuring arrangements of administrative organizations, in terms of the dilemmas which can occur between alternative arrangements in functional space. The same thing can occur with the conceptual classifications of cases and categories in administrative operations. A case illustrating this problem, the British wartime Purchase Tax/Utility scheme, is described at the end of this chapter.

One way of handling alternatives which cannot be espoused simultaneously is to take them sequentially.[58] For example, rather than having a single fixed capital city, early medieval kings typically had a 'travelling centre', which avoided the problem of where to locate the seat of government. Pettigrew suggests that 'incompatible requirements in social structures lead to recurrent reorganizations',[59] but in fact clear examples of sequential solutions to functional or spatial dilemmas are rather hard to find. Still, it may be that some reorganization cycles, both at the level of patterns of administrative organization and of actual policies pursued, may be interpreted as oscillations between contradictory alternatives. But we will not dwell on this point, because it once more introduces a time dimension.

A final type of 'incompatibility' which may arise is not between logical alternatives but between different 'levels' in an administrative system, for example in reconciling 'internal' and 'external' languages. It is easy to find relatively superficial cases of this, such as the familiar difficulty of translating the internal language of some administrative area, such as income tax or social security, into something resembling common speech at points where the 'lay public' have to give information or to fill in forms: hence the persistent complaints about the complexity and unintelligibility of such forms. The problem also arises in cases such as slum clearance or compulsory purchase procedures for land where local authorities' stress on legal correctness make official forms seem 'obscure and peremptory' to the general public.[60] The same thing may occur, of course, where forms are geared to an automatic data processing system.

There is also a 'deeper' sense in which incompatibilities between the languages of 'levels' or of horizontal groups may arise. It is pointed out by authors approaching the problem from the point of view of cybernetics, such as Dunsire[61] or Pelikan,[62] who see the problem of reconciling languages as one of the critical bottlenecks in administrative processes. Highly simplified, the argument proceeds in two stages.

First, the discriminatory power of any single administrator is finite, for either or both of two reasons. In the first place, there are limits to absolute judgment, which we have already mentioned. In the second place, there is limited time. An individual or group can either discriminate finely within a restricted area of commodity space, or discriminate shallowly over a wider area. It is a common enough observation that languages, particularly in simple societies, tend to allocate space to items according to social importance: if pigs are important, there are many words to denote the different types of pigs; if cattle are important, there are many words for cattle; and so on.[63] But a language which distinguished many sub-types of all objects could scarcely be spoken by an ordinary person. An individual cannot 'pan' and 'zoom' at the same time. His indexical span is limited.

The problem of central control then arises in terms of relating one type of 'shop talk' to another type of 'shop talk' and of relating all types of 'shop talk' to the language of common speech, which by definition is the highest common factor of all types of shop talk. In Pelikan's case of economic planning, the central allocation agency must apply its indexical span to deal with broad aggregates and thus it cannot issue precise orders to the units working within each category. As Török puts it

'necessarily laconic general definition cannot express all aspects of a given technical term as used in practice, and not even a general definition reflecting all aspects can directly be applied to all concrete spheres'.[64]

Moreover, the problem logically cannot be solved by importing into the central agency 'expertise' on each minute area, since this would make the central agency itself so large that another agency would be needed to co-ordinate the first one, and the problem would then occur at another level. Downs calls this the 'Law of Imperfect Control.'[65]

Stated baldly, this argument is by no means new, and it is closely similar to the arguments advanced against 'reductionism' in science, the idea that all scientific phenomena can be reduced to the language of physics or chemistry. In large part, it reinforces an argument put forward by cybernetic theorists, that attempts at synoptic command processes are likely to be either ineffective or self-defeating, except in fairly simple systems, for example where materials are very restricted, as in the British World War II utility schemes which will now be briefly described.

The Life and Death of the British Purchase Tax/Utility Scheme

The British utility schemes encountered a number of the categorization problems which have been discussed in this chapter. The schemes were introduced in the early 1940s, when physical rationing of materials had encouraged manufacturers to concentrate on high-quality, high-price articles (expecially in clothing) and thus created shortages of the cheaper types of necessary goods. The utility schemes were based on strict specifications of materials for 'standard' goods of a 'necessary' type. Design specifications were also included in the case of furniture, since timber was in particularly short supply. These physical specifications were accompanied by two other elements, that is, price control and exemption from Purchase Tax, a heavy direct tax on a wide range of goods which was introduced in 1940 and was collected from wholesalers or manufacturers. Exemption from Purchase Tax was the 'carrot' for manufacturers to produce goods to utility specifications, and with rigid specifications for goods, it was relatively easy to control prices.[66]

The system threw up many difficulties even in the wartime context. For example, such workaday garments as Wellington boots and industrial protective clothing were excluded from the utility schemes and carried Purchase Tax, whereas scarcely 'necessary' goods like evening clothes and dance shoes were utility and therefore free of tax. Similarly, the economic balance between closely competing alternatives, or firms, could be severely distorted by the side of the Purchase Tax/Utility line upon which they happened to fall. For example, oil cloth is normally cheaper than the cheapest types of cotton cloth, but it happened to fall on the other side of the utility line (for purely fortuitous reasons) and therefore carried Purchase Tax of $66^2/3$ per cent.

There was also a 'lumpiness' problem. The arbitrary cut-off point for tax exemption, which was implied by the price controls on utility goods, penalized goods which were produced at just above the maximum price, which meant that non-utility goods were excessively dear. This had export implications in the post-war period. Moreover, the relative position of this cut-off point differed unfairly between products. For example, in footwear the utility (and tax exemption) price maximum was very high, whereas it was very low in the case of men's trousers.

In the post-war period, these difficulties became much greater. The reason was the greater quantities and varieties of raw materials which became available, the existence of a greater variety of manufacturing processing alternatives owing to the release of machinery from war production, and the expansion of foreign trade. The basic problem was that the grant of utility status to a product was an automatic key to Purchase Tax exemption. As a result, the Board of Trade faced an increasing flood of applications from firms for the inclusion of more products under utility schemes. These applications were hard to resist because of considerations of equity, as in the cases of anomaly which were described in the previous paragraph. Consequently, the Board of Trade had to produce more and more specifications of nearly-similar products. For example, by 1952, there were over 1,000 specifications for non-wool cloth, 531 for boys' underpants and 781 for men's shirts.

Such pressures became so great that strict specification began to be abandoned in the late 1940s, for example in footwear and furniture design in 1948 and in hosiery and knitwear in 1950. Strict specification was replaced by broad descriptions of products, allowing a considerable range of variation. This change removed the linch-pin of the utility schemes, severely weakening the price and quality control machinery and making the whole system increasingly difficult to police adequately. There also developed the additional threat of reciprocal trade discrimination by many of Britain's trading partners, who regarded the Purchase Tax/Utility scheme as an unfair means of taxing imports. As a result of all of these pressures, the link between the Purchase Tax system and what remained of the utility schemes was severed in 1952.[67] Instead, Purchase Tax was levied on a range of specified goods of both utility and non-utility types. In fact, the tax was charged on the excess, if any, of the value of the article over a tax-free limit, which also removed the 'lumpiness' problems which were described earlier. In practice, this was the end of the utility system.

This case is one of many which could have been taken to illustrate the 'structural plateaux' which can be reached by administrative categorizations. There are some relatively 'objective' and fixed limits of categorization, notably the 'furniture arrangement' dilemmas which we discussed earlier. But there are also limits of categorization dependent upon particular circumstances, in particular the changefulness and hostility of the system under control. Once limits of the second type begin to operate, the problem ceases to differ from that of the effectiveness of administrative control systems in general, which we will discuss in Part 3: control becomes a matter of motivation and of the manipulation of roles rather than of 'correct wording'. Hence the apparent paradox that some taxes are able to operate without strictly defining the object to be taxed at all. 'Income', the basis of the Income Tax, and 'bets', the basis of the Betting Tax, have never been statutorily defined in Britain.

Conclusion

We have discussed five main limits of categorization in this chapter — lumpiness, slippage, the time required for recategorization, mutually incompatible categorizations and problems of reconciling internal and external languages. These problems have been very little examined in a general way. Arguments about limits to administrative processes arising out of limits to communications channels in an *engineering* sense, are now fairly well-established. But the possibility that there might be semantic (and semantic-type) limits to administrative processes, has hardly been explored. This is strange: 'lumpiness', 'slippage' and incompatibility of categorization are immediately familiar as administrative problems and would be even in an imaginary world which offered no resistance to administrative authorities — one of the requirements of 'perfect administration' in Chapter 1. When one adds the element of deliberate human ingenuity in resisting the categorizations of the authorities, it is clear that many categorizations rely in large part upon the stupidity and inertia of their potential enemies.

As we mentioned earlier, it is very difficult to discuss 'time problems' and 'space problems' independently. Many supposedly 'spatial' problems are in large part a function of time. For example, as Betrand Russell pointed out, central—local problems arise basically because messages travel faster than men.[68] In the next chapter, we will look more carefully at the time dimension. As we will see, the effect of overlaying 'time' on 'space' in many cases is to narrow further the limits of categorization in the context of recalcitrance.

Notes

1. Gaus, J., *Reflections on Public Administration*, University of Alabama Press, Alabama, 1947.
2. Legendre, P., *Histoire de l'Administration de 1973 a Nos Jours*, Presses Universitaires de France, Vendôme, 1968.
3. Wells, H. G., 'A paper on administrative areas read before the Fabian Society' (1903), reprinted in A. Maas, *Area and Power*, The Free Press, Glencoe, 1959.
4. de Jouvenel, B., *The Pure Theory of Politics*, Cambridge University Press, Cambridge, 1963, pp. 208—210.
5. cf. Giglioli, P. P. (Ed.), *Language and Social Context*, Penguin Books, Harmondsworth, 1972.
6. Downs, A., *Inside Bureaucracy*, Wiley, New York, 1967.
7. Randall, R., 'Influence of environmental support and policy space on organizational behaviour', *Administrative Science Quarterly*, 19, 1974.
8. cf. Simon, H. A., *Administrative Behaviour*, 2nd ed., Free Press, New York, 1965.
9. cf. Mitchell, J. D. B., *The Contracts of Public Authorities*, G. Bell and Sons, London, 1954.
10. cf. Stringer, J., 'Operational research for multi-organizations', *Operational Research Quarterly*, 18, 1967; J. K. Friend and J. M. H. Hunter in 'Multi-organizational decision process in the planned expansion of towns', *Environment and Planning* 1970, Vol. 2, pp. 33—54.
11. Peterson, E. N., *The Limits of Hitler's Power*, Princeton University Press, New Jersey, 1969.
12. Vajda, S., *The Theory of Games and Linear Programming*, Science Paperbacks, London, 1967; T. H. Naylor and E. T. Byrne, *Linear Programming*, Wadsworth Publishing Co., Belmont, 1963.
13. March, J. G., and H. A. Simon, *Organizations*, Wiley, New York, 1958.
14. Butler, Sir Harold, *Confident Morning*, quoted in F. M. G. Willson and D. N. Chester, *The Organization of British Central Government 1916—1965*, Allen and Unwin, London, 1957, p. 82.
15. Dunsire, A., 'The passing of the Ministry of Transport and civil aviation', *Public Law*, 1961, pp. 150—164, cf. the discussion of reorganization in W. J. M. Mackenzie and J. Grove, *Central Adminstration in Britain*, Longmans, London, 1957.
16. cf. Willson, F. M. G., and D. N. Chester, *op. cit.*
17. cf. Cresswell, M. J., *Logics and Languages*, Methuen, London, 1973.
18. cf. Greene, J., *Psycho Linguistics*, Penguin Books, Harmondsworth, 1972; Y. Bar-Hillel, *Language and Information*, Addison-Wesley, Reading, Mass., 1964, p. 224.
19. Birdwhistell, R. L., *Kinesics and Context*, Allen Lane Penguin Press, London, 1971; T. Schwenk, *Sensitive Chaos*, Rudolph Steiner Press, London, 1965.
20. Giglioli, P. P. (Ed.), *op. cit.*, p. 326.
21. Dunsire, A., 'The theory of the superior—subordinate relationship in a bureaucracy', paper presented at Warsaw Conference of the European Group of Public Administration, Internationsl Institue of Administrative Sciences, 24—28 June 1975, p. 9.
22. cf. Miller, G. A., *The Psychology of Communication*, Penguin, London, 1963.
23. cf. Schwenk, T., *op. cit.*

24. Keynes, J. M., *A Treatise on Money*, 2 vols., Macmillan, London, 1930, p. 291, fn. 1.
25. Grant, A. T. K., *The Strategy of Financial Pressure*, Macmillan, London, 1972, p. 112.
26. Reynolds, L. G., *Economics: A General Introduction*, R. D. Irwon Inc., Illinois, 1963, p. 474, quoted in G. Dalton, *Tribal and Peasant Economies*, The Natural History Press, New York, 1967, pp. 280–281.
27. Empson, W., *Seven Types of Ambiguity*, Chatto and Windus, London, 1930.
28. Dorfles, G., *Kitsch: An Anthology of Bad Taste*, Studio Vista, London, 1969.
29. Austin, J. L., *Sense and Sensibilia*, Clarendon, Oxford, 1962, p. 2.
30. Gottlieb, G., *The Logic of Choice*, Allen and Unwin, London, 1968, p. 49.
31. Winograd, T., *Understanding Natural Language*, Edinburgh University Press, Edinburgh, 1972, p. 26.
32. cf. Barker, Sir E., *Traditions of Civility*, Cambridge University Press, Cambridge, 1948, p. 125, fn. 1.
33. Cresswell, M. J., *op. cit.*
34. cf. Mackenzie, W. J. M., *Power Violence Decision*, Penguin Books, Harmondsworth, 1975.
35. cf. Empson, W., *op. cit.*, p. 319.
36. cf. Giglioli, P. P., *op. cit.*, p. 222.
37. cf. Hoggart, R., *Speaking to Each Other*, Chatto and Windus, London, 1970.
38. cf. McGhie, A., *Pathology of Attention*, Penguin Books, Harmondsworth, 1969.
39. cf. Feit, E., 'Insurgency in Organizations: A Theoretical Analysis', *General Systems Handbook*, 1969, pp. 157–168.
40. Von Clausewitz, C., *On War* (Ed. A. Rapoport), Penguin Books, Harmondsworth, 1968.
41. cf. Barker, Sir E., *The Development of the Public Services in Western Europe, 1660–1930*, Oxford University Press, London, 1944.
42. Stassinopoulis, M., *Traité des Actes Administratifs* (Preface de Rene Cassin), Athens 1954, p. 149; C. S. Shoup, *The Sales Tax in France*, Columbia University Press, New York, 1930.
43. Dowell, S., *A History of Taxation and Taxes in England*, Longmans, London 1884, 4 Vols.
44. *The Times*, 7 March 1973.
45. *The Times*, 6 January 1969.
46. Brown, J. A. C., *Techniques of Persuasion*, Penguin Books, Harmondsworth, 1963.
47. Gowers, Sir E., *Plain Words*, HMSO, London 1948, pp, 6–10.
48. Quoted by Sir E. Gowers 'Mainly about the King's English', *Public Administration*, Vol. 7, 1929, p. 191.
49. Quoted by P. Legendre, *op. cit.*, p. 463.
50. Lord Justice Emslie, 'The role of judges in society in Scotland', Address to the Aviemore Conference of the Law Society of Scotland, 19 May 1974.
51. cf. Mitchell, S. K. (Ed. S. Painter), *Taxation in Medieval England*, Yale University Press, New Haven, 1951.
52. Hope-Jones, A., *Income Tax in the Napoleonic Wars*, Cambridge University Press, Cambridge, 1939.
53. Cuny, H., *Ivan Pavlov: The Man and His Theories*, trans. P. Evans, Souvenir Press, London, 1964, Chap. 4, pp. 114–117.
54. Crombie, Sir J., *HM Customs and Excise*, Allen and Unwin, London, 1961 (New Whitehall Series).
55. cf. Gottlieb, G., *op. cit.*
56. Carroll, L., *The Annotated Alice* (Ed. M. Gardner), Penguin Books, Harmondsworth, 1970, p. 99, note 8.
57. For the 'Necker cube', see R. L. Gregory, *Eye and Brain*, Weidenfeld and Nicholson, London, 1966, p. 12, figs. 1–4.
58. cf. Cyert, R., and J. March's discussion of the 'sequential' treatment of conflicting goals in *A Behavioral Theory of the Firm*, Prentice-Hall, Englewood Cliffs, 1963.
59. Pettigrew, A., *The Politics of Organizational Decision-Making*, Tavistock, London, 1973.
60. Norman, P., and J. English, 'An appraisal of slum clearance procedures in England and Wales', *University of Glasgow Discussion Paper in Social Research*, No. 4.
61. Dunsire, A., *op. cit.*
62. Pelikan, P., 'Language as a hidden parameter: some notes on the pattern of centralization vs. decentralization' unpublished paper, Prague School of Economics, 1968.

63. Giglioli, P. P., *op. cit.*, p. 314.
64. Török, L., *The Socialist System of State Control*, Akademiai Kiado, Budapest, 1974.
65. Downs, A., *op. cit.*
66. *Report of the Purchase Tax/Utility Committee*, Cmd. 8452, 1952.
67. *Report of the Purchase Tax (Valuation) Committee*, Cmd. 8830, 1953; *Report of the Committee on Tax-Paid Stocks*, Cmd. 8784, 1953.
68. Russell, B., *Power: A New Social Analysis*, Unwin Books, London, 1960.

Chapter 5

Learning and Counter-Learning

'That things not only alter but improve is . . . the boldest of evolution-
ary conceptions . . . but I for one imagine that a pterodactyl flew no
less well than does an albatross and that Old Red Sandstone fishes
swam as well and easily as the fishes of our own seas.' D'Arcy
Wentworth Thompson, *On Growth and Form*, abridged edition by
J. T. Bonner, Cambridge University Press, Cambridge, 1966, p. 201.

In the last chapter we considered some of the problems of administrative
categorization in space, conceiving space as relatively 'timeless' for the purpose of
simplification. But it was impossible to avoid introducing time into the discussion
at various points. For example, many of the ambiguities which were discussed can
only work themselves out in time.

The impact of the time dimension will now be examined more explicitly. Perfect
administration, as we saw in Chapter 1, requires the absence of time pressure. In
reality, time pressure and rapid change are a dominant feature of many
administrative processes, and it is a cliché that 'we live in an age of rapid change'.[1]
What problems does the relaxation of the time requirement of perfect administration introduce? In Chapter 2 we discussed some of the ways in which the time
element can limit administrative capacity, particularly the 'leads' and 'lags' problem
of administrative adaptation and reorganization problems.

A time dimension is not *always* a handicap in administration. In some cases it is
an advantage: it offers possibilities of adopting incompatible alternatives sequentially, of improving knowledge or performance through time, and of using delaying
tactics (such as file-passing or hair-splitting). Delay is often described as one of the
most powerful administrative weapons. But in this chapter we will concentrate on
the ways in which administrative activities can be hampered by the time factor, and
indeed all the weapons which the time dimension affords to administrators are
double-edged. For example, we will see later that delay can be used against
administrators as well as by them, particularly by the use of judicial or
administrative appeals machinery as a means of 'buying time'.[2]

Models of Administrative Learning

The general problem of change, adaptivity, learning and 'unlearning' dominates
much of the modern literature on organization and administration. To a large
extent this reflects the historical context of the late twentieth century. On the one
hand, there has been the development of organizations which are very large by

historical standards in the spheres of production and of general administration; on the other hand, there has been an accelerating pace of socio-technical change as measured by indicators such as population, communications, ability to travel at speed and so on.[3] Everybody has their own favourite example of this process. One is the development of military rifles and the adoption of armies of new types of rifle. Formerly, this pace was extremely slow: as Thayer remarks, it took a century for the match-lock rifle to be replaced by the wheel-lock, 200 years for the wheel-lock to give way to the flint-lock, and another century for the flint-lock to be replaced in turn by the percussion cap rifle.[4] Nowadays a military rifle may be obsolete in a decade.

So widespread is this process of exponential change that the older style of discussing piecemeal the specific reforms in organization which are demanded by a particular set of changed circumstances (for example, the adaptation of tax administration to an increasingly national rather than localized economy, in which information about a person's financial affairs becomes decreasingly likely to be contained within the confines of a single parish) has been supplemented by a body of writing discussing adaptivity as such. For example, Simon,[5] Bennis,[6] Cyert and March,[7] Vickers,[8] Mackenzie,[9] Beer[10] and others have all argued that maximum flexibility must be the watchword in a situation where omniscience is unattainable. One could almost speak of a 'cult of adaptivity', which clearly to some extent is a reaction to an earlier cult of long-range planning.

In exploring the possible mechanisms by which organizations might 'learn' or adapt, writers have taken various analogies to use as models. The two most powerful ones are the model of adaptation by competition and the model of individual organisms as learning systems. Both of these analogies have been presented in various forms as prescriptive models as well as guides to understanding. We will encounter both kinds of model again when we come to discuss control systems in a more general sense in Part 3.

The first model is drawn from the effects of competitive social processes through successive time-periods, such as in the process of natural selection in biological evolution or in the process of competitive markets in economics. Adaptive mechanisms of this type are clearly relatively weak in bureaucratic structures of the classic type and particularly in public administration, owing to the relative absence of market control and of competition, except by war and by international competition. The application of economic 'market-type' analysis to administrative processes by writers such as Downs[11] and Tullock[12] has brought out this point sharply, and many such economic analysts see the faults of 'bureaucracy' as basically derived from the lack of exposure to an adaptive medium of the market type. These ideas, of course, have prescriptive implications. For example, Niskanen[13] and Wagner[14] advocate the reversal of the bureaucratic doctrine of avoiding competition and overlapping under all circumstances, as a means of promoting adaptation through competition.

Such models have received little explicit challenge. But in fact there is a group of arguments stressing that the adaptation brought about by market processes may be 'dysfunctional' in some circumstances, particularly where markets are in some way 'imperfect'. A fairly recent example is Hirschman's analysis of 'exit voice and loyalty',[15] which applies particularly to organizations providing services of a collective kind, such as insurance, public transport or postal services. As a means of improving the performance of such organizations through time, consumer behaviour of a purely market type (switching to another supplier) rather than 'protest and loyalty' may be negatively effective. If people respond to failure by seeking alternative sources of supply in sufficient numbers, performance may worsen, not improve. Prices rise, standards drop, a vicious circle develops between desertion by consumers and worsening performance, and there are circumstances in which such changes can be irreversible. Probably this kind of 'dysfunctional adaptation' is largely confined to economic processes, but cases of a similar type have been known to take the place in biological adaptation, for example, where 'demands' for greater sexual attractiveness compete with other functional 'demands', as in some cases of tail plumage.[16]

The alternative 'model' to that of competitive social processes is the analogy of learning by individual organisms or machines. A set of concepts which can be applied equally to the operation of animals or of machines is provided by cybernetics, a generalized science of feedback systems and of statistical patterns of information flow, originally drawn largely from telephone engineering.[17]

'Organic' models using the vocabulary of cybernetics are influential in thinking about administrative adaptation, particularly in the analysis of the engineering limits of informational channels. The key to such analysis is known as the 'Law of Requisite Variety' or 'Shannon's Tenth Theorem'.[18] Very simply put, this law states that control in an informational sense can only be fully effective where the 'channel capacity' of the controller matches that of the object of control. By analogously regarding an administrative system as a telephone circuit or a computer programme, it can be shown that a simple command system is likely to be self-defeating in a system of any scale or complexity, and that large adaptive systems therefore have to be very largely self-controlled.[19] One can also arrive at the same conclusion from economic theory, based on a similar analysis of the binomial expansion of complexity.[20]

The implication, then, is that 'bureaucratic organizations', in the sense of multi-level hierarchical systems, are severely handicapped as adaptive systems.[21] In cybernetic terminology, highly stratified control systems have very narrow channel capacity limits and are therefore poorly equipped as 'appreciative' systems as a result of mechanisms such as departmentalism, narrow mission assignments, pyramidal command structures and so on.[22] This, too, has prescriptive implications and has generated enthusiasm for messy, non-hierarchical, 'organic' systems of organization of the type described by Burns and Stalker in the early 1960s[23] and popularized by later writers.

It is interesting to note that the same conclusions about the limited adaptive capacity of bureaucracies can be reached by the two wholly different theoretical paths of cybernetics and economics, although the prescriptions to which these paths lead are rather different. And the cybernetic model in particular suffers from two drawbacks as a means of understanding administrative adaptation. One is that it is indiscriminate. We are offered a 'model' of learning without much guidance as to how circumstances will alter cases. The other is that administrative adaptation does not consist simply of intra-organizational processes. We have to consider the administered object as well as the administering subject in order to understand the whole learning system.

As a means of further exploring the administrative problem of adaptation, let us begin by ignoring the internal processes involved in administrative learning and simply consider some different types of administrative response to a variety of learning situations. This will give us a clearer idea of the limits which the time dimension can present, while still assuming control resources to be unlimited. For the moment, we will define learning simply as the relation between changes in inputs and changes in outputs, and, where there is some relation, as the gap between perception, decision, action, outcome and perceived outcome. Four learning systems can then be considered.

Three Conventional Types of Learning System

Logically, we should begin by looking at 'non-learning systems', or situations in which changes in inputs produce no changes in outputs. It cannot be taken as axiomatic that organizations 'learn' or that all organizations learn equally well. 'Non-learning systems' are plentiful. For example, the Carolingian monarchs in France operated reasonably effectively on the basis of Roman land tax registers, as did their counterparts in Spain and Italy, and there are more modern cases of non-adaptive organizations which survive successfully. As Katzenbach remarks, in the context of the survival of horse cavalry in the twentieth century

'History . . . is studded with institutions which have managed to dodge the challenge of the obvious.'[24]

There is, of course, a school of writers, of which C. N. Parkinson[25] is the most famous, who take the view that organizations in general tend to develop according to inner dynamics, like the embryo from the egg, rather than to adapt to outside forces.[26] This is in a sense a 'non-learning' view of organizations, since embryo-type development and learning are mutually exclusive.

As opposed to a 'non-learning' system, a learning system is defined by Stafford Beer[27] as a mechanism which

(a) is aware of something happening, labels it and recalls relevant similar experiences.

(b) alters its internal state until the effects of the disturbance are offset.

Following this definition, there are two other conventional types of learning system which can be added to the 'non-learning' type.

The first is the case where the environment is static, while the system learns. The 'pure case' of this is in fact very rare, though it can be simulated. A simple example of this process is learning to play a musical instrument: the increase of knowledge and proficiency to a maximum is in principle limited only by the normal processes of human forgetting and physical decomposition. Where an administrative agency rather than an individual performs such a learning task, there is, of course, an additional limit constituted by the rotation and replacement of officials. Everyone has heard tales of the chaos which can be created by the absence of departure of a key experienced official.

The second case is that of learning against a changing environment, like learning to hit a moving target. A greater element of uncertainty now creeps in, though it can be limited in principle by sufficiently sophisticated prediction and anticipation. Failures to predict future developments are so well known as scarcely to need illustration: unforseen changes which cause large, carefully-planned projects to fall flat on their faces are a classic administrative banana-skin and we saw several cases of this in Chapter 3. Failures of this kind are comparable to the division of labour problems which were discussed in the last chapter, in that they become more costly the more (literally) concrete the wrong predictions are. An example is the British new towns and municipal housing estates of the 1940s, which failed to anticipate the advent of a motorized working-class and thus became technically obsolete quite early in their physical life. Another case is the gross over-estimates of future demand for higher education in Britain, which were made in forecasts of the early 1960s. Typically what happens is that the responses of the authorities lag behind the movements of the 'target', either because of inadequate perception or because of a gap between perception and action. Donald Schon characterizes government structures in general as a 'monument to past problems'.[28]

There are two further problems in this type of learning situation. The first is that even where the eventual response is not 'erroneous' in a clear-cut sense, there is a point at which delayed response can render the whole operation futile, as in Dickens' famous parody of the English legal system in *Bleak House*.[29] By the time that the case of *Jarndyce v. Jarndyce* was eventually concluded, not only had the disputed estate been largely swallowed up in lawyers' fees, but most of the disputants were dead. Pressman and Wildavsky make a similar point.[30] There are circumstances in which delay is failure.

The other problem is related to our discussion of the 'horse-shoe-nail' problem in Chapter 2. Administrative processes are so concrete that 'near misses' in anticipation are often as useless as forecasts which are very far wide of the mark. For example, before World War II, the British government had in fact anticipated the problem of bombing attacks and accordingly the fire services in the early part of the war were centralized and expanded. But these expanded and improved fire services were often of limited use in bombing attacks in practice, because the authorities had expected incendiary bombing, not the heavy structural bombing which in fact occurred. In such bombing raids, the water mains were usually knocked out quickly, which meant that there was no water for the fire services to use; and in cases such as the famous Coventry bombing raid of 1941, fire crews raced engines to the city from some hundreds of miles afield, only to find when they arrived that there was little that they could do.

A changing environment, of course, is the typical administrative situation. But environments can change in two quite different ways. One is as a result of conscious reaction to administrative movements, which is discussed below as the fourth and perhaps least conventional kind of learning system. The type of learning system which we have just been discussing, deals with relatively 'autonomous' social change, such as population change. Many of the skills of administrative adaptation lie in this type of learning system, the ability to spot 'niches' of potential administrative leverage when they emerge. One famous case is that of stamp taxes. Invented by a Dutchman, Johannes Van den Broeck, in 1623, these are a clear example of administrative reaction to social changes which were almost wholly autonomous. Simply by making contracts unenforceable in the law courts unless stamp duty was paid on the relevant documents, the duties harnessed the growth of contracts and written documents which were replacing an earlier oral (=audit) system of justice and administration, partly as a result of the invention of printing. Many military innovations belong to the same type of learning process. A classic example is Lynn White's description of how in the eighth century the Franks revolutionized medieval warfare and social structure (and later conquered England) by grasping the military implications of the invention of the stirrup.[31] This made possible a new type of mounted warfare and greatly widened the strategic gap between horse and foot warriors.

Reciprocal Learning

The fourth case of learning is perhaps less familiar. This is the case of learning against an environment which is also learning. Where such an environment is co-operative or sympathetic, the result is symbiosis. But where, as is the typical case in administration, the environment is hostile, the outcome can be very different. Downs, in his 'Law of Counter Control', states that the greater the effort made by a top-level official to control the behaviour of subordinate officials, the greater the efforts made by those subordinates to evade or counteract such control[32] (though he does not state what determines the outcomes of such a reciprocal learning process). Similarly, as we will see in Part 3, the effectiveness of many types of control is eroded simply by time. Pesticides are a clear example of this. Similarly, Schelling has observed that children, animals and inmates of mental hospitals tend to learn habits which minimize their susceptibility to threats.[33] This is by no means a trivial administrative problem.

The cybernetic writings on control and learning do not refer much to this type of learning, but it is commonly observable and it is a familiar process wherever there is an element of hostility between controller and controlled. 'Planning' in this sort of context is strategy in the strict sense, that of planning against an opponent. As Bailey remarks

'Not only may the plan fail to take into account all the relevant *natural* circumstances; it may be thwarted by the action of those who have a different plan.'[34]

As we will see in Chapter 10, the administration of betting and gaming is an elegant case of this type of learning system. As early as 1541 reference is made in an English statute to 'subtill and inventative and craftie persons' who had evaded the earlier gaming statutes by inventing new games.[35] Over four centuries later, the same process was at work. In 1970 the British Gaming Board reported that, over the previous decade

'Whenever a method of operating commercial gaming which purported to be legal was found by the courts to be illegal, other methods appeared to take its place.'[36]

In many other fields of regulative administration, the same sort of 'regulation—response cycles' can be found. In counter-insurgency the problem is almost too familiar to need illustration. Examples of evasive tactics are the routing of mail through 'innocent' third parties to avoid surveillance by political police, the development of scramblers to foil telephone tappers, or the acquisition by rioters of gas masks to foil CS gas attacks by the security forces, as happened in Northern

Ireland in the early 1970s. Similarly, the distribution of cash benefits or subsidies[37] and the administration of prisons or taxes is a continuous struggle against fraud and the discovery of escape routes or loopholes. Some years ago the British Inland Revenue Department stated its problem as follows

'Legal avoidance has become a science with its own inventors and practitioners. The Income Tax . . . is . . . a war between the experts who have devised schemes to enable their wealthy clients to reduce the burden of their tax and the legislature seeking constantly to frustrate them . . .'[38]

Thus, just as the Window Tax resulted in people bricking up their windows and the Land Tax encouraged people to express their income in money, so money taxes encourage them to express it is kind with astonishing ingenuity. Other examples of this kind of reaction are the popularity of bearer bonds such as Eurodollar bonds, where ownership is not registered and therefore taxation is difficult, or the invention of 'dividend stripping' in Britain in the 1950s. Dividend stripping was mentioned briefly in Chapter 1. It was a method of making artificial tax losses by setting up two companies and draining the resources of one by paying dividends to the other. By the mid-1960s this had become such a problem that the whole profits tax system had to be changed and the liabilities of corporations separated from those of shareholders.[39] Even now the distinction is fuzzy round the edges.

Types of Reciprocal Learning

Reciprocal learning processes permeate the relationships within and between humans, animals and plants. Whether one should add machines to this list is problematic, but there is certainly a sense in which machines can be said to 'learn'. Certainly, the process of counter-learning is not unique to administration. Different types and levels of the process can be observed in other contexts.

One familiar type is the process of natural selection, where the need for self-preservation causes mutual adaptation by the various members of a food chain, resulting in a moving equilibrium. Such processes may be found in the reciprocal development of predators and prey within the animal kingdom, and even in animal—plant relations. An example of the latter case is the development of the teeth of grazing animals for greater grinding power and the reciprocal development of defences by nutritional plants (such as harder thorns or the storage of silicates) to prevent themselves from being eaten.[40] Everybody has heard of 'symbiosis', but processes of this kind are perhaps not so well known.

Some of these processes are directly relevant to administration in some contexts. For example, the 'flu' virus seems to change fairly radically approximately every decade in order to 'outflank', so to speak, the antibodies which the human population has built up against previous viruses. Another familiar example is the development of 'super-rats' which are immune to Warfarin (a 'final solution' to the rodent problem which was introduced in 1956). New 'super-poisons' are now being introduced for those immune rats which have broken through the 'poison cordon', but this introduces the risk of developing 'super-super-rats'. 'Super-lice', 'super-mosquitoes', 'super-mice' and so on, have similarly developed in response to the introduction of poisons and pesticides by man. The faster the breeding curve, the more rapidly does adaptation have to take place on both sides. In the context of bacteria, for example, whether relating to medical treatment or to food processing (particularly milk), antidotes have to be continually varied, so rapidly do the products of natural selection snap upon the heels of human technology.

The level of *social* adaptation involves a rather different set of learning processes. The brown rat, man's most successful biological opponent, owes its position partly to social processes: the fact that rats transmit their experience to subsequent generations, thus achieving cumulative knowledge.[41] Many social learning processes operate through rather ill-defined processes of information dissemination, with reciprocal learning built into it. Consider the development of fashion. As some new style disseminates through the whole population, so the 'vanguard' of fashion abandons it in favour of something else. 'Private languages' operate in much the same way. For example, in youth or underworld argot, words and phrases are discarded as they enter into common use and become clichés. In both of these cases, a special group is using the time-lag between the introduction and general dissemination of a style, for 'cover'.

In markets, the mechanism is different, though there are similarities in the underlying process. Markets in information work by progressively discounting information relating to likely future performance by changing odds or stock prices as the information is disseminated among the relevant population. If such a market is fully competitive, there will come a point at which once relevant information about future performance has become so diffused that any special gains from holding such information will be removed. When everyone knows the secret password, it ceases to have any value as a security device. Similarly, if everyone backs the favourite in a horse race, no one will gain anything if it wins (except possibly the Exchequer) because the odds will have become infinity to one on. Stock markets are similar in that if you buy a successful stock too late, your gains are likely to be small or negative. Indeed, some economists have argued on this basis that buying stocks on the basis of their past showing will produce results no better than selection based on spinning a roulette wheel, and have therefore tried to test 'random walk' theories of stock-market prices.[42] But there is an element of self-fulfilling prophecy in the stock market case which does not apply to the case of betting markets — the amount of money staked on a horse is only a symptom, never a cause, of its probable success.

All of the processes which have been described here may impinge on the relationship between administrators and administered and some, such as the case of private languages, may be used as a 'screen' against the authorities. On top of that, there is a further level at which the process can operate, that is, within the administrative apparatus itself. Downs' Law of Counter Control, which we mentioned earlier, refers to this level of counter-learning, and it can be illustrated by the reaction of agencies to financial targetry, the 'new rationalist' techniques of budget control and project appraisal,[43] and other 'quick technological fixes'[44] of the same kind; such agencies quickly develop counter-strategies of 'cost-benefitmanship', 'PPBS-manship' and other 'numbers games'. 'Plan fulfilment' controls in the Soviet Union seem to attract a similar response,[45] in that managers learn to play the system by lobbying for low initial targets, not exceeding such targets too far for fear of harder targets being set in the following year and so on. Such strategies are quite familiar in the process of intra-company targeting in large private firms. Nor is it only 'numbers games' which provoke this kind of counter-learning response. For example, the attempt to screen job applicants by 'personality testing' in the 1950s in order to 'smoke out the psychological mess' had similar results.[46]

Finally, it is at least logically possible to conceive of hierarchies of regulation—response cycles involving a number of the levels or types of process discussed here. For example, the internal administrative learning process might trigger off an 'external' regulation—response cycle, or there might even be hierarchies of 'external' effects. An example of the latter process might be fisheries regulation, in which government regulations (such as closed seasons) trigger responses from fishermen (such as more intensive fishing within the seasons which remain open), which in turn may provoke responses from the fish population, and so on through the whole biosphere.[47]

Outcomes

The learning processes which we have described could logically have a wide variety of outcomes. One extreme case would be a progressive advance to the point of perfect administration. In cybernetic terms, this would be the point of maximum entropy and minimum information.[48] In the case of our second type of learning system (the static environment case), the attainment of this point would be a question simply of time, other things being equal. The opposite extreme would be the outcome where administrative control is steadily weakened to the point of total ineffectiveness.

To these two extreme cases, two intermediate ones can be added, equilibrium and stalemate. The first is where some sort of equilibrium is established between the first two extreme cases — the system settles down somewhere between 'perfect administration' and complete ineffectiveness. The location of such an equilibrium is not necessarily fixed and it could move in either direction. This outcome is similar to the equilibria which we discussed earlier in terms of balance between predators and prey. For example, the last lions would have died of hunger long before they had killed the last pair of antelopes or zebras:[49] there are analogous 'economic-type' limits in administration, as we have already discussed.

The second intermediate case is narrower and more 'elegant'. This is Donald Schon's case of 'dynamic conservatism'. Dynamic conservatism means complete equilibrium, stasis, stalemate, in a situation where both (or all) sides are continually adapting to the other(s) in order to maintain exactly their relative positions. Edward Feit, in the context of insurgency situations, calls this 'institutionalized conflict',[50] but it does not only occur in situations of overt conflict. It could arise in some of the odd cases of 'consumer behaviour' which were discussed in Chapter 1.

Of these outcomes, the third is clearly the normal case, the others being rare or limiting cases. What determines these outcomes? We will consider three possible influences: technology, time-span and public sector status. The impact of technology deserves examination because people at one time seriously feared that developments in technology would make for all-powerful governments (outcome one). George Orwell's *1984* is the most elegant expression of this idea, taking a 'black' view of the process.[51] Others predict the same trend, but take a more favourable view. Can this thesis be sustained?

The Impact of Technology

Some writers, as was mentioned above, see technology, and particularly the 'data processing revolution', as bringing about an administrative millenium, whether of a 'black' or of an utopian kind. D. C. Hague, for example, observes in a well-known textbook

> 'As time goes on, information systems will *obviously* improve steadily as managerial knowledge improves and as better data-processing equipment (especially computers) is brought into use.' (Italics mine)[52]

Other authors have considered 'technological fixes' of the same kind.[53] For example, in a study of revolutions, Peter Calvert suggests that with developments in psychology and in the computing sciences, governments might be able to detect characters who might be disposed to promote revolutions, and accordingly act to deter them. At the same time, he notes that at present governments find it difficult enough to keep a proper check on those who are known to be likely to sell state secrets to foreign powers:[54] and J. B. Rule comes to much the same conclusion in his study of surveillance systems.[55]

There is a basic weakness in the 'technophile' and 'technophobe' argument that technological developments will create all-powerful administrative systems. Such arguments are based on the assumption of an autonomously changing or static environment (our second and third types of learning system). The argument ignores the case of reciprocal learning. It is true that a new development in technology, particularly if it is very costly, may *initially* advantage the authorities relative to the administered. Everyone has heard the story of the arrest of the murderer Dr. Crippen on his way from England to Canada in the liner *Montrose* in 1910, which was achieved as a result of a radio message. This was the first time that radio had been used to track down a criminal in this way. But it is typically difficult to prevent the dissemination of a new technique, except, in some cases, by forswearing the use of new devices at all, as with the former prohibition of photocopying machines in the Soviet bureaucracy for fear of security leaks and of the dissemination of seditious propaganda by these means. Technical warfare in World War II affords a range of examples, particularly the counter-development of radar by Germany to match the initial British lead. Later, the British developed techniques for blinding German radar by dropping strips of silver paper from bombers, but the use of these techniques was held up for months, lest the Germans in turn should use them against British radar.

At a lower level, developments in transport and communications (cars, walkie-talkies, copying and 'bugging' devices, telephones and so on) have helped criminals at least as much as the police. Likewise, Kitson asserts that modern technology of this kind disproportionately advantages insurgents *vis-a-vis* governments.[56] For example, we are told that small nuclear weapons will soon be freely and fairly cheaply available. Experts in security companies, too, often admit that the technology of the high-level thief is on a par with their own.[57]

It would therefore appear that technological development will only lead to a progression towards perfect administration (outcome one) in our second and third types of learning situation. Technological development in the context of our fourth type of learning (reciprocal learning) is more likely to lead to our third and fourth outcomes. This is, of course, implicitly recognized by many writers, and perhaps one should add to the 'technophile' and 'technophobe' points of view an emerging school of cosmic technological pessimists who consider that technology plus reciprocal learning may even lead to our second outcome, a progressive weakening of administrative control. Sir Geoffrey Vickers, for example, considers the 'paradox of the Western World' to be that

> '. . . it grows less controllable with every advance in the techniques of manipulation and less predictable with every advance in the techniques of information handling.'[58]

Counter-learning is one important limiting factor which the technophile/ technophobe case ignores, but it is not the only one. There are also limits in terms of the sheer capacity to handle information, both of mechanical capacity and of human capacity. We have already mentioned problems of mechanical capacity in the earlier discussion of cybernetic models of learning. The full analysis of comparatively simple systems may turn out to require computer 'brain space' not only greater than at present exists, but also greater than could ever conceivably exist. Stafford Beer, for example, has argued that even the capacity which would be possessed by a computer the size of the Earth and running for as long as the age of the Earth would still only be adequate for a full specification of a decision-making system of fairly moderate complexity.[59]

The technophile/technophobe case perhaps tends to underestimate such purely mechanical limits. Moreover, there is the other capacity limitation of the 'span of attention' of administrative systems: the *human* processing required to translate increases in 'data' pouring out of machines into increases in administrative information in the sense of knowledge useful for action. Data may increase, but the information derived from it by a human scanner may not increase. For example, there is the familiar case of 'data overload', where to be 'over-informed' has the same effects as being under-informed. This is in fact sometimes used as a weapon in bureaucratic processes: it may be easier to conceal potentially damaging information from busy people by issuing a thick pile of papers than by attempting secrecy. Human scanning is typically a recurrent rather than a once-for-all process, so there is a 'queuing' element too. If a data-processing system has a fixed (or at least limited) span of attention but faces a 'data environment' which is larger than the system's span of attention in any given time period, and if the rate of input of new data into the environment is equal to or larger than the system's span of attention, the system cannot properly cope with the available data in any finite time. These conditions are in fact not very rigorous, even though in practice it is not easy to tell the exact point at which 'overload' is likely to occur.

So both human and mechanical limits to data-processing have to be balanced against the argument that modern communications make people in general and administrative authorities in particular, better 'informed".[60] As individuals, we overcome our very sharp limitations on absolute information-processing by intuitively recoding information (into 'chunks', in one psychologist's phrase),[61] but this interpretive process is difficult if not impossible to reproduce mechanically. The notion that perfect systems of administrative surveillance and data-processing can be achieved through machinery is therefore a very dubious one, particularly in the case of the fourth type of learning system. But this does not necessarily imply accepting the 'pathetic' approach of Vickers and others who believe that a data overload crisis is approaching because of the recent exponential growth in mechanical information processing capacity. Such an approach ignores the parallel exponential increase in skilled manpower and the resulting specialization which keeps individual 'span of attention' within manageable bounds.[62]

The Impact of Time Span

A second determinant of the outcomes of adaptation processes is the pattern of change and the time-span within which change is occurring. As we have already mentioned, if the pace of change is sufficiently slow, non-learning systems can maintain a slowly deteriorating equilibrium position, and if the pattern of change is cyclical it may even be a fluctuating equilibrium. Clearly, it is major rapid or linear changes which are likely to spell disaster for such systems, as with the fate of the dinosaurs (though with a total period of existence of 140 million years or so, the dinosaur species was a relatively successful biological system).

In the case of the second type of learning system, we have already remarked that in principle, time is the only obstacle to a 'perfect' outcome. In the case of the third type of learning system, the effect of cyclical and linear patterns of change on adaptation processes has already been discussed in Chapter 2. Fishing policy provides an interesting case of administrative adaptation in the face of a cyclically changing environment. The British Herring Industry Board, seeking a means to dispose of surplus herring in the era of abundant post-World War II catches, built four herring meal and oil factories in the UK in the 1950s. But by the time that these reduction factories were finished, herring catches were falling and the Scottish Office (within whose jurisdiction two out of the four reduction factories fell) had altered its subsidy policy. Worse, the fishmeal boom in Peru, which started in the early 1960s, knocked the bottom out of the world fishmeal market, with Peruvian fishmeal selling in the UK at not much more than half the price of British herring meal. Having been rejected by the British government in attempts to secure an import levy on herring meal, the Herring Industry Board was obliged to abandon the reduction factories policy as hopelessly uneconomic. But by the time that the factories had been sold, the world fishmeal market was picking up again.[63]

Two further problems deserve attention in the case of the third type of learning system. The first is the problem of arbitrariness which is presented by action in a changing environment. We saw in the last chapter how difficult it is to avoid ambiguity when drawing lines in 'space', whether on a map or between different conceptual categories. The same problem occurs when drawing lines in time. In any changing situation, the introduction, abolition or change of an administrative measure will advantage different groups of people according to its exact timing. Recall the 'banding' problem which was discussed in the last chapter. For an analogous case in the time dimension, suppose that there is an annual vehicle tax based on engine capacity groups and that this tax is raised at a given point in time. Not only does such a tax cause inequities within each 'band' as we discussed in the last chapter (the man with the 1098 cc car who is classified in the 1000—1500 cc class, for example). It also creates inequities between those who have just paid their tax at the old rate just before the change, and those who have to pay immediately afterwards.

We will see this problem clearly in the land tax case in the next chapter. Whenever you have legislation which is not retrospective you have to have an interim period, and, as we will see, such an interim period can create particular difficulties in the case of developers who buy up building land for many years in advance. The problem also occurs dramatically in the case of incomes policies. Wage bargaining occurs through successive settlements by different groups in a series of 'rounds'. It is therefore scarcely possible to impose a wage freeze, restriction or derestriction without advantaging or disadvantaging those groups who have already settled against those who have yet to do so. There is always the case of the 'last-minute' settlement before a wage freeze, for example. It is impossible to avoid this kind of arbitrariness in timing, but in some cases it may be possible to minimize the damage. To take a lower-level example, if the peak month for moving house is April, the worst time to revise the telephone directory is in March; and similarly the most dangerous time to introduce wage restrictions is immediately before a pay settlement of a powerful wage group.

Things become more difficult where there are *multiple* peaks or powerful groups, for example when the peak removal months are April *and* September, or when wage settlements by powerful groups are evenly distributed throughout the year. The problem then becomes a pure dilemma: there is no way out of it. In such cases, timing could just as well be decided randomly or by considerations such as the availability of staff, as by 'strategic' considerations.

The other problem in the case of the third type of learning system is that of the pace of change. Unlike the case of the non-learning system, it is not the absolute pace of change in the environment which matters, but rather the environment's pace of change relative to the pace of adaptation by the learning system. The most familiar case arises where there is a 'lead time' problem. For example, it takes eight to ten years to build a major hospital, but by the time that such a project is completed it will already be obsolete to some extent owing to the development of medical technology (in the recent past this has applied to fields like renal dialysis and open heart surgery). The same applies to aerospace and weapons systems, and in Chapter 2 we have already mentioned the 'great leap forward' syndrome, in which attempts to take time by the forelock and to counter the process of obsolescence have counter-productive results. We also encountered this kind of learning problem in the case of contracting and procurement in Chapter 3. But it should be noted that the lead-time problem does not only arise in the context of accelerating social change. It can also apply in cases such as crisis or sudden major disaster where the time-scale is very short and where the relevant resources (funds, firepower, supplies and so forth) have to be brought to the right place very quickly if they are to be effective.

Turning finally to the case of the fourth type of learning system, it is again the *relative* speed of response by participants which matters. If other things are equal, if both sides have an identical speed of response to initiatives by the other and command equal resources, then their relative positions will remain constant, even though their absolute positions are constantly changing. On the other hand, if either side achieves a faster rate of response than the other, its advantage may become cumulatively large. It is relevant to note that promotion in the British Inland Revenue recently depended to a large extent on the size of arrears of work (measured in terms of years) in any given tax office.[64]

Of course, it is not simply 'response times' which will determine outcomes, but also the 'quality' of response in some sense. This is harder to analyse, but in some cases the quality of response is simply a function of time. Even in the basic learning problems presented to rats in a psychologist's laboratory, there will be some statistical pattern of chance successes and sudden flashes of genius, but typically the rats will learn by experience in time which is the 'food' button or how to get through the maze. In administration, too, quality of response and time are typically related. It is often necessary to reduce the quality of response in the interests of speed.

In fact, in a typical short-term situation in which there are either an infinite number of cases or stimuli per time period or a limited number of cases capable of absorbing unlimited time (in investigation, litigation, search and so on), the *only* variable in the system is 'service time', or the quality of administrative outputs. This is because the stock of personnel and equipment is fixed by definition in the short term. It is thus the inverse of 'Parkinson's Law' which applies in such a case. If the number of cases is infinitely large in any given time period and the stock of personnel is by definition fixed in that period, the only means of preventing the development of an infinite queue (or in queuing theory terms, keeping the 'traffic intensity' of the system equal to or less than one) is to adjust 'service time'.[65] Again, this is a real problem in tax administration. For example, during the whole of World War II, virtually no 'back duty investigation' (that is, checking up on suspected tax fraud) took place in Britain. The problem also applies to policy fields such as health administration, where the scope or demand is in principle unlimited.

The Impact of Public Sector Status

Public sector status, too, will have an impact on the quality of response in a learning process. Thus, apart from time, the other main influence on quality of response is probably the quality of employees. Every policy area involves some stock of people competent in the relevant skills. It is safe to assume that this stock is fixed in the short term; and the more qualified the relevant personnel in terms of number of years of experience or training, the longer the 'short term' becomes. In the longer term, however, two problems may develop. The first is the learning problem which is created by the deliberate rotation of officials as a security device, a control system which will be discussed in Part 3. The other problem is that the relative shares of the 'stock' of relevant policy skills as held by the authorities and by the administered, may change. This can occur through various possible mechanisms: influencing officials by bribery or its diminutives, 'wastage' in the sense of poaching officials by offering more attractive terms of employment elsewhere, or competition at the 'pre-entry' stage in terms of competitive bidding for skilled or high-quality personnel.

Wastage, too, will be discussed more fully in Part 3; it is mentioned here because it is an obvious mechanism by which reciprocal learning processes can take place between public sector agencies and their clients. For example in the Land Tax case, described in the next chapter, wastage from the Valuation Department of the Inland Revenue played a part in hindering the 1909 tax, since some ex-District Valuers went over to the 'enemy' and waged a relentless war against the tax. It would seem that the more 'professionalized' the policy field, the more the effectiveness of the authorities will tend to depend on the division of the relevant policy skills. Such skills are likely to be scarce by definition. One of the defining characteristics of professionalism — indeed, *the* defining characteristic, in the opinion of many writers — is the self-limitation of numbers below the 'Malthusian' limit at which the market for the relevant skills is flooded. Similarly, the more professionalized the policy field, the more likely it is that no net advantage will accrue to either side if the ratio of division of the relevant skills remains constant.

There are three further handicaps which are suffered by public or large-scale organizations in reciprocal learning processes. First, their moves cannot be arbitrary. One of the obvious strategies for coping with learning systems of the fourth type is very rapid, randomized switching between alternative courses of action. This is the way that cleaning systems for milk processing plants operate to beat bacterial adaptation. But this kind of response typically cannot be mounted in public administration. It is true that there is the case of 'unacknowledgeable means', another device which will be explored more fully later. For example, some time ago in Brazil a number of supposed criminals were unofficially murdered by supposed policemen off duty. But unacknowledgeable means is in fact the exception which proves the rule. Public authorities cannot openly respond to insurgency by lawless violence of a similar kind without incurring very heavy costs.[66] It is not only a rule of equity, but also a pre-requisite of corruption-free administration, that like cases should be treated in like manner and that field officials should not be allowed to make purely arbitrary decisions.

Accordingly, in any large-scale public organization dealing with a ramified clientele, comprehensive rules have to be drawn up, revised, approved, disseminated. This process not only builds in an extra element of delay in adaptation, but in the process of promulgating the rules to field officials, such rules will inevitably find their way into the hands of the 'enemy' as well, even if an attempt is made to keep them secret, as sometimes happens. For example, this happened some time ago in Britain over the 'office instructions' for Supplementary Benefit allocation.

As a result of these handicaps, large-scale administration can rarely, if ever, enjoy the strategic advantage of surprise. This problem is not, of course, confined to the authorities, but also confronts their opponents. Small guerilla operations planned by word of mouth and with ephemeral communications techniques are very hard for the intelligence agencies of the authorities to deal with. Such operations begin to suffer the same vulnerability as the authorities themselves once they acquire permanent staff, records, files and radio.[67]

The second problem is related to the first. It is that the accumulated experience represented by a large or public organization may be balanced or outweighed by the time constraints under which it is working. Writers such as Etzioni have argued that large organizations are in fact superior to individuals as learning systems,[68] in that such organizations may have many times more aggregate skill, cunning and experience than any individual or small-scale opponent. One human brain cannot understand itself. But a set of human brains (the scientific community) can understand 'the brain'. On top of the advantage of pooled or cumulated information can be added the theoretical advantage that public administrators can change the rules to benefit themselves. For example, as can be seen from both the tax cases in this book, tax administrators often try to introduce short Parliamentary bills containing clauses nullifying decisions in certain court cases which the revenue authorities do not like (these are known as 'Somerset House Bills' in Britain, *bris de jurisprudence* in France).[69]

But there are two major handicaps which Etzioni's theory ignores. The first, as pointed out by Wilensky, is that in any finite time the big organization may not be able fully to mobilize its resources. The second is that the individual case or small opponent may have much more time in which to prepare his moves than his large adversary. This may be a real advantage, especially in a defensive situation in which in order to win it is only necessary not to lose. For example, the British local planning authorities cannot move quickly against illegal 'fly-by-night' car park operators who use demolition sites because of the appeal procedures which have to be gone through against enforcement notices under the planning laws. Temporary car park operators can thus move from cleared site to cleared site with impunity.[70] Most 'fly-by-night' operations enjoy this kind of strategic advantage, and it is the other edge of the weapon of bureaucratic delay which was discussed earlier.

The third handicap for public authorities is the problem of multi-organizations which we discussed in Chapters 2 and 4. This problem is particularly intractable for public administration because of the scale and scope of its operations. Not only will 'multi-organizationality' inevitably slow down the authorities' speed of response to a situation because of the time required for inter-agency bargaining, as analysed by Pressman and Wildavsky. Multiple agencies may also introduce an element of reciprocal learning within the public sector where the objectives of such agencies are conflicting, as was discussed in Chapter 2. Metcalfe and other writers suggest that after a point such an inter-organizational environment may become 'turbulent' and uncontrollable.[71]

Summary and Conclusion

In this chapter we have examined the inroads which are made into perfect administration by the introduction of a time dimension. We considered four simple types of learning situation and four possible types of outcome. We explored some of the possible influences on these outcomes, beginning with technological development. We found that the technological argument for growing central administrative control is based on restrictive implicit assumptions about the nature of the learning situation involved. In exploring adaptation, it is essential to look at whole learning systems rather than at merely intra-organizational characteristics, because what looks like linear organizational change in one context may look more like a moving equilibrium in another. The problems of adaptation in tax administration are a clear example of this.

Time-span is another influence on learning outcomes, but in many cases it is the relative rather than the absolute speed of response which is the key factor. Finally, there is the problem of structural characteristics, in particular that of public sector status. The argument lying behind the quotation which forms the epigraph to this chapter is that there are structural limits to the process of improvement by evolution: purely 'engineering' limits to the size of a giraffe's neck or of a horse's backbone, for example. Can one apply this kind of analysis to the limits which are imposed by public sector status on adaptability? The impact of public sector status might take a variety of forms. Among them are the adjustment of 'service-time' in the context of unlimited administrative scope and highly limited available time; the

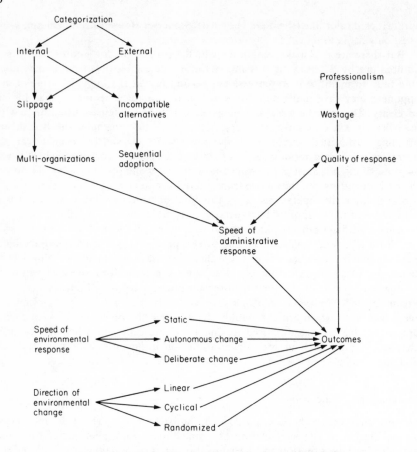

Figure 2. Some problems of categorization and learning

problem of wastage as a mechanism of reciprocal learning; and the inability to act quickly or randomly owing to rule-boundedness. These problems apply in large part to all big organizations; but the public sector is particularly handicapped by the problem of 'multi-organizationality' and by the problem of confronting small-scale 'fly-by-night' operations.

This discussion of adaptation in time is far from exhaustive, but no further complication will be attempted here. Figure 2 gives the components of the adaptation processes which have been discussed in this chapter, by showing the interrelation of the issues which have been discussed. It also relates these to some of the problems of language and categorization which were discussed in the last chapter. When we combine space and time problems we get a clearer picture of the limits of administration. Not only are we arbitrarily cutting into systems in space, we are also arbitrarily cutting into systems in time. Many of these problems will be recognizable from the case of contracting and procurement, which was explored in the last chapter.

There is still, of course, a missing dimension in all this. In exploring the administrative problems which can be created by 'space' and by 'time', we have assumed that control is otherwise unlimited. The artificiality of this assumption can easily be seen from the case studies of contracting in Chapter 3: even where administration is not handicapped by limited capacity to specify key terms or to cope with rapidly changing situations, the sanctions available are limited in number and often severely limited in effectiveness. What we have so far explored is the information, but not the 'energy', limits of administrative control, and we will explore the energy side of control more broadly in the next part. But before turning to the 'perfect control' conditions of perfect administration, we will look at a case of policy implementation which has a particularly unhappy administrative history, the attempt to tax 'speculation' or 'profiteering' in land. This case serves to illustrate some of the points made in Part 2, particularly the analysis of the last chapter.

Notes

1. Spann, R. N., 'Cliché in political science', *Journal of the Australasian Political Studies Association*, Vol. 1, May 1966.
2. Zeisel, H., *Delay in Court*, Little Brown, Boston, 1959.
3. See, for example, Beer, S., *Brain of the Firm*, Allen Lane, The Penguin Press, London, 1972.
4. An example given in Thayer, G., *The War Business*, Weidenfeld and Nicholson, London, 1969.
5. Simon, H. A., and J. G. March, *Organizations*, Wiley, New York, 1958.
6. Bennis, W., *The Planning of Change*, Holt Rinehart and Winston, London, 1969.
7. Cyert, R., and J. G. March, *A Behavioral Theory of the Firm*, Prentice-Hall, Englewood Cliffs, 1965, p. 101.
8. Vickers, Sir G., *The Art of Judgment*, Chapman and Hall, London, 1965.
9. Mackenzie, W. J. M., *Power, Violence, Decision*, Penguin Books, Harmondsworth, 1975.
10. Beer, S., *op. cit.*
11. Downs, A., *Inside Bureaucracy*, Wiley, New York, 1967.
12. Tullock, G., *The Politics of Bureaucracy*, Public Affairs Press, Washington, 1965.
13. Niskanen, W. A., *Bureaucracy and Representative Government*, Aldine Atherton, New York, 1971.
14. Wagner, R. E., *The Public Economy*, Markham, Chicago, 1973.
15. Hirschman, A. O., *Exit Voice and Loyalty*, Harvard University Press, Cambridge, Mass., 1970.
16. Lorenz, K., *On Aggression*, Methuen, London, 1966, p. 32.
17. For a brief introduction, see M. Trask, *Cybernetics*, Studio Vista, London, 1971.
18. Shannon, C. E., and W. Weaver, *The Mathematical Theory of Communication*, Illinois University Press, Urbana, 1949, p. 37.
19. cf. Beer, S., *op. cit.*
20. Starbuck, W. H. (Ed.), *Organizational Growth and Development*, Penguin Books, Harmondsworth, 1971.
21. Wilensky, H., *Organizational Intelligence*, Basic Books, New York, 1967; J. Hage, 'An axiomatic theory of organizations', *Administrative Science Quarterly*, Vol. 10, 1965.
22. A vintage model of this is M. Polanyi, 'Planning and spontaneous order', *The Manchester School*, Vol. 16, 1948, pp. 237–268.
23. Burns, T., and G. M. Stalker, *The Management of Innovation*, Tavistock, London, 1961.
24. Katzenbach, E., 'The horse cavalry in the twentieth century: a study in policy response', *Public Policy*, 1958, pp. 120–149.
25. Parkinson, C. N., *Parkinson's Law*, Penguin Books, Harmondsworth, 1965.
26. Haire, M. (Ed.), *Modern Organization Theory*, Wiley, New York, 1959, pp. 272–305.
27. Beer, S., *Decision and Control*, Wiley, New York, 1966.
28. Schon, D., *Beyond the Stable State*, Temple Smith, London, 1971.

29. Dickens, C., *Bleak House*, Chapman and Hall, London, 1890.
30. Pressman, J., and A. Wildavsky, *Implementation*, University of California Press, Berkeley, 1973.
31. White, Lynn, Jr., *Medieval Technology and Social Change*, Clarendon Press, Oxford, 1962.
32. Downs, A., *op. cit.*
33. Schelling, T., *The Strategy of Conflict*, Harvard University Press, Cambridge, Mass., 1960, p. 17.
34. Bailey, F., *Stratagems and Spoils*, Basil Blackwell, Oxford, 1969, p. 111.
35. Chenery, J., *An Introduction to the Law and Practice of Betting and Bookmaking*, Sweet and Maxwell, London, 1961, p. 6.
36. *First Report of the Gaming Board for Great Britain*, HC 208, 1970, p. 13, para 24.
37. cf. *Report of the Committee on the Abuse of Social Security Benefits*, Cmnd. 5228, 1973.
38. Memorandum of Evidence from the Inland Revenue Staff Association to the Royal Commission on the Taxation of Profits and Income, 1955, *Vols of Evidence*, Document 243.
39. Stanley, O., *A Guide to Taxation*, Methuen, London, 1967.
40. Lorenz, K., *op. cit.*, p. 18.
41. *Ibid.*, p. 137.
42. Cootner, P. H. (Ed.), *The Random Character of Stock Market Prices*, Massachussetts Institute of Technology, 1964.
43. cf. Heclo, H., and A. Wildavsky, *The Private Government of Public Money*, Macmillan, London, 1974; J. R. Schlesinger, 'Systems analysis and the political process', RAND, Santa Monica, 1967 (Mimeographed); G. Beneviste, *The Politics of Expertise*, Croom Helm, London, 1973.
44. Weinberg, A., 'The technological fix' in N. Cross, D. Elliott and R. Roy (Eds.), *Man-Made Futures*, Hutchinson, London, 1974, pp. 281–288.
45. Berliner, J. S., *Factory and Manager in the USSR*, Harvard University Press, Cambridge, Mass., 1957.
46. Glasser, R., *The New High Priesthood*, Macmillan, London, 1967.
47. cf. Morehouse, T. A., and J. Hession, 'Politics and management' in A. R. Tussing, T. A. Morehouse and J. D. Babb (Eds.), *Alaska Fisheries Policy*, Institute of Social, Economic and Government Research, Alaska, 1972, pp. 283–285.
48. Feit, E., 'Insurgency in organizations: a theoretical analysis', *General Systems Yearbook*, 1969, pp. 157–168.
49. Lorenz, K., *op. cit.*, p. 18.
50. Feit, E., *op. cit.*,
51. Orwell, G., *1984*, Secker and Warburg, London, 1965.
52. Hague, D. C., *Managerial Economics*, Longmans, London, 1969, p. 18.
53. cf. Cross, N., D. Elliott and R. Roy (Eds.), *Man-Made Futures*, Hutchinson, London, 1974.
54. Calvert, P., *Revolution*, Pall Mall Press, London, 1970, p. 105.
55. Rule, J. B., *Private Lives and Public Surveillance*, Allen Lane, London, 1973.
56. Kitson, F., *Low Intensity Operations*, Faber and Faber, London, 1972.
57. Russell, G., 'Shutting the stable door', Financial Times, 31.8.72, p. 12.
58. Vickers, Sir G., *Freedon in a Rocking Boat*, Penguin, Harmondsworth, 1968, p. 90.
59. Beer, S., *Brain of the Firm*, Allen Lane, The Penguin Press, London, 1972.
60. MacLuhan, M., *Understanding Media*, Sphere books, London, 1967.
61. Miller, G., *The Psychology of Communication*, Penguin, London, 1968.
62. cf. Y. Bar-Hillel, *Language and Information*, Addison-Wesley, Reading, Mass., 1964, pp. 365–372.
63. Hood, C. C., 'The politics of the biosphere: the dynamics of fisheries policy' in R. Rose (Ed.), *The Dynamics of Public Policy*, Sage Publications, London (forthcoming).
64. Stanley, O., *op. cit.*
65. cf. Speirs, M., *Techniques and Public Administration*, Collins, Glasgow, 1975, pp. 64–70.
66. cf. Feit, E., *op. cit.*
67. Elliott-Bateman, M., *The Fourth Dimension of Warfare*, Vol. 1 (Intelligence, Subversion, Resistance), Manchester University Press, Manchester, 1970.
68. Etzioni, A., *The Active Society*, Free Press, New York, 1969.

69. Formier, L., *Les impôts en France*, Presses, Universitaires de France, Paris, 1946.
70. *Sunday Times*, 9.12.73.
71. Metcalfe, L., 'Systems models, economic models and the causal texture of organizational environments', *Human Relations*, Vol. 27, 1974, pp. 639–663; cf. E. L. Trist and F. E. Emery, 'The causal texture of organizational environments', *Human Relations*, Vol. 18, 1965, pp. 21–31.

Chapter 6

Case Study Number Two: Taxing Land Speculators

'The separate rating of ground value is, in my opinion, extremely desirable, provided that the practical difficulties can be sufficiently overcome to allow of successful administration.' Mr. G. H. Blunden, quoted in *Second Series of Memoranda and Extracts Relating to Land Taxation and Land Valuation*, Cd. 4845, 1909, p. 63.

Nowhere is the gap between the administerable and the ideal more serious than in the case of taxation, especially of land. One author speaks of land taxation as a subject of 'hideous complexity'.[1] The problems which arise, as will be seen, are very largely of the type which we discussed in Chapter 4, that is, limits to categorization and discrimination. In spite of the administrative difficulties involved, there are strong and recurrent political demands for effective measures to grapple with speculation and profiteering in land, so this case affords another opportunity to explore the limits of administration.

Background

Taxation of land speculators has attracted political interest since the beginning of the Industrial Revolution, and indeed can be traced back well beyond it. In England, attempts to tax owners whose property had increased in value as a result of public works go back as far as 1427.[2] But in the nineteenth century, the 'land problem' came up dramatically, and the 'classical' economists of that time had ample opportunity to notice that land could increase in value through no effort on the part of the owner of the land, but simply as a result of urbanization of population growth. Nowadays, of course, such an increase in value is frequently triggered by government decisions over permitted land use, but this only makes the problem more acute, since a stroke of an administrator's pen, by changing the permitted use of a piece of land from agricultural to building, can immediately increase its value many-fold.

Thus for at least 200 years, proposals to tax away that 'unearned' part of land values which is due to social change (and government decisions) rather than to individual effort, have had considerable appeal. The idea that a tax of this kind could be a 'single tax', replacing all other taxes, goes back to the French Physiocrats, but it is most popularly associated with Henry George, the American economist and propagandist, who by the early twentieth century had attracted considerable support for the idea of a land value tax, including the support of liberal-socialist leaders like Kerensky, Gladstone, Lloyd George and Sun-Yat-Sen (who proposed full land value taxation in 1898).[3]

To the leaders of the 'far left', of course, such a policy was 'tame' compared to the doctrine of outright nationalization of all forms of property, not merely of site value. Karl Marx called the single tax 'capitalism's last stand'.[4] But the idea of using taxation as a means of grappling with land 'speculation' has been of continuing appeal to those reformers who wish to retain some form of 'mixed economy', and indeed site value taxes, albeit of a very watered-down kind, have actually been introduced in a number of countries. British property taxation has traditionally been based on annual rack-rent, and in the United States and South Africa, property taxes are typically based on the capital value of land plus improvements. But by the early twentieth century individual cities like Johannesburg in South Africa and Salisbury in Rhodesia had full site value rating and cities such as Pittsburgh in the USA had partial site value rating.[5] In addition, there were a number of 'single tax colonies' established in the USA in the late nineteenth and early twentieth centuries as model communities run on Georgist lines (for example, 'Fairhope', Alabama, the 'Three Ardens' in North Delaware, 'Free Acres', New Jersey, and so on), often incorporating some of William Morris's ideas about idyllic rural communities as well. But in practice none of these 'colonies' managed to survive on a single tax basis except where they were in some way subsidized by philanthropic idealists.[6]

Site value taxation was also widely adopted in the British 'White Commonwealth', with the exception of South Africa. Thus in the late nineteenth century, taxes on the unimproved value of land were levied in British Columbia (the 'wild land' tax of 1873),[7] South Australia,[8] Queensland,[9] New Zealand and New South Wales.[10] Indeed, in some cases of newly-colonized or virgin land, the emphyteutic principle of leasehold tenure only has been applied, as in the Canberra district of Australia, most of Queensland and in Argentina in the early nineteenth century. But none of these taxes approached the Georgist scheme of taxing away the whole of site value. Few of them taxed more than 5 per cent of capital value, and in most cases these taxes were insufficient to hinder land speculation, as was demonstrated by the land boom in Western Canada between 1900 and 1914.

It is significant that few of the major European countries (with virtually no virgin land and much more complicated types of land tenure) have successfully established such a tax. One exception is Denmark, which established a national tax on increments in land values in 1933, levied annually at 4 per cent on three-quarters of the increase and assessed by local committees.[11] The other main exception is the increment tax systems of the German towns which grew out of earlier property registration taxes. A notable example is the Frankfurt *Wertzuwachssteuer* (increment value tax) of 1893, which was later copied by other German towns such as Hamburg and Cologne, and indeed was taken over by the German Imperial government from 1911 to 1913.

Such taxes attracted considerable interest in Britain in the late nineteenth century, particularly in the context of schemes for the reform of the rating system. Then, as now, local rates were levied on the annual value of property rather than on its capital value, and this was thought to encourage landowners to hold potential housing land off the market. The land value tax movement was strongest in the cities of Glasgow and London; in fact, Glasgow Corporation itself sponsored a land value taxation bill (the Land Values (Scotland) Bill of 1906) in Parliament, which was only frustrated by the House of Lords. One of the reasons for the prominence of Glasgow in the land tax movement was that the feudal system is the typical form of land tenure in Scotland and in the 1880s and 1890s the idea of taxing ground landlords had considerable appeal, since such landlords could be represented as 'parasites' on the land, and moreover in most cases they paid no rates, since they typically contracted away to the lessee or feuar any such fiscal obligations. A tax on ground rents was one of the original ideas put to the Liberal Cabinet in the tax proposals of 1909, the alternatives being a simple tax on site values or the Frankfurt-type increment tax.[12]

But the shortcomings of a ground rental tax can easily be shown. First, it is out of line with the basic rationale for taxing land ownership which was outlined above — the taxation of wealth which has been created by the community or by public works. This is because in all cases where the ground landlord has no reversion (as with feus in Scotland, fee farm rents in England, and, to all intents and purposes, 999-year leases as well), such a landlord does not enjoy any benefit from public works or economic development. Second, such a scheme would be unfair where there are a number of subordinate lessors and lessees. For example, if A (who holds the fee simple) is the 999-year lessor to B, who in turn leases on a 99-year term to C, who in turn leases on a 21-year term to D, who finally leases on a 3-year basis to E, the occupier, it would be highly unjust to tax only the 'ground landlord' A, and allow B, C and D (all of whom derive far more benefit from improvements and development than A) to go scot free. Moreover, even by the 1890s, the mythology of the typical ground landlord as an idle aristocrat living in luxury off the backs of the labouring classes, did not correspond with the reality. In Scotland particularly, feus had in many cases passed from their original owners to churches, charities, insurance companies, local authorities and the like — rather less dramatic 'exploiters' than the grands seigneurs conjured up by the reformers' rhetoric.

These objections to ground rent taxation are clearly serious; but in fact problems are also created if one admits of these objections and treats the feuar as the taxpayer. This is because the notion of 'land ownership', the apparently clear concept with which one started, begins to crumble, and one gets into one of those definitional tangles which we discussed in Chapter 5. In effect, under the Scottish feudal system, the feuar is the owner, the superior merely a creditor with first claim on the land (equivalent to a debenture shareholder); but the strict legal position is that feu duty is 'rent' and that the superior is the holder of the absolute title to the land, merely granting to the feuar the dominium utile. Commonly the estate of the feudal superior carriers with it the power to realize development value, and the feuar may have to pay the superior for a waiver of the obligations which inhibit or restrict the development of land. Similar problems arose with copyhold land tenure, which persisted until the 1920s. The 'landowner' is thus not quite so easy to identify as one might think.

In spite of the political attractions of a land values tax, indeed its claim to be a panacea for solving a wide variety of economic problems, the difficulties of implementing such a tax in a long-settled country with complex systems of land tenure are very great. Denman, for example, considers the land tenure problem to be the key explanation of the difficulty of implementing land speculation taxes.

The problem, he says, is that the land market does not in fact deal in land

> 'What is sold there are estates and interests in land, fee-simples, limited interests of various kinds, easements and other rights and privileges over land . . . a particular interest is not peculiar at any one moment to a given parcel of land.'[13]

One administrative way out of the tangle might simply be to impose heavy charges on capital gains in land transactions, and this was in fact done in Britain in 1974 as a temporary basis for a land speculation tax. But this solution has several drawbacks. Even if such a tax could be effectively enforced (which is by no means self-evident, since there is no means of 'objectively' checking the market price of a piece of land comparable to the system of quoting the values of stocks and shares in the newspapers), it would not meet the purpose. First, it would not effectively distinguish between the 'speculator' and the man who has raised the value of a piece of land by altering it in some way (for example, by reclamation). Second, it might encourage land hoarding. This has been the experience in some cases of taxes of this kind. The result is a scarcity of land on the market and consequently higher land prices — precisely the opposite of the desired objective. Third, such a tax would obviously be unjust unless there was some means of distinguishing between the value of the land proper and the value of whatever is upon it.

In order to catch the 'speculator' therefore, a land tax has to be based on the value of 'sites' or notionally cleared ground; in principle, such a tax will discourage land hoarding in or near built-up areas and falls more heavily upon the 'speculator' than upon the 'improver'. But these concepts are too subtle to serve as the basis of administrative distinctions, as can be illustrated from the case of Lloyd George's ill-fated land values taxes, which were introduced in the 'People's Budget' of 1909 and repealed by Austen Chamberlain in 1920.

The Land Taxes of 1909

The Finance Act of 1909 declared its purpose along 'Georgist' lines

> 'The guiding principle of this Act is to secure for the state a direct contribution from owners of land whose property is enhanced in value by the action of the community at large.'

But in fact, instead of a 'pure' land value tax, Lloyd George introduced four separate taxes: the Mineral Rights Duty, Reversion Duty, Undeveloped Land Duty and Increment Value Duty.[14] The Increment Value Duty was a duty of 20 per cent *ad valorem* on the increase of the site value of land over a base value at 30th April 1909, to be levied on sale, death, lease or every 14 years in the case of bodies corporate, trusts and the like. In order to avoid taxing working-class home-owners, small dwelling-houses were exempt and there had to be an increase of over 10 per cent in the value of the site before duty was payable. Moreover, no duty of ten shillings or less was in fact collected, on the *de minimis* principle (this represented a capital value of £120).

In the last chapter we examined the 'base line' problem of drawing lines arbitrarily in time, and the base line of the Increment Value Tax was a problem of this type, bearing hardly on individual cases. For example, the town of Leicester had gone through a boom at its height about 1904 and subsequently suffered a depression which was at its worst in 1908—1910. In cases like this, people could be taxed on increment values from 1909, while making large overall losses on land transactions. As a result, a 20-year rule was introduced (following the Frankfurt *Wertzuwachssteuer*) under which people who had paid for property up to 20 years before 1909 and had subsequently seen it fall in price could claim the actual purchase price as the base value. The same applied to sales of leases for Reversion Duty (for example, the case of a Mr. John Lindsell of Willesden, who bought a lease for £280 in 1906 and sold it for £250 in 1911),[15] though many people were unaware of this concession and cases of 'injustice' were mistakenly publicized.

The second tax, the Undeveloped Land Duty, was intended to prevent the 'hoarding' of land needed for industrial or housing development. No duties were imposed on agricultural land as such, but all land exceeding £50 per acre (which was thought mainly to involve land in the vicinity of cities which would in the course of time be developed) was subject to a tax of one-half penny in the pound each year on the difference between £50 per acre and the development value of the land, with a fresh valuation every five years.

This tax raised a host of definitional problems. It included all sorts of odd cases such as urban allotment gardens, which were particularly awkward since they were commonly let at less than the economic rent and hence the tax in practice fell on the tenant rather than on the owner.[16] But the Inland Revenue Department considered that allotments could not be exempted from the tax, since it would then become impossible to refuse exemption to all agricultural land, and moreover it would have been possible for any land 'speculator' to avoid duty on undeveloped land by letting it (perhaps only nominally) as allotments. As it was, the Undeveloped Land Duty contained generous exemptions (for example, for private houses with large gardens), some of which tended to defeat its object. For example, landowners were exempted from duty on account of expenditure on roads and sewers at the rate of one exempt acre for every £100 of expenditure. This exemption in practice tended to remove from charge the 'ripe' land which was in immediate demand for building, while 'ripening' land which had only a prospective building value remained liable to the duty.[17] A separation of the tax treatment of 'ripe' and 'ripening' land was repeatedly urged, but the Inland Revenue officials considered that no distinction could be made which would stand up in the courts.

Various other problems of the same type arose in connection with Undeveloped Land Duty. For example, there was the case of glebe land (part of a clergyman's stipend).[18] A clergyman's powers of disposing of glebe land were typically fairly limited, but he might nevertheless be taxed upon the capital value of the glebe land while his income was limited in practice to its annual value. Indeed, in cases such as glebe land, where potential building land was let as agricultural land, Undeveloped Land Duty could amount to 50 per cent or so of the annual income from the land. Another problem was that the duty offered no incentive for agricultural improvement, because even if by improvements the agricultural value of land was raised to over £50 per acre (say to £80), the landowner was still being taxed on the difference between £50 per acre and the development value of the land.[19] There were always a few cases of hardship here, and the problem received more attention in the context of attempts to stimulate food production in World War I, but in fact nothing was done about the problem.

In order to prevent avoidance of Increment Value Duty by resort to leasing, the third duty, Reversion Duty, was levied on leasehold property. This was a 10 per cent tax on the benefit accruing to the lessor by the determination of a lease (that is, the 10 per cent was charged on the excess of the capital value of the land over the rent payable capitalized at 25 times annual value). It was not payable in the case of agricultural land, where the original term of the lease was less than 21 years, or where a reversion had been purchased before 1909 with less than 40 years to run. Small lessors very often did not render accounts to the tax officials, and the bulk of the revenue came from London and from the rich (for example, more than two-thirds of the Reversion Duty revenue from London in 1913 came from only three taxpayers, the Duke of Westminster, the New River Company and the Ecclesiastical Commissioners). For such taxpayers it was obviously worthwhile to seek every possible legal loophole and in fact by 1919 the Reversion Duty had been 'killed for all practical purposes' (in the Inland Revenue's words)[20] by a decision of the Court of Appeal in the case of *Ecclesiastical Commissioners for England v. the Inland Revenue Commissioners.*

Finally, the Mineral Rights Duty, the simplest of the four taxes, was a special tax of one shilling in the pound on the rental value (or imputed rental value, in the case of owners working their own land) of the rights to work minerals. This did not involve valuation of land and did not cover unworked minerals, which were covered by Increment Value Duty and by Reversion Duty. As a result, this Duty caused few administrative problems and was retained long after the other three had been swept away.[21] But even this tax did not entirely escape the categorization problem, because 'mineral' is by no means an unambiguous term. For example, felsite, granite and whinstone were borderline cases involving court judgments, and there were other even more difficult ones: for example, was brine a 'mineral'?[22]

The taxes presented few problems of control in a general sense because they were stamp duties payable by the transferor or lessor, and therefore all transfers of land and leases were invalid unless stamped with the Increment Duty stamp. Illegal transfers of land thus presented little or no problem. The real administrative problem was the problem of valuation, since all of the duties with the exception of Mineral Rights Duty involved valuation. To cope with this task, the Inland Revenue Department expanded its Valuation Department and set up a new field organization of valuation officials, called District Valuers, in 130 areas based on groupings of Income Tax parishes and working with Ordnance Survey maps.[23] By 1914 there were almost 5,000 valuation officials, and these officials had by then provisionally valued about 79 per cent of the total land area of Great Britain and about 86 per cent of the (approximately) ten million 'hereditaments' involved.[24] The income-tax machinery was used to trace landowners and to send out tax returns. Provisional valuations were made on the basis of these returns, and owners disagreeing with these valuations could appeal either to the courts, or to the Inland Revenue's Board of Referees (consisting of qualified surveyors), or both. By 1917 there had been nearly 1,700 appeals to the Board of Referees.[25]

The administrative machinery survived the abolition of the taxes and the abandonment of the valuation:[26] the District Valuers have subsequently been used for purposes such as Estate Duty valuations, wartime requisitioning and compensation work and local authority rating (in England and Wales) as well as the later attempts to levy taxes on land speculators in the 1940s and 1960s. But the taxes themselves were a spectacular failure, with the sole exception of Mineral Rights

Duty. The land taxes cost far more to collect than they ever brought in, and even in 1914, the high-water-mark of administrative success, the cost of collecting the taxes (£2.17m) was more than twice the revenue involved (£612,000). The total receipts down to the repeal of the duties in 1920 were £1.3m and the total cost in connection with the valuation, administration and collection of the duties was estimated at £5m. [27] Table I tells this story.[28]

The expense of the valuation could have been greatly reduced if the valuation had also been used for local authority rating, and both Lloyd George and the Chief Valuer of the Inland Revenue (Sir Edgar Harper) were keen on the idea of site value rating, which was seriously considered just before World War I.[29] But there was a multi-organizational problem: at that time local authority rating was administered by local assessment committees (a system which was notoriously uneven, especially in rural areas) and local authorities were jealous of local rating assessments being made by a central department.[30] Some top Treasury officials were also opposed to the scheme.[31] There were more technical problems as well. For example, Increment Value Duty and Reversion Duty were only leviable on certain 'occasions', whereas local rating is an annual tax and obviously would have required a continual up-dating of the 1909 valuation. Also property belonging to public utility companies was not valued for the land value taxes, though it was subject to local rates; and fixed charges were deductible for the land taxes but not for local rates. Besides, the 1909 valuation could not have been used for rating purposes until at least 1916 — by which time the advent of World War I had killed the scheme.

Valuation

The dominant administrative problem in these taxes was that of valuation. Such problems could have been lessened by setting an arbitrary (and therefore inequitable) uniform acreage value as the base value, but they could not have been eliminated. Valuation for these taxes threatened to take administrators into the realms of high metaphysics of the type which we discussed in Chapter 4, because the problem is to value the site notionally cleared of buildings, but nevertheless with such buildings still upon it. The majority report of the Royal Commission on Local Taxation (England) of 1901 considered this to be a nonsensical idea

'The only ultimate basis of a valuer's knowledge is his experience of actual market values, and as the land and the houses upon it are sold and let together, no such basis can exist for a separate valuation of the two things.'[32]

The Select Committee on the Land Values Taxation (Scotland) Bill of 1906 came to much the same conclusion. They considered that the value of a site considered as cleared and ready for building was an intelligible proposition, but

'... the value of a site which is to be treated as covered by the present building and no other, and yet is to be valued entirely separately from that building, is an abstraction which it is impossible to regard as an appropriate subject for taxation.'[33]

Moreover, it was difficult to avoid the problem by applying some fairly easy rule of thumb such as the deduction of the cost of buildings from the market value of the site plus buildings, since the cost of a building is not always a reliable test of the

Table I. Land tax revenue 1909–1920

Year	Increment value Est. £	Increment value Yield £	Reversion Est. £	Reversion Yield £	Undeveloped land Est. £	Undeveloped land Yield £	Mineral rights Est. £	Mineral rights Yield £	Total Est. £	Total Yield £
1910–11	20,000	127	90,000	257	280,000	2,351	700,000	506,290	520,000	509,025
1911–12	50,000	6,127	50,000	22,621	200,000	28,947	400,000	436,193	481,193	493,888
1912–13	30,000	16,981	125,000	47,974	100,000	97,852	290,000	273,915	455,000	436,722
1913–14	20,000	34,199	100,000	80,435	325,000	274,916	305,000	345,343	715,000	734,893
1914–15	55,000	48,316	130,000	19,313	230,000	8,652	310,000	337,680	412,000	413,961
1915–16	60,000	46,070	10,000	11,796	—	638	280,000	308,511	363,000	368,817
1916–17	100,000	67,088	10,000	18,009	—	196	290,000	286,405	521,000	524,138
1917–18	30,000	103,005	15,000	23,164	—	74	255,000	262,129	685,000	650,908
1918–19	110,000	183,321	25,000	39,331	—	62	270,000	252,277	664,000	709,867
1919–20	120,000	135,823	20,000	15,737	—	52	260,000	253,892	663,000	650,596

rental which it can command. Finally, there are cases in which the value of the site and the capital which has been expended on improvements can hardly be distinguished, as in the case of land reclaimed from the sea. This problem will be discussed further below.

For the Increment Value Tax of 1909, the notional 'site value' of all the land in the country had to be valued as at the same time (30th April, 1909) and this valuation had to take place at the same time as the assessment and collection of the duty was being carried out. The original scheme was for valuation to be made by owners and merely checked by government officials at relatively small expense,[34] but this was later changed into a complete official valuation, securing greater efficiency at the expense of much greater cost and delay, since it depended in practice upon a small core of trained valuers who had to train other officials while also carrying out the base-line and 'occasion' valuations. The size of the task to which these very limited administrative resources had to be applied, can hardly be exaggerated. No valuation on this scale had been carried out in England since the Domesday Book of 1086,[35] and the obligation to value property on the 'occasions' on which tax fell due (death, sale, reversion or lease) meant that the valuers could not work systematically across their territories.

The basic difficulty of identifying owners of property and units of land was less acute in Ireland and Scotland, owing to the system of land registration in Scotland through the Court of Sasines and Burgh Surveyors and to the fact that there had been a Commissioner for Land Valuation in Ireland since 1810. Land registration at least removed some of the initial difficulties of implementing the tax in these countries, and the existence of similar land registration systems in German towns may well have facilitated the introduction of the Frankfurt increment value tax which was mentioned above.

The Irish valuation, however, was by no means plain sailing, since it was particularly badly handled. The names of owners had not been obtained before sending out assessment forms, no records were kept of what was building land and what was agricultural land, and in fact no visual inspections whatever were made at first. In many cases, assessment forms were not sent out at all, which meant that fixed charges were not included in the original valuation and so the first valuation was entirely useless. On top of this, shortages of trained staff, inaccurate records and an arbitrary 10 per cent deduction from Dublin 1909 site values on the orders of the Valuation Commissioner (which thereby increased the Increment Tax payable on occasions) created a tremendous muddle, especially in the city of Dublin and in the townships.[36]

These and other valuation problems meant that arrears steadily built up and the problem of establishing the base value (as of 1909) became more difficult as time elapsed and the original valuation was still uncompleted.[37] This was worsened by the fact that the valuers tended to tackle the easiest problems first, working inwards from the outskirts of towns and cities; and though over three-quarters of the total hereditaments were in fact valued (at least provisionally), it was the most difficult ones which remained.[38] As a result of this experience, Philip Snowden proposed to begin the work of valuation some two years before tax was leviable[39] when he introduced another land values tax in 1931 (this tax in fact perished in the National Government of 1931 and was abolished in the 1932 Finance Bill).[40]

A general problem of valuation is the time element — units of landownership are not stable. Single units of property are divided into separate units, separate units are aggregated into single units, and as time elapses the problems of apportioning increment values become more difficult. Moreover, different results will be obtained according to whether units of occupation or units of ownership are taken as the valuation unit. Units of ownership might seem to be the more logical choice, but in fact for the 1909 duties and for the taxes proposed in 1931, units of occupation were used, presumably because this fitted in more easily with the Income Tax machinery upon which the tax was based. This arrangement could create severe inequities, for example where adjacent properties, commonly owned but separately leased with leases close to termination, were valued at the sum of their individual values, which might well be much less than the value of the whole property as a single unit (for industrial or office development, for example), and thus set different values on identical units of ownership.

An inherent problem with taxes based on notional values rather than on actual market values is that they create all kinds of absurdities which seem to fly in the face of common sense — another problem which is beginning to be familiar to us. For example, in the 1909 taxes, several cases arose in which there had been no rise, or even a fall, in the price of land, but in which an 'increment value' was deemed to have arisen. This could happen in cases where the official valuation of buildings was less than the actual cost or market price of those buildings, and thus the deduction of the value of the buildings from the value of the site plus buildings revealed a site value higher than the true market price of the site. This could even happen in cases where identical adjacent sites were still on offer at prices lower than the official valuation of the neighbouring site, making it quite plain that no actual increment in site value had taken place. A fall in the cost of buildings could have the same effect.[41] The result in such cases was that the tax fell on builders' profits or individual improvements to land — the very thing, in fact, which such a tax sets out *not* to do. There were also awkward cases where builders made profits on land but losses on building (for example, where they sold land separately and then contracted to erect buildings upon it, making a loss on the second transaction). Moreover, since there was no allowance for losses in the 1909 tax, cases could have arisen (though in fact they did not) in which builders of an estate sold some properties at 'abnormal' profit and others at a loss, making a low overall profit, but nevertheless rendering themselves liable to heavy Increment Value Tax.

The most celebrated 'builder's case' arose in Newcastle-on-Tyne in 1910 concerning a shop sold by a builder (a Mr. Lumsden), where an increment value was revealed in spite of the fact that the site value had demonstrably not increased. The Lumsden case went as far as the House of Lords, which divided equally on the matter and thus upheld the Inland Revenue. The revenue authorities defended their position over the Lumsden case on the grounds that the Increment Value Tax did not fall on 'normal' building profits, but on 'abnormal' profits such as Lumsden had made; that price was not equivalent to market value, and that it would be absurd to let the speculator in land off all Increment Value Tax simply because he happened to be a builder.[42]

The Lumsden decision, however, attracted considerable ridicule. For example, Lord Justice Moulton in the House of Lords case said that in future a 'catechism on the laws of England' would read thus

> Q. What is the increment of the site value of land where the value of the site has not changed?
>
> A. It is the difference of opinion between two sets of Government Valuers as to the value of the owner's total interest in the estate.'[43]

Political pressures too, built up over this issue. The depression in the property market and in the building trade were blamed on the tax (though in fact property values were definitely beginning to recover by 1911), and a tax falling on either the building trade or the working-class home-owner was the opposite of what the government had intended. Since Lumsden threatened to become a kind of 'builders' Hampden' and withheld payment of his tax (£22 plus £249 costs), the Prime Minister, Mr. Asquith, himself promised to reverse the Lumsden judgment by a Bill providing that sites used for building should have their site values estimated on a valuation basis rather than by reference to actual sale price (but see the post-war story for experience with this type of system). This legislation never in fact materialized because of World War I; and instead all cases of the Lumsden type (for example where the value of buildings was greater than the value of the site) were simply held in abeyance from 1915 onwards.

Other valuation problems were less abstruse. Any kind of valuation raises the problem that like cases will be treated differently as a result of some people being lazier and more ignorant than others. Some people failed to appeal against valuation; others ignorantly thought that under-valuation of the base value of property was to their advantage (as it would be for local authority rating, for example), whereas in fact it was to their disadvantage in this case. The result was that in a series of identical adjacent properties some could have higher valuations of site values than others, which again flies in the face of common sense.

Lloyd George, reflecting on his experience with land values taxation at the time that Snowden's proposed tax was being discussed in 1930, observed

> 'We have learned by experience that the only way to make a valuation of that kind effective for taxing purposes is to make it as simple and direct as possible . . .'[44]

Certainly, the ill-fated Snowden tax was to be much simpler than the 1909–1920 duties, since it simply involved an annual tax of one penny (d) in the pound on the site value of every unit of land in Great Britain (including agricultural land and small landholdings, which had been exempt under the 1909 tax), with various exemptions. But this tax would still have involved a complete simultaneous valuation of all the land in the country, and it is difficult to see how the knotty questions relating to site valuation which arose over the 1909 taxes, could have been avoided.

Multiple Types of Land Tenure

The second major class of problems in the 1909 taxes arose from the complications of mutiple types of land tenure. In most of the other countries where site value taxes were introduced, the White Commonwealth countries and the cities of Hamburg and Frankfurt, freehold land ownership was the typical form of land tenure. But in Britain there have traditionally been many different forms of land tenure, such as freehold, customary freehold, freeholds subject to perpetual ground rents (common in the North of England, normal in Scotland), copyholds, 999-year leases, building leases and occupation leases. As a result, it is very difficult to frame regulations in such a way as to prevent inequities between different types of land tenure. For example, Reversion Duty was levied on the difference between the value of a property at the end of a lease and the value of a property at the beginning of a lease, but when a lessor purchased his freehold, he had to pay Reversion Duty on the *entire* value of his property.[45] There were also problems related to multiple occupation of a single site, as in the case of flatted property or office property.

The problem was that many types of flatted property would strictly have a nil site value under the 1909 tax. Worse, minus site values could arise in the case of copyholds and where the fixed charges were heavy, as in the Scottish feudal system. Negative site values would arise because, in order to tax equitably the freeholder, the copyholder, the feudal tenant and so on, there had to be some means for deducting the encumbrances or fixed charges attached to the site or the cost of enfranchisement in the case of copyholders (tithe rent-charges were, however, excluded for some reason under the 1909 tax), and the capitalized value of these charges could exceed the value of the site unencumbered.

Thus in the 1909 duties, 'assessable site value' represented the price which the cleared site would fetch if the permanent burdens remained and none of the outlay of the owner in developing or in otherwise improving the site had been expended. Therefore if, as was common in Scotland at this time, a builder obtained a plot of land by a feuduty set at 5 per cent of the capital value of the site and added to it a ground annual of an equal sum, the capital value of the added ground annual (at 20 to 23 years' purchase) would have to be deducted from the value of the site in assessing site value. This deduction would be likely to make the value of the notionally cleared site negative if the value of land had not changed, since the capital value of the feuduty deducted from the capital value of the site would by definition be nil.[46] Indeed, it was possible generally to avoid or mitigate the effects of Increment Value Duty by creating ground burdens which would reduce the selling price of the site, though how far this took place as a deliberate tactic of avoidance is difficult to tell.

Apart from negative site values, nil site values could arise in the case of flatted property or offices. In Scotland particularly, many flatted houses were owned separately and unless otherwise determined by title, the *solum*, area and back green belong to the lowest heritor (subject to a right of common interest in the upper heritors enabling them to resist any injurious alteration); and the result was that the owners of the upper floors would escape liability in Increment Value Duty and the whole burden would therefore be thrown on to the ground-floor owner, the other flats having no 'site value'. This was particularly inequitable in the case of basement flats and flats built on two levels, where flats above 'ground level' might nevertheless lead off into a street (a glaring case of this arose on the George IV Bridge in Edinburgh).

Difficulty of Separating Land Value from Improvements

Another basic categorization problem in taxing 'site value' is to determine what a 'site' entails. In principle, as has already been mentioned, the idea is to distinguish the value of the ground from the value of the improvements which have been carried out on it, but in practice there is no easy dividing line. What is assumed to be on the 'site'? Only the 'natural fertility of the soil', a notion of classical economics? But how is 'natural' fertility to be distinguished from fertility obtained by investment in drainage and fertilizers? In practice under the 1909 tax, gates, culverts, stone walls, 'dead fences' of all descriptions (but not hedges), ditches, dykes, farm roads and land drainage were included in what purported to be the unimproved value of land. Problems arose over whether stone walls were 'buildings', but 'buildings' were held to constitute more than one wall and a roof. But this dividing line, not surprisingly, proved to be too arbitrary to hold the position. Indeed, there was in fact some ambiguity between Section 25, sub-section 4 and Section 24, sub-section 2 of the 1909—1910 Finance Act on this point (the first stating the allowable deductions for arriving at assessable site value, the second defining site value).[47] In February 1914 a High Court case, the 'Norton Mal-Reward case' (*Lady Smyth v. Commissioners of Inland Revenue*) overturned this basis of valuation by establishing that the value of crops, unexausted manure and all 'vegetable growths' should be included in unimproved value (but illogically, in a later case decided by the same judge, the value of sporting rights was *not* to be included in unimproved value).

This court decision effectively sabotaged the valuation effort, since it rendered illegal all valuations which had been made up to that date and introduced a principle of valuation which, whatever its logical merits, was scarcely of practical application. Not only would it have been almost impossible to ascertain in 1914 the exact position of tillage in every farm in the country at 30th April 1909, but the value of land in January, when corn or hops were not above the ground, would be less than the value of the same land in July, when the corn and hops were near maturity. Legislation was introduced to reverse this decision in 1914 (the same bill which was to have reversed the Lumsden judgment), but owing to the war emergency it was never passed, and consequently the taxes, particularly the Undeveloped Land Duty and the Increment Value Duty, were virtually held in abeyance pending the necessary amending legislation.

The Problem of a Two-price System in Land

A final administrative problem which is inherent in many schemes for taxing increments in land values is that they invite the development of 'two-price systems'. This can happen in two ways. One is that the prices of land acquired for development by public authorities may differ widely from land sold in private transactions, a problem which has arisen in the post-1945 planning machinery and which will be briefly discussed later. Second, and more generally, there are 'two-price' systems in the sense of 'under the counter payments': the 'official' price which is notified to the authorities for the purpose of Stamp Duty or other taxes is much lower than the price which is actually paid. This problem might well have arisen if the 'Lumsden amendment' to the 1909 Finance Bill had been carried through, and it has certainly affected seriously the post-1945 British attempts to grapple with the 'land speculation' problem, notably the Development Charges scheme under the Town and Country Planning Act of 1947 and the Betterment Levy of 1967.

Indeed, this problem can only be averted by a tax based wholly on official valuation (and we have seen some of the problems which that can create) or by moving away from taxation as a means of administration towards provisions such as direct state control or nationalization of land. This is certainly the trend of more recent attempts to deal with the 'land problem' in Britain, which we will now briefly discuss.

Post-1945 Schemes

It is not our purpose here to give an account of the growth of the machinery for town planning, compulsory purchase powers for local authorities and so forth. Obviously these developments in the nineteenth and twentieth century are closely related to other means of dealing with 'unearned' benefits accruing to landowners from social and economic development, and are to some extent alternatives to taxation. But they have been adequately discussed elsewhere[48] and so will not be dealt with here. Nor will we describe the British post-war spatial planning machinery which was created in the late 1940s, except for those measures which dealt directly with land values.

The main way in which the existence of a physical planning machine affects the administration of taxes on land speculation is that the granting of planning permission or re-zoning can be used as the tax point, and this was the means used in the 1947 Town and Country Planning Act. The government nationalized the 'development value' (but not the 'existing use value') of all land in the UK, and made a fund of £300 m available to compensate landowners for the loss of development rights. The Act followed in large part the recommendations of the 1942 Uthwatt Committee Report on Compensation and Betterment,[49] itself the result of unsatisfactory experience with the compensation and betterment provisions of the 1932 Town and Country Planning Act. As from 1947, people who wished to develop their land had to pay the government for the privilege, paying the whole of the difference between 'existing use value' and 'development value' of the site as a development charge. The revenue accruing from such development was to be used to finance schemes of land development undertaken by the Central Land Board, an administrative body which was also responsible for assessing development charges and claims for compensation out of the £300 m.[50]

This scheme obviously had grave deficiencies from a pure 'Georgist' point of view, though it avoided the problem of simultaneous valuation of all the property in the UK to some extent, since the onus rested on landowners to claim compensation for loss of development value, and development charges only involved valuing a limited number of properties in any given year. But various problems of categorization and discrimination, similar to those encountered in the 1909—1920 duties, immediately emerged. One case of arbitrary dividing lines concerned the distinction between 'existing use' and 'change of use': there is in fact a very fine line dividing the two, and moreover cases in which there was no significant change of use might nevertheless constitute a 'change of use' for administrative purposes. For example, 'light industry' fell into three or four use categories under the 1947 Act. These problems resulted in some unhappy administrative experiences, such as long delays in granting authorization for some very trivial change of use;[51] and many of the finer discriminations in planning categories were abandoned in 1950.

There were also problems of control in a more general sense rather than of categorization. The basic problem of this type has already been mentioned, namely that the actual prices paid for land in the private sector were far above the official basis of existing-use value. Indeed, this was scarcely surprising, since with a notional development charge of 100 per cent, a premium payment of some kind was obviously necessary in order to persuade an owner to sell other than by compulsory purchase.[52] Thus, far from alleviating the 'land problem', the development charge system actually drove development costs up in all cases other than compulsory purchase projects — once more achieving the reverse of the desired objective. The Central Land Board could not effectively grapple with the problem since it had no systematic information about land prices. This is because actual purchase prices did not have to be notified to the Board when development charges were being assessed, and even if such disclosure had been compulsory, there would have been no means of checking on its veracity, since both seller and purchaser would have had a common interest in under-reporting. In spite of this problem of weak administrative control and no incentives for complying with the law, the Labour government seems to have set its face against a development charge of less than 100 per cent (the Uthwatt Committee had in fact recommended 75 per cent) or an alternative proposal for variable development charges devised to benefit the depressed regions.

A third problem was that the process of assessing development charges suffered from the general problems of taxes based on valuation; that is, delays, uncertainty (there was no statutory basis of valuation) and the difficulty of guaranteeing equity in the face of a multitude of special cases, particularly small cases — the 'back garden' developments which in some cases were scarcely distinguishable from 'rebuildings and enlargements' (exempt from charge). The same problem was later to plague the Land Commission, as we will see. A typical case was that no development charges were incurred in cases where houses were sub-divided vertically, but where any form of 'lateral' conversion took place (for example, by taking down the walls dividing adjacent houses which had formerly been 'semi-detached', in order to form horizontal flats) development charges were payable, and in some cases this generated absurdities.[53]

In 1951 the Conservatives returned to office and in 1953 development charges were abolished. In practice, this meant no funds and a vast apparatus of restrictive control. The £300 m for compensating property owners for loss of the development value of their land was never paid out; instead, compensation was paid only if and when a landowner suffered from planning restrictions which resulted in the loss of development value. Moreover, in order to prevent such compensation from becoming prohibitively expensive (a problem which had arisen under the 1932 Town and Country Planning Act), compensation was only applied to the 1947 development value, based on the claims to the £300 m. Compulsory purchases were on the basis of existing use values plus the assessment of 1947 development value, if any. All other land transactions were in effect returned to a free market.[54]

The result once more was a 'two price' system in land values as described in the previous section, but this time it was of a formal kind between compulsory purchase value and private market values. This produced glaring anomalies in some cases, resulting, for example, in a suicide in one well-publicized 'back garden' case of 1954. As a result of such anomalies, compensation after 1954 was changed to a 'market value' basis, but nothing was done about the problem of betterment (improvement in property value through public works or planning decisions). The Central Land Board itself lingered on until 1959 to complete the assessment of claims on the £300 m made by landowners, which was being used as the basis of compensation for all planning restrictions.[55]

Returned to office in 1964, the Labour Party once more prepared for an assault upon the land problem.[56] Measures taken in the first '100 days' included the restriction of office building in central London (which succeeded only in driving rents up); and later the government announced proposals for a tax on betterment,[57] though these plans did not in fact materialize until 1967. The new system in many ways went back to the Uthwatt proposals of 1942, and the government rejected the 1947 approach of attempting to collect the whole of the difference between existing use value and development value of land. Instead, only 40 per cent of this difference was to be paid as tax and 'existing use value' was calculable in a variety of ways, the taxpayer being able to select that tax base which most benefited him. The Land Commission, a central administrative body, was created to operate the tax and was given powers of compulsory purchase. The Commission was intended to acquire land for housing and other needs, particularly in the 'pressure areas' of London and the South East, the West Midlands and the North East of England.

On the second objective, the Land Commission was not very successful. Basically, there was a 'multi-organization' problem of a type described earlier. The Land Commission was subject to local planning authorities (though the relationship was never quite clear) and in the 'pressure areas' the planning policies of local authorities were typically directed to the containment of urban growth and to the preservation of open country.[58] In fact, Denman argues that such planning policies, rather than land 'speculation', are the root of the shortage of building land in such areas.[59] As a result, the Commission's early estimates of vast available stocks of land waiting to be acquired for housing dwindled, and at one point central government waded into the arena on behalf of the Commission. Mr. Kenneth Robinson, Minister of Land and Natural Resources, attempted in 1968/9 to direct local authorities in the South East to release enough land for 20,000 houses, to be built under the auspices of the Land Commission. But this attempt met with determined opposition from the local planning authorities.

Most of the land acquired was therefore in the North of England and in Scotland, where the pressure was least, and only 16 acres of building land were in fact acquired by the Land Commission in London and the South East, though there was a little more success in the Midlands and in the North West.[60] In fact, the Land Commission repeatedly claimed that its activities resulted in land being brought on to the market for development without having to use its compulsory purchase powers, though it is difficult to assess how far this was true.[61] Certainly one of the results of the conflict between the Commission and local planning authorities was that the Commission became something of a 'land speculator' itself, buying up land in the hope of gaining planning permission for building on it. Moreover, the disposition of what land the Commission did acquire was not an easy task, since such land was to be disposed of at lower than market values, and consequently there were inevitable charges of 'favouritism' over land disposal.

So far as the tax itself was concerned, the 'two-price' problem once more appeared. Builders had also restocked with land before the 'first appointed day' for the operation of the levy; this restocking activity, plus exemptions which applied to projects begun before the introduction of the Betterment Levy in 1967, combined to exempt from levy about two years' supply of building land, in the Commission's judgment.[62] This was probably a very conservative estimate, since in the South East, it appeared that many of the major builders had bought up land even further ahead than planning authorities had looked in the Development Plans. A further problem was that the land boom of the early 1960s had collapsed by the time that the Commission began operations, and the land market was stagnant. Exactly the same problem had befallen the 1909 taxes.

For the technical process of collecting the levy, the Commission had difficulty in recruiting sufficient professional staff (particularly Estate Officers and Lawyers) and moreover — another familiar problem — the levy procedure was very slow. The process leading from the transaction to the collection of levy could take up to seven months even in an absolutely straightforward case, and much longer in the event of disputes. Indeed, such were the complexities that levy assessments might involve, that the Commission was allowed to take up to six years to prepare its tax demands, and payment of levy might thus come long after actual development had taken place. Perhaps because of the uncertainties which such delay involved (causing landowners to build generous allowances for possible tax liabilities into their calculations), the Land Commission machinery did not succeed in its objective of bringing land prices down. Indeed, there is some evidence that the levy, like the earlier development charges system, in fact pushed land prices up, and for the same reason (that is, levy was added to the sale price).

Moreover, the Land Commission, like the Central Land Board before it, suffered from the problem of small developments — 'back garden' cases. Originally, such small cases had deliberately not been excluded from levy in order to prevent tax evasion by fragmentation. In Chapter 4 we discussed the problem that cut-off points exempting small cases from administrative schemes may result in fragmentation as an evasive tactic. In this case, there were fears that exempting small plots of land from tax would result in collusive sub-division of properties, joint occupation, collusive sales, evasion through the formation of companies and so on (such problems had been experienced after the exemption of small properties from the New Zealand site value tax of 1893).[63] For the same reason, the Commission refused to exempt charities from the Betterment Levy in 'Case B' dispositions (taxation of the capitalized value of leases, leviable at the time when a tenancy was granted, comparable to the Reversion Duty of 1909—1920); and this provoked considerable protest. Instead of exemption, the Commission tried to cut out some of the small cases by adding 10 per cent to the existing use value as the assessable base value and thereby narrowing the margin between development value and existing use value. The 1909 duties had, of course, operated the same procedure, though the similarity was probably not deliberate.

But this 'eleven-tenths' rule was not sufficient to cut out the small cases, and as a result the Commission had to grapple with a string of awkward cases involving widows, grandchildren, pensioners and small businessmen facing unexpected and heavy demands for levy payments. Particularly in the North East of England, problems arose with old-age pensioners selling off allotment gardens and spending the proceeds, in happy ignorance of the heavy tax demand which was to follow. A typical case, well publicized, involved a £40 demand from the Commission to an old-age pensioner.[64] In addition, there was a storm of protest from owner-occupiers who had not perceived themselves as the 'land speculators' against whom the Betterment Levy was ostensibly directed, but who were collectively responsible for a large part of the total revenue in the early years. For example, in 1968—1969, some 40 per cent of the levy came from cases involving levy charges of less than £10,000. Moreover, these cases were often worsened by the problems of inequity through ignorance and laziness which we discussed in relation to the 1909—1920 taxes. As a result of such problems, the government decided to exempt small cases from levy in 1969.[69] An administrative by-product of this, of course, was to cut out much of the laborious procedure of levy collection, and this caused a considerable decrease of work; but at the same time risked the evasion which had been originally feared.

As it turned out, there was not time to test whether or not the removal of 'red tape' over small cases would lead to evasion of the levy, because the Land Commission became moribund immediately after the Conservative victory in the 1970 election and was finally swept away in 1971.[66] The loss in revenue was comparatively small, since most of the transactions in land which were subject to Betterment Levy would otherwise have been covered by the general tax on capital gains, and in fact only £30 m or so was actually collected over the three years of the Commission's existence.

But the 'land problem' remained, with an exceptional property boom which reached its peak in 1972. As a result, the Conservative government in early 1973 announced proposals for charges on land hoarding which later turned into plans for a Development Gains Tax, an extra capital gains tax on land transactions. This tax was in fact introduced by the succeeding Labour government in Spring 1974 (in the middle of a collapse in the property market), with later plans for nationalizing all 'development land' — in effect returning to the 1947 position. The process was to begin with an 80 per cent development gains tax on capital values accruing from local authority planning decisions (the Uthwatt proposals of 1942), the proceeds of which were to be shared between central and local government. Local authorities were to be enabled to purchase land net of development gains tax (on the Land Commission principle), and at some time in the future local authorities were to be enabled to purchase land at existing use value (in effect, the 1953—1954 position) with the intention that all 'development land' should eventually be handled by local authorities.[67]

At the time of writing these proposals are tentative and it is impossible to predict the success or failure of the scheme. All of these measures have been tried before, though not in this exact combination and in circumstances which were more or less 'special'. In an attempt to avoid the multi-organization fiascoes of the Land Commission era, the idea of using the planning machinery as the tax point was made much more explicit, and thus the local authorities were to be the taxing authorities, the earlier expedient of a central body having been rejected (though there is to be a central 'back-up' organization to ensure uniformity of tax treatment between areas — no easy task). But in fact the physical planning machinery is now moving away from the very detailed physical planning which would be required for the purposes of taxation, and moreover it is quite possible that the conflict between land taxation or acquisition agencies and the physical planning machine will reproduce itself within the local authority structure. This is particularly true of Scotland, where land acquisition would be mainly handled by the District authorities, whereas planning powers largely rest with Regional Authorities. Areal divisions of local authorities may also cause conflicts, particularly in England. Problems of allocating the land which is acquired by local authorities under this scheme will theoretically be eliminated by disposing of it at market prices, but in practice this is bound to create problems. Moreover, few of the categorization problems encountered in earlier land taxes will be altogether eliminated, and there will be the 'small cases' problem — the cut-off point is to be very low, to prevent evasion, and some of the Land Commission's experience will inevitably be repeated as a result.

Conclusion

Is taxation of land speculators an 'administrative impossibility'? In spite of the administrative problems which are undoubtedly involved, the evidence is in fact highly ambiguous. Even the repeal of the land values duties of 1909 cannot simply be explained in terms of administrative failure. The intervention of World War I and the subsequent coalition government with a Conservative Chancellor who had opposed the introduction of the taxes in 1909, obviously played a large part. The administrative difficulties which had crippled the duties by 1914 made it easier for the opponents of the land taxes to destroy them, but these difficulties might possibly have been overcome or at least mitigated had it not been for the war. Similar ambiguities surrounded the abandonment of the post-war schemes up to 1974.

Moreover, many of the administrative limits involved are basically quasi-administrative limits in that they are rooted in dilemmas between administerability and political acceptability. For example, we noted earlier the tendency for governments to move away from taxation to direct control as a means of controlling land speculation, and there are various ways that direct control might be applied. Consider three alternatives

    (a) the nationalization of all land,

    (b) the nationalization of 'development land'

    (c) government monopoly over all trading in land, i.e. a provision that land could only be sold to the government.

The problem is, as in many other policy issues, that the most 'administerable' solution (in this case (a)) is probably politically the least acceptable in a mass democracy in which approximately 50 per cent of all families are 'landowners' in some sense. But the politically more acceptable half-way-house solution, i.e. (b), is least likely to be administratively successful. The attempt to distinguish 'development land' from other types of land raises a host of discrimination problems similar to those created by the distinction between 'ripe' and 'near-ripe' land for Undeveloped Land Duty in 1909–1920.

As we have already mentioned, most of the administrative problems in the case of land value taxes lie in the lack of fulfilment of the fourth 'internal' condition of perfect administration and the corresponding limit of language and categorization, aggravated by reciprocal learning of the type which we discussed in the last chapter. Examples of these problems are the difficulties of valuation, problems contingent on multiple types of land tenure, the distinction of 'ripe' 'near-ripe' and 'unripe' land, the base-line problem, and the necessity to grapple with small cases in order to prevent evasion. But there were also problems of administrative control in general, for example in applying the capital gains tax practice to land transactions and the general difficulty of avoiding a two-price system in cases where price rather than valuation is taken as the basis for tax. Indeed, the key to successful taxation is administrative control, and in the next Part we will explore the difficulties of 'perfect control', the final set of conditions of perfect administration.

Notes

1. Mellows, A. R., *Taxation of Land Transactions*, Butterworths, London, 1973.
2. *Papers relating to taxation of unimproved value in Queensland*, Cd. 3890, 1908; *The Land Commission*, Cmnd. 2771, 1965.
3. Brown, H. G., H. S. Buttenheim, P. H. Cornick and G. E. Hoover, *Land Value Taxation Around the World*, Robert Schalkenbach Foundation, New York, 1955; S. B. Cord, *Henry George: Dreamer or Realist?* University of Pennsylvania Press, Philadelphia, 1965; H. George, *Progress and Poverty*, 5th ed., Kegan Paul, Trench and Co., London, 1883.
4. Cord, S. B. *op. cit.*
5. Madsen, A. H., 'Land value taxation in practice', appendix to G. L. Record, *How to Abolish Poverty*, G. L. Record Memorial Association, New Jersey, 1936.
6. Brown, H. G., *op. cit.*
7. *Papers on the Working of Taxation of the Unimproved Value of Land in Canada*, Cd. 3740, 1907.
8. *Papers on the Taxation of Land Values in New Zealand, New South Wales and South Australia*, Cd. 3191, 1906.
9. Cd. 3890, *op. cit.*
10. *Papers on Land Taxes in Miscellaneous Foreign Countries*. Cd. 4750, 1909; *Second Series of Memoranda and Extracts Relating to Land Taxation and Land Valuation prepared for the Chancellor of the Exchequer*, Cd. 4845, 1909.
11. This replaced the old Danish *hartkorn* tax which was based on the fertility of the soil and collected whether the land was used or not; the *hartkorn* thus had some features of a land value tax, but it took no account of betterment.
12. Cabinet papers, CAB 37/98.
13. Denman, D. R., 'Lessons From the Land Commission', *Three Banks Review*, no. 98, 1971 (March).
14. For details, see *44th Report of the Commissioners of Inland Revenue for the Year ended 31st March 1911*, Cd. 5833, 1911.
15. Treasury papers T171/39.
16. T172/84.
17. T171/64.
18. T172/84.
19. T172/100.
20. T171/64.
21. T172/1038.
22. T171/39.
23. T171/8.

24. *Report of the Committee on Land Values Taxation*, HC 243, 1919; Cmd. 556, 1920.
25. Records of these are preserved in the Public Records Office, (Long Room) London.
26. *Fifth Report of the Select Committee on National Expenditure*, (Land Valuation Department) 1920, HC 172, 1920, pp. xxxv–xxxvii.
27. HC Deb. 26 April 1920, c. 860; R. B. Yardley, *Land Value Taxation and Rating*, W. H. Collingridge Ltd., (for Land Union) London, 1929.
28. Source: *64th Report of the Commissioners of Inland Revenue for the Year ended 31st March 1921*, Cmd. 1436 1921, p. 153, Table 98.
29. T171/69; CAB 37/117.
30. T172/156.
31. T171/71.
32. Cd. 4750, *op. cit.*, p. 256.
33. *Report of the Committee on the Land Values Taxation etc. (Scotland) Bill 1906*, HC 379, 1906.
34. T171/39.
35. Cd. 5833, *op. cit.*
36. T172/53.
37. Cmd. 918, *op. cit.*
38. CAB 37/117.
39. HC Deb Vol 252, 1930, c. 46; vol. 251, 1931; c. 1409–11.
40. *75th Report of the Commissioners of Inland Revenue for the Year ended 31st March, 1932*, Cmd. 4196, 1933, p. 90, para 66.
41. Cmd. 556, *op. cit.*; T172/100; T171/39.
42. T171/28.
43. T172/100.
44. HC Deb Vol 237, c. 2938.
45. HC Deb Vol XXI (Lords), c. 928.
46. Cmd. 556, *op. cit.*, p. 5.
47. T172/88.
48. See, for example, Ashworth, W. H., *The Genesis of Modern British Town Planning*, Kegan Paul, London, 1954; or J. B. Cullingworth, *Town and Country Planning in Britain*, 4th ed., Allen and Unwin, London, 1972.
49. Cmd. 6386, 1942.
50. *Report of the Central Land Board for the Period to 31st March 1949*, HC 223, 1948–9; *Ministry of Housing and Local Government Progress Report 1943–51*, Cmd. 8204, 1951.
51. HC Deb Vol. 476, 1950, c. 151.
52. Cullingworth, J. B., *op. cit.*; HC 223, 1948–9, *op. cit.*, p. 11, para 43.
53. HC Deb. Vol. 476, 1950.
54. *Report of the Central Land Board for the Financial Year 1952–3*, HC 201, 1952–3; Cmnd. 8699, 1953.
55. *Report on the Work of the Central Land Board 1958–9*, Cmnd. 908. A total of £16.9 m. was collected in development charges.
56. This had considerable academic support. Cf., for example, P. Hall (Ed.), *Land Values*, Sweet and Maxwell, London, 1965.
57. *The Land Commission*, Cmnd. 2771, 1965.
58. Land Commission, *Report and Accounts for the Year ended 31st March, 1969*, HC 371, 1968–1969, p. 4, para 13.
59. Denman, D. R., *op. cit.*
60. Land Commission, *Report and Accounts for the Year ended 31st March, 1970*, HC 69, 1970–1971, p. 3, para 15.
61. Land Commission, *Report and Accounts for the Year ended 31st March, 1968*, HC 358, 1967–1968, p. 7, para 29.
62. *Ibid.*
63. Cd. 4750, *op. cit.*, p. 73.
64. HC Deb Vol. 780, 1969, c. 1319.
65. HC 69, 1970–71, *op. cit.*
66. Land Commission, *Report and Accounts for Period 1st April 1970 to 30th April 1971*, Cmnd. 4874, 1971.
67. Cmnd. 5730, 1974.

Part 3

Authority and Control

Chapter 7

Types of Administrative Control

'Hierarchic control, whereby instructions are passed down the line, is
not the only dimension of control.' S. Beer, *Brain of the Firm*, Allen
Lane the Penguin Press, London, 1972, p. 138.

In Part 2 we examined the conditions of perfect administration relating to time
pressure and to the ability to categorize and discriminate. The problems which arise
would largely occur even in a situation where control presented no problem and
was simply a question of 'passing instructions down the line'. In this Part, we turn
to the central problem of administrative control. What are the basic forms of
administrative control, and what are the limits of such controls? Perfect
administration, it may be recalled, requires either perfect obedience or perfect
control. Perfect control requires (*a*) unlimited control resources, and (*b*) no
incompatibilities between levels or types of control. In Chapter 2 we briefly
discussed the limits which arise when these conditions are relaxed, and in the
following chapters this theme will be developed.

In this chapter we will explore the control resources which are available in
administration by classifying the major types of administrative control, but
avoiding lengthy discussion about the limits on the use or effectiveness of such
controls. The second issue will be explored in the next two chapters. The first of
these chapters examines some of the literature on administrative control, the
second adds some further analysis which largely consists of developing themes
introduced in earlier chapters. After exploring the development of betting taxes, a
particularly interesting study in administrative control, we will return to our
opening question about the limits of administration.

Unlimited control resources is a requirement which could have either or both of
two possible meanings. One is that there is an infinite variety of different types of
control. The second is that any given control can be 'stretched' infinitely in the
sense that one can go on adding extra units without limit and without loss of
effectiveness. The second possible meaning will not be considered here; we will
merely look at the variety of types of control system that are most commonly
found in administration.[1] We will begin with the crudest 'mechanical' forms of
control, but will ignore the techniques of control which operate only in small
informal groups. As we explained in Chapter 1, administrative control involves
some minimum level of scale and formality, and this distinguishes it from 'social
control' in a broader sense, except insofar as 'social control' relates to administrative control.

Ergonomic Controls — Physical Structuring of the Environment

We begin with a set of controls which can be called 'ergonomic' controls.[2] This term refers to the deployment of physical force, or, more generally, to the manipulation of the physical aspects of situations. In its simplest form, manipulation of this kind can be seen as an 'economics' of compliance per unit of threat, force being readily perceived and directly applied. Herman Kahn's 28 levels of nuclear war[3] is a surrealistic example of this kind of economics, but it can also be applied at a more low-key level.

Similarly, ergonomic control can take place *indirectly* by the physical structuring of environments, as with those cases where organizations are built round a computerized process or machine-paced work. Such devices can range from a simple turnstile to the intricate social system which is engendered by the structure of a warship: in Wouk's *The Caine Mutiny*, one of the characters remarks that a warship is 'a system designed by geniuses to be run by idiots'.[4] But the classic example of indirect ergonomic control is the legend of King Arthur's round table, at which his knights never needed to come to blows, because there was no 'head of the table' and therefore no scope for quarrels about placing; also it was so large that no-one needed to be excluded.[5] 'Round table discussions', of course, are still held today; in fact, furniture arrangement is by no means a trivial case in administration and has attracted some interest from social psychologists.[6] A more modern example is the introduction of a new type of swivel chair in British social security offices' interview cubicles, which has been designed to make it harder for irate claimants to attack the interviewing officer. There is the possibility of similar arrangements for road 'furniture' by the development of parking meters which automatically trap cars which have parked illegally or beyond the alloted time, only releasing their grip when fee and/or fine is paid.[7]

Sophisticated ergonomic controls of this type have the advantage of being impersonal and relatively automatic. Marcuse[8] (and others) has noted that our society distinguishes itself by containing recalcitrance with technology rather than with terror: how far this is in fact true as a historical proposition seems doubtful, but it is certainly a goal which has long been desired by those in authority. For example, Hughes quotes a feudal lord in 1484 advocating a tax system

'... providyng as it weare of some sewers or channelles to drawe and sucke from them theyr money by subtyle and indirect means to be handled insensiblye ...'[9]

In the extreme case of ergonomic control, there are thus no overt 'controllers' at all: the controlled is simply like a lunatic in a padded cell. But at a more typical level, ergonomic control involves policing physical bottlenecks, such as airports or seaports, and there are two main ways in which this can be done. The first is to parade forces *visibly* for the purposes of surveillance or in the hope that they will act as a deterrent (for example, the policeman on the beat). This may be coupled with the technique of making periodic 'examples' of offenders *pour encourager les autres*. Such a system may operate either through exhaustive surveillance (as in those countries where customs officials search every suitcase) or through detailed spot checks, either selective or randomized or both. The other main method of policing bottlenecks is to locate the authorities' forces *invisibly*, so as to catch offenders unawares, as with radar speed traps for motorists, the use of closed-circuit

TV cameras to detect shoplifting in large stores and so forth. Very commonly there is a range of 'trade-off' between the two strategies of detection and deterrence, and this applies both to specialized policing (such a factory inspection) and to general-purpose policing.

The 'bottleneck' system is of course the traditional form of tax system, and societies contain many 'threat systems' of this kind, operated both by public authorities and by outlaws, such as criminal protection rackets and political criminals. For example, in the inter-war years, the great American criminal tycoons like Benjamin Siegel, 'Lucky' Luciano, Al Capone and so on, derived the bulk of their money from the Trans-America and Continental racing wire services which they controlled. This was a highly effective control system because, as we will see in Chapter 10, bookmakers have to subscribe to a wire service in order to avoid being 'past-posted', i.e. accepting bets after a race has begun. But reliance on physical bottlenecks is precarious in the context of economic change and development, which is — almost by definition — a 'de-bottlenecking' process involving the production of a range of substitutes for previously scarce goods. In this way, the development of suburbs killed the *octrois*, the old French town-entry taxes which were originally imposed at the gateways of walled towns; and similarly the development of the steam-pump killed Western European salt taxes, because with the advent of such a pump, salt might be produced anywhere on the coast, instead of at a small number of easily policed brine springs.

Bottlenecks, as with ergonomic controls in general, may be 'natural' or 'contrived'. Famous examples of contrived bottlenecks are Bentham's *panopticon* prison design, and Haussman's reconstruction of Paris in the 1860s so that artillery could be used against rioting mobs.[10] More modern examples are automatic car-park barriers and the increasing use of large convex mirrors in retail stores to increase the areas which can be policed by a single official watching for shoplifters. Scanning mirrors and see-through mirrors are beginning to appear, as 'second-generation' deterrents. More abstractly, the concept of artificial bottlenecks may be extended to include 'fees' where official support is needed to enforce contracts. We discussed the development of Stamp Taxes in Chapter 5, and exactly the same mechanism operates with the enforcement of rights of inheritance in return for payment of estate duty. Such fees are, of course, sometimes paralleled by extra-legal levies in the form of 'speed money' and the like.

In fact, ergonomic control in the administration of modern society is more pervasive than one might think, and in some fields, such as town planning, increasing emphasis is once more being placed on the need for ergonomic control. The conventional town planning doctrines of the recent past, of separating traffic from people in towns in order to speed up traffic, and of moving people out of city centres to outlying suburban areas with more surrounding space have had the unforseen effects of creating major possibilities of sabotage (such as children playing 'chicken' on urban motorways or throwing bricks at rapidly moving vehicles) and very great difficulties of policing, because the new structures do not incorporate the important self-policing elements of overlooked city streets.[11] Similar problems arise with new high-density central-heated housing blocks which are outside the official police beat and which often attract meths drinkers and tramps (dog patrols have been used in London as a deterrent in such places). The tower housing block is, of course, the extreme case of such problems, since it has to be open to everyone, if only for reasons of fire access, and there is no means of distinguishing residents from intruders. As a result of such problems, there has been a 'counter-revolution' against the conventional planning doctrines by writers such as Jacobs and Newman, observing that 'the new physical form of the urban environment is possibly the most cogent ally the criminal has in his victimization of society'[12] and advocating 'ergonomic' concepts of 'defensible space' (that is, architecture involving 'privatization' or territoriality in its allocation of space and providing capacity for surveillance of all parts by the inhabitants).

However widespread, ergonomic control is not a panacea. In Chapter 5 we pointed out some of the flaws in the simple assumption that technology will always work to the authorities' advantage, and the same point applies here. Even writers such as Newman recognize that suitable architecture must be combined with appropriate social norms in order to be effective. The crudest types of ergonomic control — the application of direct force — can be costly to operate and presuppose credibility if the threat of their use is to be effective. At this level, too, the application of force can easily be counter-productive, as in the familiar situation where an increment of threat results in a negative increment of compliance. The more sophisticated indirect ergonomic controls are typically very much more effective. As Schelling remarks, tenants are more easily evicted by shutting off services like water and electricity than by direct ejection.[13] Similarly, instead of using security forces to protect trunk telephone lines with hundreds of vulnerable manhole covers, the authorities in Britain built a microwave communication system for security purposes in the early 1950s which simply involves giant concrete towers — very difficult for insurgents to sabotage.[14]

Informational Circuits and Accounting Systems

Our second major type of administrative control is that of accounting and audit systems. Dishonesty and corruption is a spectre hovering over the entire field of administration, particularly at the point of direct contact between administrators and the administered. The basic technique of accounting systems is to divide the information held by people in 'combat' positions into separate compartments, a system which enables only those higher up or somewhere else to see into all the compartments at once, as it were. For example, at one time it was forbidden for English Surveyors and Collectors of Taxes to lodge in the same house. The same principle applies to the traditional separation of 'contracts', 'supply' and 'finance' divisions in government purchasing organization, though this is a system which seems to be more prone to breakdown than the tax examples. Such controls are a standard feature of bureaucratic checking systems, which we will explore more fully in Chapter 9.

Accounting systems of this type are 'threat systems' in the same way as ergonomic control systems in that there is no direct element of reciprocation of benefits in return for compliance.[15] But this type of control is to be distinguished from simple 'ergonomic' controls as discussed in the last section, in that it employs *symbolic* monitors. Literacy, numeracy and mechanized accounting are three very decisive milestones in bureaucratization.

Balzac remarks (in *Illusions Perdues*) that: 'Les idées sont binaires ... il n'y a que Dieu de triangulaire!'[16] But accountability is certainly a 'triangular' concept. It is a checking-up process which logically has to involve at least three separate officials or units. Such triangular controls are illustrated by the traditional system of comptrollers (originally from the Latin *contra-rotulus*)[17] in public administration, for example in the operation of the ancient cross-checking system of jerquers and landwaiters in the Customs or of the central and local officials involved in the collection of direct taxes. Another example is the old army system of contracting out military supply functions to colonels (in France, England and the United States) which was notoriously prone to corruption and mismanagement, and hence 'mustermen' were sent from the King to check regularly that regiments were up to strength.

As in the last example, the basic triangle of accountability logically precedes strict numeracy, though 'accounting' is now virtually identified with numerate control systems. The most familiar forms in modern business practice are the matching of prior costing with operational accounts (first used extensively in the nineteenth century)[18] and the traditional triangle of double-entry book-keeping systems and accounting systems. Until the nineteenth century, the mechanics of this process in the English public accounts was the system of multiple-locked chests and carved wooden tally-sticks, a cumbersome but highly sophisticated process[19] (the accounts balanced to a ½d in 1273).[20]

Nowadays, of course, the completion of the accounting triangle is increasingly mechanized, and here the borderline with ergonomic controls becomes difficult to distinguish. The cash register is perhaps the most obvious example (referred to cynically by F. P. Dunne's Mr. Dooley as 'the crownin' wur-ruk iv our civilization')[21] and the next development is to link cash registers directly to computers in order to further reduce fraud by checkout operators. In Chapter 10, we will see how this type of control system has established itself in bookmaking. 'Black box' flight recorders and monitoring devices fitted to lorries work on similar principles. Even so, many accounting systems in practice still offer enormous scope for petty graft, for example by buyers sanctioning under-delivery of goods by suppliers in return for a percentage 'drop', and by sellers operating similar practices (for example, by over-reporting bad debts, a 'fiddle' which it is very difficult wholly to eliminate).

Symbolic and numerate monitors are increasingly used as monitors of performance as well as their more traditional use to prevent 'the gentle art of scarpering with the ackers'. Indeed, a variant of the 'technophile' argument which we examined in Chapter 5 is that the older forms of administrative control may be rendered less necessary by the development of 'rational evaluation' and numerate targetry. The problems brought out by experience with these techniques are by now fairly well known and they will only be briefly summarized here. There are five main points. First, those techniques which depend on the specification of objectives or targets are ambiguous in those cases (most) where objectives are multiple, conflicting and/or unacknowledgeable. As Boyle has remarked, to say, 'First define your objectives, then you can solve your problems' is really no more than to say, 'First solve your problems, then you can solve your problems'.[22] Second, 'partial rationality' tends to result in the kind of cost shuffling and sub-optimization which was discussed in Chapter 2 in relation to multi-organizations.

Third, 'judgment by results' in its various forms encounters the problem of 'concomitant variations' as J. S. Mill put it.[23] That is, it is difficult to trace some 'result' (good or bad) to a single cause when more than one thing is changing at once.[24] This problem applies to the sub-units within an organization, for example in weighing up the effects of planning, sales and personnel departments in contributing to overall success or failure. It also applies between organizations in the public sector, in weighing up how far the good or bad performance of Agency A depends on the good or bad performance of Agency B. We have already mentioned this problem in Chapter 2 and in the discussion of contracting problems in Chapter 3, since the performance of contractors is very often interdependent.

Fourth, numerate control is only as good as the data on which it rests. In any such system, 'hard' arithmetic must at some point be joined up to verbally-expressed concepts and hence becomes subject to the problems of categorization which were discussed in Chapter 4. The result is often what Coddington has called 'soft numbers',[25] that is, measures which contain casuistic or potentially disputable judgments or unrealistic degrees of precision. This can arise either through more or less dishonest manipulation and loophole-hunting or through 'honest perplexity'. It is by no means unusual in public administration to erect fantastic structures of calculations upon very shaky data bases (as with the wartime price control and Excess Profits Tax system described in Chapter 3) or even to solemnly subtract one totally arbitrary figure from another, as in the case of the old British Purchase Tax 'D' scheme, the financial control of the nationalized industries, or the profit formula for the remuneration of government contractors.

Finally there are two problems inherent in any numerate performance monitoring system. First, as we discussed at the close of Chapter 5, information is not energy: people may 'irrationally' defy rational control, or (more likely) there may be genuine scope for argument about what the figures mean. Second, there is the danger that the thing may turn into a reciprocal learning process: raising the stakes of 'rationality' may be dangerous if it triggers an increased propensity to hunt for loopholes and anomalies and thereby weakens the (apparently) less 'rational' ethics of fair dealing, word of mouth contracts and the like. In the context of health planning, Eckstein remarks that the most probable result of the attempt to make society substantively rational is the breakdown of rational conduct altogether,[26] and at the level of 'pathological rationality', writers like Schelling and Rapoport have invented situations like 'brinkmanship' in which 'rationality' involves behaving like a maniac; a neat paradox.

The problem is partly due to the fact that ignorance may be socially beneficial:[27] for example, the common observation that if people had perfect information about their potential marriage partners, very few people would get married. But it also derives from the basic conflicts involved in trying to equate 'collective rationality' with an aggregation of individual rationality in the sense of exclusive pursuit of self-interest (a problem examined by writers such as Downs and Olson). A very elegant attitude of individual rationality was expressed by Sir Robert Walpole: he

'laughed at and ridiculed all notions of public virtue and love of one's country, calling them the "chimerical schoolboy flights of classical learning", declaring himself at the same time "No saint, no Spartan, no reformer!" '[28]

Enlightened as such views may be, few forms of control in public or private administration could operate effectively if individual rationality of this kind was sufficiently widespread.

Control through Intermediaries

We now move from simple 'threat systems' to systems in which administration operates through intermediaries and usually confers some benefits on its agents. Control through intermediaries might be described as 'the fourth dimension of administration' in the same way as guerilla and insurgent warfare has been called the fourth dimension of warfare.[29] Control through intermediaries is pervasive, if only because policing forces in practice are always relatively scarce: there are never enough police to go round. Societies and organizations therefore depend heavily on 'unofficial police' which can enjoy varying levels of recognition from the authorities. As Hughes puts it 'Government in practice depends on the devolution of unpopular tasks . . . .'.[30]

One example of the use of intermediaries in control processes can be taken from prisons. The process is formalized in the case of prisoners of war, but it is also used in other cases. In Northern Ireland in the early 1970s, terrorists and internees were imprisoned in compounds according to each political group (Ulster Defence Force, Ulster Volunteer Force, Provisional IRA and official IRA) under the absolute authority of a 'commanding officer' prisoner for each group. This officer's authority was required for items such as visits, interviews with the prison governor or receipt of parcels. Less formally, children act as police in all societies by punishing the unconventional or 'odd' adults: they are explicitly used as police in communist countries. Then there are 'hired guns': the protection of property by ordinary police in western countries is increasingly being supplemented (if not replaced) by aggressive private security forces using savage dogs.[31] But a problem arises here in terms of 'monitoring the monitors', and security firms are now being hired to check up on other security firms. This kind of unofficial policing has to be distinguished from simple informers and from ginger groups, though both may be related to it, as in the British automobile testing system, where licensed garages test the roadworthiness of vehicles as a precondition of licensing them. Unofficial policing can arise in three main ways, by blackmail, by 'letters of marque' and by professionalization.

First, blackmail. People can be browbeaten into policing their own behaviour under (credible) threat of confiscation or of external regulations. Bonding systems are a traditional stand-by of financial administration, such as in the old French *taille* or in the Greek and Roman practice of using slaves for financial matters so that they could be tortured. Less dramatically, the British Metropolitan Police entered into fidelity bonds up to 1927 and there was also a bonding system for tax collectors up to the twentieth century. The problem is that it becomes harder to find bondsmen whose worth in cash is equal to that of the amounts they guarantee. Hence the increasing use by companies of 'fidelity bonds' guaranteed by insurance companies, for high-risk employees such as cashiers or delivery roundsmen; this tactic also pushes the onus of deciding an applicant's suitability for a job on to a third party.

Nowadays, bonding is mainly found in forms such as petty deposits on returnable articles or the 'retention moneys' bonding system in construction and civil engineering contracts. It is also to be found in the legal system of bail, more weakly in the Accounting Officer system in the civil service and the legal doctrine that local authority councillors are surchargeable for unlawful expenditure; and moreover it is widely used in taxation, as with the collection of excise taxes from producers in advance of retail sale, the system whereby employers are accountable to the Inland Revenue for Income Tax deductions and retailers are accountable for collecting Value-Added Tax from customers. Obviously, any kind of bonding system can only be effective where people have 'something to lose', and in many large business corporations there is an element of deliberately manipulating executives into expensive patterns of living or of indebtedness so that they will be more amenable to this kind of pressure.[32] Control over drug addicts by their source of supply is a more sinister example.

This type of control can operate through institutions as well as through individuals. For example, the British Board of Film Censors, an unofficial and therefore disavowable, censorship body,[33] the Press Council and the TV complaints machinery (set up in 1971 after allegations of bias in reporting events from Northern Ireland) were all set up under threats from the British government that if the relevant 'houses' were not set in order, official measures would be taken. Similarly, there are 'codes of conduct', laid down by unofficial bodies like the City Panel on Takeovers and Mergers and by the National Association of Bingo Clubs. The basic technique is ancient. Historically, 'voluntary' taxes were often paid in lieu of pillage, as when Ye-lin Tch'on-ts'ai offered 500,000 oz of gold, 80,000 pieces of silk and 400,000 sacks of grain in the face of a threat by Genghis Khan to exterminate the entire population of China.[34]

After blackmail, the next device of control through intermediaries is 'letters of marque' in which the authorities grant 'rights' to outsiders, usually in return for some *quid pro quo*. Letters of marque are not quite the same as the use of 'unacknowledgeable means', because unacknowledgeable means by definition are operations where no explicit authority has been conferred by the authorities.[35] Indeed, the basic reason for operating through such agents is to conceal the identity of their masters. This applies, for example, in espionage, sabotage, *agent provocateur* and guerilla operations, illegal or 'shady' arms deals and in some fields of police operations.

Tax-farming is probably the 'purest' example of administration by letters of marque. In its modern form, this mainly takes the form of the granting of franchises for operations on government property, as with the exploitation of oil and natural gas fields. The award of franchises can take the form either of a formal auction to the highest bidder (running a risk of collusive tendering) or of stipulating a fixed sum and thus allowing the concessionaires to retain any surpluses. In both cases, the authorities act only as policemen in the last resort.

Relationships of a tax-farming kind are apt to be ambiguous and it is sometimes difficult to distinguish form from substance. Even in a system of nominally direct administration, local directors may be quasi-independent 'bosses', as when regional commissioners 'milked' the taxes of medieval Europe in between periods of tax farming. The same applies to Roman governors, Turkish pashas, Persian satraps and so on, in the old empires. On the other hand, the tax farming of early modern

France and England, although formally similar to the medieval set-up and to the independent tax-farmers of ancient Greece and republican Rome, in practice resembled far more closely a rudimentary central banking system. The element of risk to the financier had virtually disappeared and the tax farm had become a continuously functioning bureaucracy leased with the fiscal rights. Hence the paradox that Louis XV of France was one of his own tax-farmers.[36]

It is often difficult to distinguish outright tax-farming from its 'diminutives', such as paying officials wholly or in part on a poundage basis, or granting rights to certain fees and perquisites. Similarly, land revenues have traditionally been linked up with land tenure systems as a rule, and earmarked taxes are also sometimes policed by those whom they benefit. In England the navy was traditionally paid from the customs revenue and the army was paid out of the proceeds of the hated excise taxes, which gave the soldiers an extra incentive to help quell excise riots (such riots were common in the early stages of the tax).

In the same way, fees and gratuities were endemic to British administration in the eighteenth century and are still so to-day in many parts of the world. For example, eighteenth-century Customs officers were entitled to 50 per cent of the value of goods discovered and Surveyors of Taxes received 10 per cent of surcharges until the nineteenth century. Vestiges of this still survive in Europe: at least until recently, French *préposés* received a share of the receipts from contraband goods which they had helped to seize and Spanish Financial Inspectors claimed a percentage of the taxes whose collection they supervize.[37] In private business, of course, such techniques are very common and they even occur in voluntary organizations; for example, many trade union shop stewards receive a percentage of the membership dues which they collect. The letters of marque system may also involve turning 'poachers' into 'gamekeepers', as with the former Mexican system of recruiting rural police from criminals and bandits, and sometimes amounts to little more than high payments to informers. A British example of the poacher—gamekeeper process is the legalization and licensing of off-course betting in 1960, which is described in Chapter 10.

Perhaps a more sophisticated variant on the same theme, mentioned in the previous discussion of accounting, is to gear the system to the interest of quasi-independent professions. For example, the Income Tax and other taxes are a fruitful market for a variety of financial and legal experts and their employees. There are some historical parallels for this, particularly 'professional form-fillers' in illiterate imperial societies (such as the census-scribes in Roman Egypt).[38] A system of this kind works a little like the famous firm of Spenlow and Jorkins in Dickens' *David Copperfield*, with the authorities playing the minor, but indispensable, part of Jorkins — the unseen sleeping partner who can always be invoked as the source of delay, expense and unpopular decisions.[39] The working of the British tax system already depends on the original calculations of tax performed by non-official professionals, to which the officials themselves only apply checks; and accountants, lawyers and professional tax experts are in effect guaranteed work by the complexity of the tax system and by the Companies Acts which prescribe the form of accounts to be published by limited companies.

Such professionals thus have no real interest in a radical simplification of the tax system (although they undoubtedly complain about the excessive complexity of the system) and, perhaps more important, they have as much interest as the tax authorities themselves in preventing fraud in the form of falsification of tax returns. This is because it is only possible to sell tax *avoidance* to people who are unwilling or unable to *evade* taxes, and also to build up favourable relations with their opposite numbers in the tax offices. The system of 'self-assessment' of taxes, as practised in the USA, West Germany and in certain British taxes, merely carries the process one stage further by exporting from 'government' to 'individuals' (in practice, to tax accountants) the responsibility for calculating their tax liability as well as for simply supplying the information upon which such calculations are based.[40] The tax offices thus become a purely checking mechanism, not a mechanism for performing routine calculations.

On this model of control, the game is manipulated into existence, a relatively small cadre of officials watch for 'fouls', and tax is drawn out almost as a by-product. Whether this exercise can be conducted without limit in a modern economy is hard to say. It can only control effectively those who are unable to conceal their assets from the authorities, in particular those with many servants or employees, because the total cost of buying the silence of such employees outweighs the cost to the tax authorities of buying the relevant information from any one individual. Interestingly, the same mechanism seems to operate for men with many wives in polygamous societies.[41] Employers with a sizeable number of clerks are therefore helpless to evade taxes, and so over 80 per cent of British taxes are collected through corporations: the internal audit system helps the tax officials, and in some cases revenue supervision itself works as a supplement to internal audit systems, as we will see in the case of the Betting Tax.

The basic mechanism is to harness the maximization of the tax yield or the minimization of subsidy wastage to the self-interest of someone other than the original recipient or donor. A common means of doing this is for governments to double up private and public money in 'matching grants' or in joint projects. And this tactic is by no means confined to governments: for example, the problems of the political vulnerability of the subsidiaries of expatriate American multinational firms in developing countries have led many of them to rediscover the old Portuguese tactic of using *compradors*.[42] This involves linking up with local capital (Levinson claims that in 1970 only 40 per cent of US subsidiaries abroad were wholly-owned, as against more than 70 per cent in the early 1950s)[43] and even to foster a system of auxiliary indigenous businesses around their own activities in order to protect themselves against attack by governments.

Professionalization

Professionalization is in effect a hybrid of the two types of control which have been discussed above. This is because, on the one hand, the enforcement of professional standards by governments is a form of 'letters of marque', since it involves the exclusion of the under-capitalized or unqualified. On the other hand, profession-alization also opens up the possibility of 'blackmail' or 'free riding' by the authorities, as in the case of accountants operating as 'tax informers' which we discussed above. Another case can be taken from the administration of fishing subsidies in Britain. In the case of deep-sea fishing, subsidies have been largely based on audited accounts, since deep-sea trawlers are mostly operated by large companies who employ professional accountants and auditors. On the other hand, the inshore fishing subsidy, which is paid mostly to individuals or to family firms with rudimentary accounting systems, has to be based on simple tangible indices on the physical 'bottleneck' principle (the indices used are days at sea or weight of fish landed, both of which are fairly easily verifiable by inspectors at the fishing ports).

We will be discussing some of the 'costs' of professionalization in administration in Chapter 9. What interests us here is simply the use of 'professional impartiality' as a device of control. Examples are the use of independent forensic science laboratories for criminal and accident investigations, and the role of auditors and management consultants in industry. As has often been noted, management consultants are often used (like Royal Commissions in government) as delaying devices or as 'hatchet men' in reorganizations, that is, as a means of sugaring the pill of executive dismissals while keeping top management smelling sweet. But the other side of professional impartiality is professional loyalty, particularly in cases where professionals have to do battle with one another on behalf of their respective organizations. This blunts the edge of conflict, particularly in cases such as tax accounting and the law, where professions straddle public–private boundaries. Montesquieu once remarked that kings should so make war as to have done one another the least possible damage when peace was restored, and a similar maxim might apply to professional conflict.

A dilemma which applies to all of the techniques of control discussed in this section, and which we will be taking up again in Chapter 9, is that controlling the populace *through* intermediaries rests on control *over* intermediaries. The old problem of vassalage is that the stronger the middleman's control over the populace, the weaker tends to be the control of central authority over the middleman (though not necessarily vice versa).[44] The position of shop stewards the local plant officials of British trade unions, is a classic case of the problem.[45] Similarly, a very large part of public expenditure in both Britain and the USA is accounted for by bodies outside central government, and, as we saw in Chapter 3, effective control over such intermediaries presents many problems. Thus the dilemma of vassalage keeps cropping up in new forms, although it is of very ancient origin. The essential problem for the authorities in such a situation is to invent middle-range penalties which are effective but not so heavy that they can never be used. A military analogy is with the development of 'miniaturized tactical nuclear weapons' or other forms of limited war which are not so powerful that they cannot be used without causing a holocaust. We will be returning to this theme in Chapter 9.

Patronage and Segregation

Patronage is difficult to classify *a priori* either as a 'threat system' or as an exchange system of the middleman type. Patronage can sometimes be quite altruistic; more commonly, it consists of manipulative gifts designed to put people under obligations. In Mauss's classic study, domination is established by giving more than can be returned: 'To accept without repaying more is to face subordination'.[46] Patronage is mentioned here for completeness, but it largely overlaps with the letters of marque technique which was discussed above, since at the margin there is no useful distinction between direct gifts of valuables and grants of exploitation rights such as exclusive dealerships and production monopolies. No separate discussion of patronage will therefore be attempted here.

Another technique of control which it is difficult to classify in terms of the categories used in this chapter but which falls somewhere between 'professional-ization' and 'patronage' is the technique of segregating officials from the populace at large, either through privileges or through physical isolation in 'total institutions' as a means of ensuring their loyalty. A well-known case is the institution of barrack life in the eighteenth century in order to isolate soldiers from 'subversive' home influences.[47]

Hereditary offices (whether *de facto* or *de jure*) are historically a common form of this technique. Examples are Indian *zamindari*, the traditional system of Northern Nigerian local government (as elsewhere in Africa), English salt officers and customs officers in the eighteenth century. Similarly one may note the use of celibate clerks, tonsured and with benefit of clergy, for royal administration in medieval England, a rule to which Geoffrey Chaucer was a notable exception. Parallel cases are the use of eunuchs in the sultanates from approximately the first millenium BC, the use of priests and slaves in oriental despotism, the janissaries of the Ottoman Empire (again, usually recruited from socially rootless strata) and the famous Chinese Imperial Censorate. The technique was also used in the overseas empires of European states in the nineteenth century, where colonial armies were often recruited from small and 'marginal' tribes. The French *noblesse de robe* is a similar, though weaker, case. The basic idea is at least as old as Plato's *Republic*: prolonged isolation in this way is intended to reinforce the solidarity of the administrative group *vis-a-vis* the outside world and to reduce the likelihood of administrators switching to another occupation.

Judicial-type Systems: Mediation, Arbitration, Regulation

The distinction between administrative systems and judicial systems is always blurred at the edges. Indeed, as Dunsire points out, the traditional view was that the enforcement of the government's will needed no machinery other than the law, since the law enforced itself through court cases and informers (plus, of course, a minimal administrative machinery in the form of gaolers, tipstaffs, bailiffs, sheriff officers and the like).[48] Similarly, many administrative bodies like the English Exchequer were originally courts of law[49] (indeed in the French *Cour des Comptes*, there is still a vestige of judicial audit), and in many countries administration is still discussed largely in legal terms. Moreover, there is often a two-way traffic of functions between legal institutions and administrative instituti-ons, although to 'de-judicialize' something does not necessarily mean to make it 'administrative'.

What interests us here is that administrative bodies often follow judicial *processes* as a technique of control. One strategy for authority is to do nothing but wait to be called to arbitrate in disputes and to push the onus of advocacy and initiative on to others. This strategy is 'tutiorism', in de Jouvenel's theological terminology,[50] or *Public Inquiries as a Form of Government*,[51] to quote the title of a book. Much of colonial administration was clearly of this type. For example, Malthus quotes Captain Cook's account of his experience in Queen Charlotte's

Sound

'If I had followed the advice of all our pretended friends, I might have extirpated the whole race; for the people of each hamlet or village by turns, applied to me to destroy the other.'[52]

Control by judicial processes has two main forms, intra-organizational and extra-organizational. So far as the 'intra-organizational' type is concerned, the 'bridging' technique is found in all types of organizations from groups of three upwards, in some form. Simmel noted this in his classic analysis of triads,[53] and other writers have observed the same processes in small groups. For example, one of Berne's *Games People Play*[54] is the situation in which the individual partners of a marriage use an outsider as a 'court of appeal' in judging complaints about each others' shortcomings. In the simplest form of 'bridging', the 'boss' acts as court of appeal to his subordinates' subordinates in order to avoid becoming the prisoner of his immediate underlings. An early example is the use of the King's courts as a channel of appeal over the heads of the barons. Similarly, Louis XIV forbade his ministers to meet without him so that he would always be able to act the role of mediator. More recently, the World War II coalition government in Britain encouraged trade union leaders to take their problems and complaints direct to Ministers rather than to operate through union-sponsored Members of Parliament, a tactic which has been continued in the post-war period.[55] In a highly ramified field administrative system (such as the US Forest Service as described by Kaufman),[56] the facilities for appealing against decisions made by field officials are of key importance in the control of functionaries by their superiors.

In fact, the technique of using appeal procedures, and the giving of handouts to the 'populace' over the heads of subordinates, while at the same time employing an almost impenetrable screen of satellite personnel for punitive purposes (including blocking access)[57] is a very ancient part of 'statecraft' and it is to be found in most organizations. Sometimes, as mentioned in the last paragraph, an organization may even be set up deliberately to produce clashes between groups for top officials to arbitrate, as with the case of corporate planning in companies, which sets a planning unit at the top level to work against the divisional interests. Baker describes this kind of control as one of 'the primary and ancient tasks of government'[58] and notes that Herbert Simon has observed that the technique of top administrators leaving authorities inadequately defined so as to divide and rule is 'used . . . so often that it cannot be casually dismissed as poor administration'.[59]

In its second, extra-organizational, form, the 'bridging' process involves the authorities playing an 'integrative' role in the regulation of disputatious communities. This can relate to peer group types of control, which are discussed below, and it can take place on scales ranging from therapy groups to industrial relations and international disputes. For example, Hough[60] stresses the importance of the regulation of supply disputes and the like by local party organs in the Soviet Union as one of the key sources of Communist Party control over industrial enterprises. But in any such situation, an outside arbitrator can only manipulate to a limited extent. If he too blatantly advantages one group at the expense of another, he runs the risk that the losers will not accept the arbitrator's decision. If, on the other hand, the outside arbitrator's decision advantages no 'internal' group in the dispute, he runs the risk of being damned by both sides. But there is often scope for manoeuvre between these two limiting points.

Market-type Systems

Uncoupled Hierarchies

By 'uncoupled hierarchies', we refer to attempts to create 'optimal tension' by the deliberate sanction or introduction of 'artificial' breaks in chains of command by creating bargaining partners and transacting with them at 'arms length' so as to evolve contracts. In private business, leasing and contracting are a well-known technique for avoiding long-term commitments.[61] Similarly, as we mentioned in the earlier discussion of 'rational' accounting controls, many of the 'new' managerial control systems in big business basically operate by creating simulated markets. The procedure is to give executives only gross output or profit indices and linking this with incentive payment systems (or negative incentives such as dismissal in case of failure). A man is given a budget and an objective and the rest is up to him, providing that he is not caught breaking the law. So far has the uncoupling of hierarchies been taken in some US corporations which are subdivided into 'pseudo companies' that there are 'anti-trust' regulations to prevent collusion among the 'pseudo companies'.[62]

The changes in the post-war British film industry from a structure of big, integrated companies to a loose-jointed sub-contracting structure, is an example of this process in the private sector. Within the public sector, too, there is a tendency to reproduce relationships analogous to 'contracts' in a market system, in an attempt to push routine activities to administrative peripheries without loss of control.[63] But many of the theoretical benefits of this type of control disappear in practice, as we saw in Chapter 3, where some of the experiences with this type of system were set out much more fully. Contracting as an attempt to avoid the difficulties of direct administrative control becomes less useful (except, perhaps, as a political handout) the more recurrent and the less definable the job and the fewer the number of suppliers; and there are few 'procedural' ways of getting round these problems. But the 'uncoupled hierarchy' may still be useful for unacknowledgeable and semi-unacknowledgeable means, for example in administrative out-flanking operations, cloak-and-dagger operations and the purchase or sale of arms in dubious circumstances. A case of the latter type was the use of a phoney Norwegian—Panamanian firm to purchase five fast gunboats from France in 1969 (nominally for oil exploration, in fact for Israel's navy), thus successfully breaking the French embargo on arms sales to Israel.

Peer Group Controls or Leagues

This type of control is closely similar to the last one, but it operates through groups, not individuals. By withdrawing the locus of power from a peer group,[64] one may promote competition between immediate rivals, in a manner comparable to the biological process of natural selection between near kin. The strategy for the boss, like monarchs in former times who kept their nobles at court, is to prevent mobilization against himself by slotting people into micro-political arenas which absorb their energies. Paradoxically, domination may be achieved through independence of a nominal kind. Albert Hirschman has applied an analysis of this kind to the US car industry which, he says, wards off dissatisfaction on the part of its customers with the poor quality of its products by spurious (oligopolistic) competition.[65] The dissatisfied customer may not on the whole benefit from exchanging the faults of Model A for the faults of Model B, but the ability to switch within the system protects the system as a whole from attack. Indeed, parochial preoccupation is undoubtedly an important mechanism of social stability, and it is possible to see such preoccupation as the essence of a control system lying behind 'neo-colonialism' (granting spurious independence to former colonies) and industrial participation schemes (giving workers the illusion of access to power). A story illustrating the extent to which absorption in a single group can distort perspective is the answer given by the great movie magnate L. B. Mayer when he was asked if he did not think it exessive that his salary was ten times that of the President of the USA. He replied, in all seriousness, 'But look at my responsibilities!'[66]

Within a peer group, authority can be hard to locate. As Churchill once said of Baldwin, it is like fighting an eiderdown — you think that you have dealt a knockout blow, only to discover that you have made no impression at all. Or, to quote Mr. Dooley again, 'A man can't be indipindint onless he has a boss'.[67] Locked into his peer group, the individual can only escape this type of control by total apathy. The use of 'league tables' within and between states and organizations as indices of profitability, sales, growth and so on, is a familiar device for monitoring the performance of individual units. Also, as with middlemen, this gives the 'centre' an advantage in terms of information: by definition it will have a more complete picture of the total situation than the individual spokes of the wheel which it connects, and hence it can use information as a basis for research and as a 'trading commodity'.[68]

There are two basic variants of this type of control, which may be labelled 'repartition' and 'assessment by peers'. Repartition, or global assessment, involves making the rewards to each member of the group depend on the effort of all, for example in the payment of fishermen by share of the catch, or payment of piece rates dependent on the total output of a work group.[69] A more modern example is the British co-ownership housing system under the 1964 Housing Act, which makes all tenants of such a scheme collectively responsible for the mortgage repayments (to building societies and to the Housing Corporation). By this means, any 'rent strike' would be self-defeating, and all tenants have an interest in making sure that the others pay their rents.

The origin of control systems of this type is lost in antiquity. Making families, communities and corporations responsible for an individual's tax debts was a common enough expedient of taxation in ancient Rome and Egypt.[70] Of modern examples, one of the most dramatic is the growth of the 'lump' in the British building industry. The 'lump' refers to labour-only sub-contracting by gangs of men producing work at high speed without belonging to unions, paying no tax, national insurance or training board levies. The 'lump' doubled in size between 1966 and 1973, amounting to nearly a quarter of the building labour force before a 'crackdown' in 1974. The *paiement fractionnée* system of turnover tax administration (in which any given trader is liable for the full tax on his sales unless he gives information to the tax authorities about his suppliers) also belongs in this group. An extreme historical case is the ancient practice at Meroe of ensuring alertness on the part of the king's bodyguard by sacrificing all of them when a king died, *irrespective* of whether that death had occurred from natural causes or otherwise.[71]

The other main variant of 'peer group control' — assessment of individuals by peers — involves making people judge their nearest rivals, as with the traditional system of jury assessment of tax. This is similar to the British Research or Arts Councils' expedient of channelling a lump sum through a hierarchy of scientific committees (commonly decisions are made in fact by an oligarchy of overlapping committee members). The theory is that projects can be judged before a forum of expertise which ordinary bureaucrats could not match, and that geese are therefore less likely to be mistaken for swans in such a system. But, as Bruce Smith has pointed out,[72] interdisciplinary projects or large institutional grants cannot be handled in this way, and this is an important limit to this type of control. Similarly, like arbitration, this technique will only work within limits. For peer group controls to function, there must be an element of mutual adjustment. That is obvious. But the scope for manoeuvre lies between two limiting cases. One is the peer 'grouping' with no reciprocal controls, each responding individually to external pressures (for example, functionally divided field administration units with no league controls of any kind or contact with one another). The other is the peer group which is engaged *solely* in mutual adjustment, often in the form of mutually self-destructive activities.[73]

Deception and Persuasion

The range of control models offered here has a 'mechanical' bias. Of course, in reality most forms of administrative control have cognitive aspects, but they are not *simply* cognitive. In some cases, however, it is possible to change the cognitive system (the system which people perceive themselves to be in) without changing the 'objective' system. Psychologists call this 'cognitive dissonance',[74] and in administration the standard 'human relations' techniques of blowing up workers' self-importance (such as telling a man who tightens 10,000 identical bolts per day that he is 'building a Chevrolet')[75] operate on this kind of principle.

Persuasion and deception are marginal as techniques of administrative control as conceived in this chapter. But they must be mentioned, because they are undoubtedly important in some circumstances. Indeed, until comparatively recently the power of persuasive techniques was conventionally thought to be so great that writers such as J. K. Galbraith gave such techniques a central place in the mechanics of the modern economy. There is in fact a variety of techniques relating to persuasion and deception. In descending order of directness, there is the straightforward use of psycho-active substances such as opium or alcohol, quite common at one time as means of control in armies and navies. Then there is simple deception (as in the case of the scarecrow), a device which is comparatively rare in its pure form. Much more common is a range of persuasive devices, the study of which stretches back to the ancient Greeks via the medieval schools of rhetoric.[76]

These devices include simple assertion (like claiming victory in doubtful circumstances), attributing motives, exaggeration and minimization. The last two involve manipulating qualitative and quantitative scales of measurement, spatial, temporal, financial and the like. Then there is chop logic, false dichotomy, the use of codes or riddles which act as involuntary mnemonics, and over-simple axioms such as essentialization or sententious generalization. Finally there is a miscellany of trick arguments, such as generalizing from particular instances or examples, circular arguments (begging the question by definition) and so on. To these might be added techniques which are neither strictly 'deception' nor 'persuasion' but which involve cognitive manipulation, such as the use of negative ionizers or the use of canned music to prevent annoyance in milking parlours, supermarkets, airports and even university libraries. Even the simple timing of announcements may fall into this category, as with the British publication of Sir Roger Casement's homosexual diaries to blunt the edge of world criticism at the time of his arrest and trial in 1916.

All of these are familiar, though they are used in continually changing contexts, and some are very marginal as 'control' devices. Assessing the importance or effectiveness of such techniques is a much more difficult question, and one which will not be tackled here. One of the difficulties is that of obtaining 'control' cases: for example, if sales go up it may not be because of advertizing. Lord Leverhulme once remarked that half of the money which he spent on advertizing was wasted, but he didn't know which half.[77] Indeed, some of the cruder forms of propaganda are clearly counter-productive, as will be discussed in Chapter 9.

Conclusion

The categorization of administrative controls in this chapter has moved, using Boulding's useful terminology, from 'threat systems' (in which there is no degree of reciprocation of benefits) through systems of interpolation in *other* ongoing systems, 'natural' or 'contrived', and concluding with the persistent problem of cognitive controls. This tells us something about the range of types of control which are available to administrators. The range contains a variety of types, but it is not unlimited, as is assumed in the model of perfect administration.

But all that we have got so far is a set of animals in a zoo. What is lacking is (to borrow a legal term) the *protases* of these models, that is, a specification of the circumstances in which controls of a particular kind are applicable and effective. The next two chapters will analyse the conditions governing the use and effectiveness of administrative controls.

Notes

1. For other discussions of administrative control see A. S. Tannenbaum, *Control in Organizations*, McGraw-Hill, New York, 1968, and R. J. S. Baker, *Administrative Theory and Public Administration*, Hutchinson University Library, London, 1972.
2. For an account of 'orthodox' ergonomics, see W. T. Singleton, *An Introduction to Ergonomics*, World Health Organization, Geneva, 1972.
3. Kahn, H., *On Thermonuclear War*, Princeton University Press, New Jersey, 1960.
4. Wouk, H., *The Caine Mutiny*, Jonathan Cape, London, 1951.
5. Recalled by M. Mauss, *The Gift Relationship*, Cohen and West, London, 1969, p. 81.
6. For example, A. Mehrabian and S. G. Diamond, 'Effects of furniture arrangement, props and personality on social interaction', *Journal of Personality and Social Psychology*, 1971, Vol. 20, No. 1, pp. 18–30.

7. *Sunday Times*, 11 May 1975.
8. Marcuse, H., *One Dimensional Man*, Routledge and Kegan Paul, London, 1964.
9. Hughes, E. E., *Studies in Administration and Finance 1558—1825*, Manchester University Press, Manchester, 1934, p. 303.
10. Chapman, B. and J., *The Life and Times of Baron Haussman*, Weidenfeld and Nicholson, London, 1957.
11. Jacobs, J., *The Death and Life of Great American Cities*, Penguin Books, Harmondsworth, 1964; J. Hillman 'Law of the Concrete Jungle', *Guardian* 6.4.72.
12. Newman, O., *Defensible Space*, Architectural Press, London, 1972, p. 2.
13. Schelling, T. C., *The Strategy of Conflict*, Oxford University Press, New York, 1963.
14. Laurie, P., 'The national guard', *Sunday Times Magazine*, 28.1.73, p. 19.
15. Boulding's, K. term: *Economics as a Science*, McGraw-Hill, New York, 1970.
16. de Balzac, H., *Illusions Perdues*, Garnier, Paris, 1969, p. 422.
17. The meaning of the French word *contrôle* (which has retained a greater element of classical purity than the English word) is largely restricted to checking-up procedures of this kind.
18. Hagen, E. E., 'The internal functioning of capitalist organizations', *Journal of Economic History*, Vol. 30, March 1970, No. 1.
19. Binney, J. E. D., *British Public Finance and Administration 1774—92*, Oxford University Press, Oxford, 1958.
20. Mitchell, S. K. (Ed. S. Painter), *Taxation in Medieval England*, Yale University Press, New Haven, 1951.
21. Dunne, F. P., *Mr Dooley in Peace and War*, Richards, London, 1899, p. 173.
22. Boyle, L., 'Politics and the Royal Commission on Local Government', *Local Government Finance*, Vol. 73, No. 10, Oct. 1969.
23. Mill, J. S., *A System of Logic*, Longmans, London, 1884.
24. Klein, R., 'The politics of PPBS', *Political Quarterly*, Vol. 43 1972, pp. 270—281.
25. Coddington, A., 'Soft numbers and hard facts', *New Society*, 1.10.70, pp. 579—581; cf. also A. Sutherland, *The Monopolies Commission in Action*, University of Cambridge, Department of Applied Economics Occasional Paper 21, 1970.
26. Eckstein, H., 'Planning: The National Health Service' in R. Rose (Ed.), *Policy Making in Britain*, Macmillan, London, 1969.
27. Moore, W. E., and M. M. Tumin, 'Some social functions of ignorance', *American Sociological Review*, Vol. 14, p. 787; H. Wilensky, *Organizational Intelligence*, London Basic Books, 1967, pp. X—XI.
28. Dowell, S., *A History of Taxation and Taxes in England from Earliest Times to the Present Day*, Longman-, London, 1884, 4 Vols.
29. Elliott-Bateman, M. (Ed.), *The Fourth Dimension of Warfare*, Vol. I, Intelligence, Subversion, Resistance, Manchester University Press, Manchester, 1970.
30. Hughes, E. E., *op. cit.*
31. Hamilton, P., 'The Security Industry and the Community', paper presented to the 1970 Bristol seminar on the sociology of the Police.
32. cf. also A. Solzhenitsyn, *The First Circle*, tr. M. Guybon, Fontana, London, 1970, p. 107.
33. Hunnings, N., *Film Censors and the Law*, Allen and Unwin, London, 1967.
34. Recalled by G. Ardant, *Theorie Sociologique de l'Impôt*, S.E.V.P.E.N. Paris, 1965.
35. Cf. Mackenzie, W. J. M., 'Unacknowledgeable means', unpublished lecture 1950; also C. C. Hood, 'The rise and rise of the British quango', *New Society*, 16.8.73.
36. Matthews, G., *The Royal General Farms in Eighteenth Century France*, Columbia University Press, New York, 1958.
37. Medhurst, K., 'The political presence of the Spanish bureaucracy', *Government and Opposition*, Vol. 4, Spring 1969, pp. 235—249.
38. Wallace, Sherman Leroy, *Taxation in Egypt from Augustus to Diocletian*, Princeton University Press, Princeton, 1938.
39. Dickens, C., *David Copperfield*, The Educational Book Co., London, 1910, p. 351.
40. Carter, A. H., 'The lesser evil: some aspects of income tax administration in the USA and the UK', *Public Administration*, Vol. 40, 1962, pp. 69—89.
41. Orewa, G. O., *Taxation in Western Nigeria*, Oxford University Press, Oxford, 1962.
42. Leys, C., 'Marxist theories of underdevelopment: an outline and some questions' unpublished seminar paper, Glasgow University, 1972.
43. Levinson, C., *Capital Inflation and the Multinational*, Allen and Unwin, London, 1971.

44. Cf. the discussion of the 'Titoist prolem of vassalage' in J. Strachey, *The End of Empire*, Gollancz, London, 1959; also J. Blondel, *Comparing Political Systems*, Weidenfeld and Nicholson, London, 1972, p. 139.
45. Goodman, J. F., and T. C. Whittingham, *Shop Stewards in British Industry*, McGraw-Hill, London, 1969.
46. Mauss, A., *op. cit.*; cf. T. Hayter, *Aid as Imperialism*, Penguin Books, Harmondsworth, 1971.
47. Postgate, R., *How to Make a Revolution*, Hogarth Press, London, 1934.
48. Dunsire, A., *Administration*, Martin Robertson, London, 1973, p. 5.
49. Binney, J. E. D., *op. cit.*
50. de Jouvenel, B., *The Pure Theory of Politics*, Cambridge University Press, Cambridge, 1963, pp. 147–148.
51. Wraith, R. E., and G. B. Lamb, *Public Inquiries as a Form of Government*, Allen and Unwin, London, 1971.
52. Malthus, T., *An Essay on The Principle of Population*, Penguin Books, Harmondsworth, 1970.
53. Rustin, M., 'Structural and unconscious implications of the dyad and triad', *Sociological Review*, May 1971, Vol. 19, No. 2.
54. Berne, E., *Games People Play*, Andre Deutsch, London, 1966.
55. Richter, I., *Political Purpose in Trade Unions*, Allen and Unwin, London, 1973.
56. Kaufman, H., *The Forest Ranger*, Johns Hopkins Press, Baltimore, 1960.
57. Krasner, W., 'How to live with bureaucracy – and win', *New Society*, 25.7.68, pp. 116–118.
58. Baker, R. J. S., *op. cit.* p. 179.
59. *Ibid.*, pp. 51–52.
60. Hough, J. F., *The Soviet Prefects*, Harvard University Press, Cambridge, Mass., 1969.
61. Cf. *Leasing in Industry*, Studies in Business Policy No. 127 from the National Industrial Conference Board, New York 1968; Cf. A. L. Stinchecombe, 'Bureaucratic and craft administration of production', *Administrative Science Quarterly*, Vol. 4, 1959–1960, pp. 168–187.
62. Bonini, P., R. Jaedicke and H. Wagner, *Management Controls: New Dimensions in Basic Research*, McGraw-Hill, New York, 1964.
63. Wettenhall, R., 'The recoup concept in public enterprise', *Public Administration*, 1966, Vol. 44, pp. 391–413; M. Home, 'The irrelevance of public dividend capital', *Public Administration*, 1971, Vol. 49, pp. 309–320.
64. Noble, T., and B. Pym, 'Collegiate Authority and the Receding Locus of Power', *British Journal of Sociology*, Vol. 21, 1970, pp. 431–443.
65. Hirschman, A. O., *Exit Voice and Loyalty*, Harvard University Press, Cambridge, Mass., 1970.
66. H.C. Deb. Vol. 458 C.2220.
67. Dunne, F. P., *op. cit.*, p. 430.
68. Cf. J. A. G. Griffith, *Central Departments and Local Authorities*, Allen and Unwin, London, 1966.
69. Follet, M. P., *The New State*, Longmans, London, 1934, p. 119, f.n.l.
70. Coffield, J., *A Popular History of Taxation from Ancient to Modern Times*, Longmans, London, 1970, p. 6.
71. Calvert, P., *Revolution*, Macmillan, London, 1970, pp. 27–28.
72. Smith, B. L., and D. C. Hague (Ed.), *The Dilemma of Accountability in Modern Government*, Macmillan, London, 1971.
73. Laing, R. D., *The Politics of Experience and the Bird of Paradise*, Penguin Books, Harmondsworth, 1967, pp. 65–83.
74. Festinger, L., *Conflict, Decision and Dissonance*, Tavistock Publications, London, 1964.
75. Hertzberg, F., 'One more time: how do you motivate employees?' *Harvard Business Review*, Jan–Feb. 1968, pp. 53–62.
76. Cooper, R. L., *The Rhetoric of Aristotle*, D. Appleton Century Co., New York, 1932; L. V. Holland, *Counterpoint: Kenneth Burke and Aristotle's Theories of Rhetoric*, New York Philosophical Library, 1959; R. Hoggart, *Speaking to Each Other*, Chatto and Windus, London, 1970.
77. Gretton, J., 'Efficiency Unlimited', *New Society*, 27.8.70, p. 357.

Chapter 8

Analyses of Control in Organizations

'The concept of control may well one day provide the elusive key to a
unified behavioral science.' A. Etzioni, *The Active Society*, Free Press,
New York, 1969, p. 39, footnote 23.

The requirements for perfect administrative control were explained at the beginning
of the last chapter. Control resources must be limitless, controls must be perfectly
effective and there must be no incompatibilities between levels or types of control.
In the last chapter we surveyed the range of administrative controls which are
available in practice, briefly commenting on each type as we noted it. In this
chapter and the next, we turn to the other conditions of perfect control, exploring
the conditions which limit the effectiveness of administrative controls. Much of
administration takes place through formal organizations, so in this short chapter we
will explore the limits of control within organizations by briefly reviewing some of
the influential writing on the subject. But administration is also a societal process in
a broader sense, and some of the wider limits of administrative control will be
considered in the next chapter.

The literature on administrative control is inevitably fragmentary. Administration is not a 'pure' science, and exploring the elements or limiting factors which
relate to the effectiveness of administrative control is bound to involve many
academic disciplines. In exploring adaptation and categorization in Part 2, we
touched on issues which belong to realms of learning as various as linguistics,
philosophy, economics and psychology; and, as the epigraph to this chapter implies,
many social (and indeed non-social) sciences relate to administrative control in a
more general sense. For example, there is economic control and psychological
control. Whether one adds 'social', 'political' or 'legal' control as separate types
depends upon how fundamental one wants to be.

Nevertheless, it is undeniable that there is a problem. As we saw in Chapter 5,
technology has not solved all the problems of administrative control; on the
contrary, what appear to be 'modern' types of control are usually only ancient
types of control reappearing in new guises. The 'golden oldies' reviewed in the last
chapter crop up again and again, and human ingenuity seems to be largely limited
to adapting them to new contexts. Cases of this are the reappearance of bonding
systems for cash-handling employees, such as delivery roundsmen; or the use of a
system of multiple locks, such as was used for the treasury chests of medieval
England, for the nuclear defence system or for the doors on state mental hospitals
for the criminally insane. Two keys, held by different officials, are needed to open
any door. In other cases, the specific techniques have changed, but the broad

principles of control systems remain unchanged, as with the development of modern accounting systems. Like football, many administrative controls seem to have been more or less spontaneously invented and re-invented in different times and places; and the basic principles of many of the controls which are used in the 'new' policy areas of public administration would have been quite familiar to a thirteenth-century tax collector.[1]

Not only does the range of administrative controls appear to be more or less limited to a range of historically recurring types; control remains problematic in the sense that well-established principles or systems often break down or turn out to be ineffective. Indeed, the problem of limits to administrative capacity has been brought into sharper focus by the recent growth of 'policy analysis' and 'appraisal research' which encourage an iconoclastic approach and which bring to light more and more cases where controls are feeble or inoperative or where the expected causal relationships turn out not to operate. For example, there is not always a clear relationship between levels of expenditure and levels of administrative performance:[2] more than money is required, it appears, to tackle administrative malfunctioning. Practical men typically explain breakdowns in control systems as occasional weaknesses, on the statistical principle that there will always be a few bad apples in every barrel.[3] Incompetent individuals are blamed, or particular circumstances. Social theorists, on the other hand, typically relate such problems to organizational structures.

In this chapter, we will consider three academic approaches to administrative control and the determinants of its effectiveness. These are models of voluntary collective action borrowed from economics, models of non-social control which are borrowed from the natural sciences, and finally some sociological theories of control in organizations. We encountered both of the first two approaches when we discussed adaptation in Chapter 5. Both of them have the appeal of relative simplicity and comprehensiveness and are influential in administrative thought.

Economic Theories

Eighteenth-century classical economics was a powerful and elegant social theory which was based on a few key assumptions of human motivation and from which sweeping deductions could be made. It was deduced that most administrative attempts to improve society would inevitably be self-defeating; most avoidable social evils could be laid at the door of government-created or government-supported monopolies, and free competition was prescribed as the cure wherever it was possible. These ideas were fiercely attacked in the nineteenth century, notably by Karl Marx, and modern economics is much less sweeping in its analyses. But the spirit of Smith and Ricardo can still be detected in the economic approach to administration which was briefly mentioned in relation to adaptation in Chapter 5. This approach is firmly grounded in 'methodological individualism',[4] on the basic assumption that it is the interests of individuals rather than the values of groups which provide the most powerful determinants of social behaviour, assumptions which economists have applied to voting and party political behaviour as well as to administration.[5]

In the case of administration, the basic assumption is that the career interests of individuals, 'rationally' pursued, will tend to determine the structure and behaviour of administrative organizations. From this assumption, Downs and Tullock have derived a number of propositions or 'laws' relating to administrative control.[6] Given rational pursuit of individual self-interest and some minimum assumption about limits to individual supervisory capacity (such as was discussed in Chapter 4), it follows that control and co-ordination of organizational activities by hierarchical bosses is bound to be seriously imperfect in any large organization, and that such control will tend to diminish marginally as the organization gets larger. That is, the overall control wielded by the top directorate may increase in absolute terms as the organization gets bigger, but the percentage of organizational activities which can be controlled inevitably gets smaller. Moreover, as was mentioned in Chapter 5, Down asserts (in the 'Law of Counter Control') that the greater the efforts which are made by top officials to control their subordinates, the greater the efforts that rational subordinates will make to evade such controls. In effect, a reciprocal learning process is sparked off, in which superiors are likely to be handicapped by the limited time available in supervizing any one individual. The propositions which have just been described are the most important ones for the purposes of this analysis, but it also follows from the central assumptions that rational administrative agencies will tend to be 'imperialistic', competing with one another for 'space', and we saw in Chapter 4 how 'imperialistic' tendencies of this kind can limit the division of labour problem beyond its purely technical difficulties. On top of this, Downs and Tullock also include a number of subsidiary themes in their analysis, but such themes are more in the nature of inferences than conditional on the basic assumption.

Niskanen[7] has concentrated on a slightly different theme, the effects of lump-sum budgeting and public ownership on the behaviour of public agencies. Niskanen assumes that bureaux are financed by a single budget allocation rather than selling output on a per unit basis, and that they are monopolists of the services which they provide. The combined effects of monopoly and of lump-sum budgeting are that under such circumstances a rational bureau will produce a greater output of the relevant goods or services than a rational non-profit-making monopoly selling its output on a per unit basis. This is because it is assumed that a high bureaucrat's perquisites, power, salary and the like, tend to depend on the total budget of the organization, so such bureaucrats are motivated to maximize their total budget rather than to relate output primarily to consumer demand expressed in terms of willingness to pay. This does not necessarily mean that the bureau produces its output less efficiently than the monopolist selling on a per unit basis; on the contrary, Niskanen assumes that bureaucrats are motivated to maximize the output from a given budget, but the 'over-production' effect still applies.

Another important element in Niskanen's theory is the effect of public ownership, which is non-transferable, on administrative behaviour. Non-transferable public ownership means that shares in the ownership of an organization cannot change hands; instead, gains and losses from the operation of public organizations are compulsorily diffused among the whole tax-paying population. Consequently, Niskanen says, there will be less pressure to search for more efficient modes of operation than under a private shareholding system, particularly in the long term. Under a scheme of private ownership, an organization which is operating less efficiently than it might be will have a share price which is also lower than it might be. There is always therefore an incentive for an individual or a group to buy a controlling interest in the organization, improve efficiency and reap a corresponding reward in terms of an appreciation in share price. No such mechanism operates automatically in the public sector, although, as we have seen, there are a variety of surrogate measures of efficiency.

All of the economic approaches which have been sketched out here are in the tradition of 'Parkinson's Law', and have the same appeal. As with classical economics, powerful deductions can be drawn from a few intuitively acceptable assumptions. Everyone wants the army to get bigger, because the bigger it gets, the more generals there can be. But the bigger the army gets, the more unwieldy it becomes, and the lower the competence of any individual general is likely to be, so overall effectiveness proportionally diminishes. It is probably no accident that this type of theory should appear after a period when economists have been drawn closely into policy advice in government and have consequently discovered that administrators are less selfless and efficient than previous economic theories tended to assume. What has been produced is an elegant axiomatic body of theory about the limits of top-level control *vis-a-vis* official self-interest in cases where administration is carried out through hierarchic, tax-financed bureaucracy.

Illuminating as such theories may be, there are some questions which remain. For example, we sketched out a range of non-market controls in the last chapter: are they all equally ineffective? Similarly, these theories are confined to control within hierarchic organizations rather than to administration as a broad societal process: do the same limits apply? To take a specific example, the 'Law of Diminishing Control', as formulated by Downs and Tullock, is based merely on organizational size. The argument, as we have seen, is that as organizations get larger, top-level control necessarily diminishes in proportional terms. But, as we will see in the next chapter, several elements unrelated to size and outside the administrative hierarchy help to determine the effectiveness of administrative control in a broad societal sense. Indeed, there are some cases in which, far from diminishing, administrative control can become 'self-sustaining' after sufficient time and resources have been devoted to policing operations. Police states largely rely on this principle, by creating an impression of all-powerful surveillance such that resistance is deterred and would-be offenders turn informer on their colleagues.

The last point raises the difficult question of how far economic theories of administration apply outside a European, or even an American, context. Almost all the 'economic' theories which have been produced so far are American, and it is probably no coincidence that public administration in the United States has traditionally been pictured as a free-wheeling, loose-jointed affair, in which the comparison of officials with entrepreneurs and of agencies with firms in a competitive market was particularly appropriate. But would the 'economic' approach be validated in other, different bureaucratic settings? Writers such as Peter Self[8] and R. G. S. Brown[9] have raised this question, though it could only be answered by detailed comparative research.

A final problem which such theories share with many others is that even if the theory is consistent with observed behaviour of a fairly general kind, that does not necessarily clinch the matter. As in medicine, the 'facts' — of bureaucratic expansion, for example — are open to a variety of explanations. For example, John Child has pointed out that 'Parkinsonian' processes of the growth of administrative personnel in organizations over time (processes which have been identified in a variety of studies) could have a technological explanation, quite apart from the expansionist tendencies of officials.[10] Similarly, as we will see in the next section, many of the conclusions reached by economists about the limits of control in hierarchies can also be reached from other academic approaches.

Cybernetic Theories

A second wide-ranging and influential body of theory about the limits of control in hierarchies is provided by cybernetic approaches to administration. Cybernetics, or 'general systems theory' is an approach which is slightly less distinctively American in origin, and which is particularly influential in Eastern Europe, perhaps because it offers a relatively 'bloodless' way of exploring administrative limits. We have reviewed the cybernetic approach in Chapter 5, and here only two brief additional comments will be made concerning the applicability of the approach to control in a more general sense.

The first problem is how one handles recalcitrance in a cybernetic account of administrative control. As we have seen, recalcitrance is at the heart of the economic approach: the rational bureaucrat seeks to evade control from above, agencies battle with one another for a place in the sun; and the same logic might be extended to those who are being administered by such bureaucrats, though we noted that in fact the 'administered' play little part in economic theories of administration. In contrast, recalcitrance plays no part in cybernetic theory; and in fact Stafford Beer, one of the main 'cybernetic' theorists of administration, recognizes that recalcitrance is difficult to handle in a theory which is based on an analogy with the workings of the human body.[11] The heart cannot deliberately refuse the brain's commands; it can only fail mechanically. The assumption is perfect obedience, as in our third condition of perfect administration.

This assumption is more or less justified in the case of those organizations, such as most business firms, which are more or less able to 'screen out' potential 'troublemakers' by recruitment procedures and other means of exclusion.[12] But many public agencies cannot screen out troublemakers, and face an environment so hostile that very coercive control mechanisms are required. The same applies to public administration as a whole: at this level hostility cannot be squeezed out of the system. All that can be done is to shuffle troublemakers round the system by 'multi-organizational' tactics. In general, the implications of a hostile environment for a cybernetic account of administration have not been fully worked out. But the more hostile the environment, the greater the resources which have to be devoted to intelligence and surveillance,[13] and the more likely it is that the system will run into 'channel capacity' limits of the type which were described in Chapter 4.

Second, the cybernetic approach deals with administrative control in an abstract and 'essentialist' way. It deals with the basic informational requirements of control systems without telling us anything about the actual mechanisms by which control is exercised. This is necessary, but it is not sufficient, for a complete discussion of the problem. Informationally, all control processes can be reduced to a common basic form. Mechanically, they are all different. For example, it is as important to understand the mechanical differences in the control systems represented by a man riding a horse and a man driving a car as it is to understand the informational requirements which both systems share. It is the mechanical level of control which we focused upon in the last chapter, not attempting to identify the 'essence' of a control system but using the concept of control intuitively and looking at different types of control. The mechanical limits of administrative control are just as important as the informational limits.

Both the cybernetic and economic approaches to administrative control are powerful and well-established analyses. As we have seen, both are particularly illuminating in their analysis of the informational problems of control in hierarchies, though they do not answer all the questions that one might want to ask. In contrast, the organizational sociology approach contains a congeries of more restricted theories of control in organizations, but many of these theories are relevant in identifying limits of administrative control. This is in spite of the fact that organizational sociology has in the past largely concerned itself with individual organizations, and private firms at that, rather than with the multi-organizational framework of public administration. Surprisingly, the science of government, political science, has contributed relatively little, in spite of Norton Long's assertion that 'organizations are governments'[14] and of the obvious pervasiveness of politics in organizations. The exploration of power and control in organizations has been largely left to sociologists.

Sociological Theories

Tentatively, we can identify roughly three generations of sociological theory relating to administrative control in this century. The first was a famous 1920 analysis of bureaucratic organizations by a Prussian sociologist, Max Weber. Weber described bureaucratic control as a single type of control and distinguished it from two other categories of social control, namely traditional government and inspirational leadership. Weber stressed the features of hierarchy, specialization and standard procedures as elements of his single model of bureaucracy, and saw this as the most effective administrative control system which could be attained in present-day circumstances.[15]

The second generation of theory, in the 1950s, was provided by a group of American writers who pointed out that many of the control systems involved in Weber's sketch of efficient bureaucratic organization could in fact hamper administrative effectiveness and thus could be 'dysfunctional'.[16] Similar arguments had in fact been put forward by earlier anti-bureaucratic theorists such as John Stuart Mill.[17] Indeed, the Prussian general staff of the late nineteenth century, often seen as an archetype of bureaucratic organization, could be used as an illustration of the negative side of hierarchy and ordered procedures, since it was an inflexible system under a senile, stone-deaf leader (Von Moltke), who only recognized one man on his staff, and called him by his predecessor's name.[18]

Enlightening as the idea of 'administrative dysfunctionality' was at the time, the concept is now fairly widely acknowledged to be unsatisfactory, for various reasons. One difficulty which has been identified by many writers is that the word 'dysfunctionality' implies a prior judgment about what organizations *ought* to be doing, whereas in practice people in organizations have multiple and conflicting objectives, and the objectives of the 'bosses' are open to challenge. In effect, this is a criticism of the first two conditions of the perfect administration model, which assume top-level authorities to be well-defined, unitary and in pursuit of clear-cut objectives. We have already acknowledged that these conditions are unreal, but it is equally foolish to go to the other extreme and to argue that the idea of organizations having 'goals' is entirely meaningless: administrative behaviour is not totally random or purposeless.

Apart from the difficulty of making prior judgments about goals, which we can in fact assume away for the purposes of this analysis, the idea of administrative dysfunctionality runs together at least three separate problems. Not all types of administrative failure produce the same kind of results; and not all types of administrative failure derive from a common basic problem. Some cases of failure can be explained simply in terms of dilemmas; but there are 'non-linearities' too. We will be exploring these different basic categories of administrative failure more fully in the next chapter.

Third, the *mechanisms* which brought about 'dysfunctional' outcomes were not adequately mapped out. Indeed, a full typology of administrative diseases has not been developed even now, as S. K. Bailey has pointed out.[19] The theorists of the 1950s identified two or three chief mechanisms of dysfunctionality. One is 'bribery and corruption' in all its forms. The other is excessive 'red tape' and a variety of processes which are usually associated with it, such as inflexible perceptions of the world, the micro-imperialism of officials, succession of goals and ritualized procedures which become ends in themselves and are adhered to, no matter how inappropriate the situation. To that should be added those types of administrative 'dysfunction' which have been located in excessive 'clientelism' and in professional fragmentation.

Certainly, 'red tape' and 'bribery' are diseases of administrative control which are familiar in most people's experience, and no-one can deny their importance in limiting administrative effectiveness. The popular caricature of 'bureaucracy' as the needless proliferation of paper for its own sake — the need to fill in, double-check and file dozens of forms, requisitions and affidavits for every trivial item — is sometimes not far from the truth. Peter Self[20] has congratulated British administration on its freedom from this kind of thing, but one should be aware of casting the first stone: for example, some years ago the Estimates Committee discovered that it needed approximately 18 separate forms to draw a spanner from army stores (this is admittedly a modest figure against some 'Third World' ones).[21] Similar examples could be drawn from social security administration. Even the humble dog licence form in Britain provides a curious example of gratuitous fact-gathering, since the 1972—1973 version required for some reason both the full Christian names of the owner (whereas initials are sufficient for a TV licence) and the hour *and minute* at which the licence was granted.[22]

The more glaring cases of 'red-tapism' make good newspaper copy, as with the apparently insane bureaucratic logic which leads British local housing authorities to smash up their own vacant property in order to prevent squatters from moving in and thus upsetting housing allocation procedures. How absurd! But when one looks more closely, it often appears that red tape and bribery are merely two horns of a dilemma which Merton,[23] in an early discussion of the problem, described as over-organization and under-organization. That is, one resorts to stringent procedural safeguards precisely in order to prevent rapacity, graft, embezzlement, special treatment for politically favoured persons and so on. One has to accept inefficiency either in the form of a leakage of resources or of money or on the other hand in the form of an excessive allocation of resources to security procedures.

Admittedly, in some cases, things are more serious than this. For example, graft may so radically short-circuit the decision process as to produce the opposite effect to that which is desired. An illustration of this, given by Ferris,[24] is the case of the money which was filched from overseas aid schemes to underdeveloped countries in the 1960s. Much of this money inexorably found its way back to Swiss banks and to investments in Nabisco and Pepsi-Cola, in effect promoting the development of the rich countries rather than of the poor ones. Worst of all, there are some circumstances in which, far from being alternatives, red tape and bribery become complementary. The only way to cut through the red tape is to pay 'speed money'. In cases like this, it is very difficult to establish whether the problems are 'internal' or strictly extra-administrative, as Riggs[25] has pointed out.

Contingency Theory

Many administrative 'funny stories' are drawn from examples of the type which we have just discussed. As explanations of limits to administrative control, such processes are plausible and attract a ready response from many people. But there are some administrative diseases for which such explanations cannot satisfactory account. In particular, what was seen to be wrong in the late 1950s was the over-general level at which the discussion was being conducted. The strategy which was effective in one setting might not be effective in another setting: 'contingent' factors had to be explored to take account of this.[26] Over the past 15 years or so, more and more typologies and contingencies affecting organizations have been identified and developed by sociologists, to the extent that sociological and quasi-sociological approaches now have the opposite virtues and defects to those of the more general theories of economics, cybernetics or of the earlier generation of sociological writers. As Perrow puts it

'We know enough about organizations now to recognize that most generalizations that are applicable to all organizations are too obvious, or too general, to be of much use for specific predictions.'[27]

Some of the most interesting sociological approaches for the purposes of this analysis are those which are concerned with tracing out the implications or 'costs' of alternative strategies of organizational control. Again, this represents a development from the earlier generations of theory, as Blau and Schoenherr[28] indicate in a comment on Max Weber, the pioneer theorist of bureaucracy

'His limitation is that he failed to make explicit analytic distinctions between different control mechanisms and subsumed them all under his ideal type.'

Examples of sociological exploration of strategic alternatives are studies by Meyer[29] and by Hickson, Inkson and Pugh.[30] Both of these studies identify two major alternatives strategies of administrative control within organizations. On the one hand, there is control through 'bureaucratization', involving elaborate rules and a professionalized staff. On the other hand, there is control by centralizing all important decisions. Of these two alternatives, the centralization strategy probably allows greater flexibility and, according to a study by Child,[31] tends to generate a lower level of conflict. On the other hand, the 'bureaucratic' model of control appears to be required for organizations which have a ramified structure of field officals. This point is also borne out by the other 'Aston' studies in comparative organization in the 1960s;[32] but Herbert Kaufman,[33] in a study of feedback mechanisms in the control of nine US federal agencies, found that few of the 'bureaucratic' checking devices were in fact used by top-level officials. Such officials tended to 'screen out' these sources of information in order to maintain relations of trust with their subordinates.

The main burden of the contingency theory approach is to identify the 'outside' or extra-administrative elements which limit the choice of effective control structures. The changeability and uncertainty of the environment, different tasks and 'technology' (with technology being defined in a number of ways) are among the contingent elements which have been identified as demanding control structures appropriate to the particular circumstances of the case.[34] It may be that a similar analysis could be applied to the level of general administrative control, in that different policy fields in public administration require different control strategies. For example, indirect taxation is an operation which has traditionally required a combination of ergonomic and accounting controls, which we will be discussing in more detail in the next chapter. By contrast, policy fields such as direct taxation, payment of subsidies and so on, combine accounting controls with market-type control systems. In foreign affairs and espionage, accounting and ergonomic controls can play little or no part; one is obliged to rely on market or judicial-type controls which came near the bottom of the list given in the last chapter. The same applies to many of the new 'social' spheres of government policy, such as the patronage of the arts, sport, broadcasting and science. But a 'contingency' analysis of administrative control in terms of policy fields will only work if one breaks down policy fields into sufficiently small pieces, because the broader the definition of policy field, the larger the spread of administrative technologies which is likely to be involved.

In some ways, the implications of the contingency approach are a little bewildering to those who expect to find one best way to control organizations. Taken over the whole gamut of organizations, there appears to be no single optimum, either of managerial structure in formal terms, or to the actual power distribution within organization,[35] from the point of view of 'best results'. Insofar as generalizations have emerged, it appears that 'bureaucratic' structures are relatively effective for routine, everyday administrative tasks, whereas less formalized and heirarchic structures are more effective for non-standardized tasks. But the studies on which such generalizations are based are largely drawn from private business rather than from public agencies, and categories within the two sides of the 'routine/non-routine' dichotomy have not yet been very firmly established. Moreover, the relation of detailed control processes to type of technology' has not yet been very satisfactorily established, in spite of some attempts to do so. In some circumstances, control is clearly built into the physical structure to a large extent; in other cases only simple and unsophisticated controls can be applied, as in the case of cloak-and-dagger operations. But there is a large intermediate category of cases where the technology permits a range of alternative control systems.[36]

Organizational Size and Level

Aside from technology, the size of the organization involved and the level of the organization within which control is operating, are other elements which may effect the appropriateness of particular types of control. This may seem obvious, but surprisingly little is known about the mechanisms which defeat administrative effectiveness in operations of large scale and scope. In recent years, there has been considerable emotional reaction against large-scale administrative structures, but we do not in fact know whether scale is the only important element which limits administrative effectiveness; or indeed whether it is important at all except isofar as failures which might arise on a smaller scale of operations are writ large.

The effects of size on patterns of administrative control have not received much attention from organizational sociologists, though their potential importance has been recognized. On a broad scale, Rule observes that the scale of different social settings vitally affects the viability of different forms of social control:[37] controls which are applicable on a small scale may be impossible on a larger scale, and vice versa. At organizational level, size has mostly been considered in relation to a long debate about changes in the relative size of the 'administrative' component of an organization's staff as organizations get larger.[38] The implication is that control becomes more formalized and institutionalized with size, and indeed Pugh, Hickson and Hinings have explicitly related growth in size over time with a move from 'line control' in a military style towards more impersonal patterns of control.[39] This is related to the observation that the larger the organization, the greater tends to be the element of 'structural differentiation', or division of labour and specialisms.

It is quite common for authors to identify the emergence of different 'stages' of control as organizations get larger.[40] An example is Whyte's exploration of the metamorphoses that a restaurant goes through as it grows from a one-man firm to a restaurant chain, observing five major changes in the control system.[41] As such an organization grows from its one-man or family origins, it will have to develop systematic accounting-type controls as it begins to employ 'outsiders', first in a menial capacity, later as supervizors. We will see this clearly in the case of bookmaking in Chapter 10. As the organization extends its operations geographically, extending into a 'chain' in the case of restaurants, accounting controls may no longer suffice. In order to adequately motivate the managers in the field units, some sort of market-type control (such as entitlement to a percentage of the takings or profits) may be introduced. At an intermediate level of organizational size, 'leagues' and 'peer groups' can be brought into play; and at some stage the operation may become too large for easy communication between the top directorate, workers and clients, resulting in the adoption of public relations or advertizing as an additional form of control. Such a development follows roughly the order in which controls were discussed in Chapter 7.

The same kind of analysis can be applied to some extent to levels within organizations as well as to overall size. The higher up the hierarchy, the more likely it is that control will have to come from outside the organization and will have to operate in relation to performance in the sense of 'outcome' rather than simply of attendance or of work done. Conversely, the lower down the hierarchy you go, the more likely it is that control will have to come from within the organization, operate according to 'output' indices rather than 'results' in a more general sense, often by techniques involving ergonomic controls of a more or less unsophisticated type, such as clocking in and out of work. But this is rather a traditional and stereotyped picture of levels of control in organizations. Organizations vary widely in type, as we have seen, and moreover the picture as a whole is changing. Many of the traditional patterns of hierarchic control are weakened in practice and in some cases they are also discredited in principle.[42] Particularly at the lower levels of organizations, there is a constant search for imperceptible and 'impersonal' types of control, and for controls which operate according to 'results'.

To some extent, analysis in terms of size and level can be applied to control systems within public agencies, which vary widely in size. Similarly, state administration as a whole has grown dramatically in size over the past century or so, and the growth of public administration from its original base in the royal household follows Whyte's pattern to some extent. But size-based concepts developed in the context of private industry are of very limited use in understanding control processes in an 'organization' as big as modern government administration as a whole.

Moreover, it is a common complaint that the implications of organizational sociology for control within society as a whole have not been adequately developed.[43] This link is important here, because administrative controls typically operate by coupling themselves to other control systems in the society. For example, metamorphoses in the control systems of business firms as they grow larger have important implications for overall administrative control, particularly in taxation. We will take up this theme in the next chapter, and the Betting Tax case in Chapter 10 illustrates how administrative controls from outside can be coupled to the control systems which operate within firms as a check on their own employees. On a broader scale, administrative control may be linked with very general social control processes. We gave an example of this in the last chapter, showing how the 'normal' activities of children can be harnessed for police purposes. An equally widespread mechanism is male dominance, still the accepted norm in social and family life as a whole; and there are some indications that administrative controls work best where this conventional pattern of social dominance is not reversed.[44] A hostile environment is expensive to control, as in those cases where administrative activities are directed against other social controls, whether organizational or of a broader kind. On the other hand, where administrative and social controls are 'congruent', administration is in effect swimming with the tide. This is an important 'contingency' for administrative control as a whole.

Conclusion

In this chapter, we have briefly reviewed a number of theories, derived from three separate academic disciplines, concerned with control in organizations and with the effectiveness of particular controls in particular contexts. All of these theories offer some insights into the limitations of administrative control processes. The economic and cybernetic theories emphasize the limitations of formal command in controlling large hierarchical organizations. The remedies offered by such theorists all tend in the direction of dismantling hierarchies by means such as competition and multiple channels of information. All this is intended to give the top directorate access to nodal points in the information system and the ability to switch within the system, avoiding paralysis in the form of lack of usable sanctions in the hands of top administrators (a disease identified by Crozier as characteristic of French administration).[45] But, given the need for hierarchies, such remedies are palliatives, not cures, since the theories imply that control can never be perfect in a hierarchical system.

Very similar analyses have been offered by some sociologists; but in general, recent sociological approaches to administrative control can be contrasted with the other two approaches in that they are more fragmented, inductive rather than deductive, and tend to emphasize that different strategies are demanded by different circumstances. Technology, size and various elements in the overall social setting, are of key importance in determining the type of organizational structure which will be effective, and indeed in determining which group within the organization will be dominant.

Clearly, a combination of the various elements which sociologists have identified as influencing the effectiveness of administrative controls would quickly become very complex. That is why we remarked earlier that sociological theories had faults and virtues opposite to those of the more 'universal' theories. Much of modern organizational sociology relates largely to 'power in organizations', a field which is at the same time narrower and broader than the larger-scale problems of administrative control considered in this book. It is broader, because it is concerned with identifying empirical patterns of power in organizations, whereas we are simply concerned with identifying what controls are potentially available to the authorities and what limits the exercise of such controls. The two questions are inevitably linked, but the first involves a debate about the empirical analysis of power in sociology and political science which we need not discuss here; for example, there may be over-arching power which is not overtly 'exercised', as in some of the subliminal controls which we discussed in the last chapter.[46] The most powerful control may be that which is invisible, as in the case of peer-group rivalries.

At the same time, the analysis of power in organizations is a narrower field than the analysis of control in administration. Public administration is an inter-organizational process, potentially covering society as a whole, and in which elements such as law and coercion must have a central place. So there are 'strategic' elements other than the structural characteristics of individual organizations which can limit or affect the exercise of administrative control in a broader sense. At the close of the last section, we showed how administrative controls can be linked with other levels of control, and we will introduce some other strategic elements in the next chapter. We also need a more explicit analysis of the ways in which administrative controls can be limited in effectiveness, and this is another question to be explored in the next chapter.

Notes

1. For the opposite view, see J. K. Galbraith, *The New Industrial State*, Hamilton, London, 1967.
2. Cf. I. Sharkansky, *The Routines of Politics*, Van Nostrand, New York, 1970.

148

3. Wilson, J. Q., 'The Police and their Problems: a theory', *Public Policy*, 1963, Vol. 12, pp. 189–216.
4. Cf. K. Popper, *The Poverty of Historicism*, Routledge and Kegan Paul, London, 1961.
5. Cf. B. Barry, *Economists, Sociologists and Democracy*, Collier–Macmillan, London, 1970.
6. Downs, A., *Inside Bureaucracy*, Wiley, New York, 1967; G. Tullock, *The Politics of Bureaucracy*, Public Affairs Press, Washington, 1965. These ideas are summarized by J. B. Bourn in *Approaches to the Study of Public Administration, Part Two: The Administrative Process as a Decision-Making and Goal-attaining System*, Public Administration Block II, Part 2, The Open University Press, Milton Keynes, 1974, pp. 49–51.
7. Niskanen, A., *Bureaucracy and Representative Government*, Aldine Atherton, New York, 1971; cf. R. E. Wagner, *The Public Economy*, Markham, Chicago, 1973, Chap. 7 'Bureaucracy and efficiency in public output'.
8. Self, P., *Administrative Theories and Politics*, Allen and Unwin, London, 1972, pp. 45–48 and p. 157.
9. Brown, R. G. S., *Approaches to the Study of Public Administration Part Three: The Administrative Process as Incrementalism*, Public Administration Block II, Part 3, The Open University Press, Milton Keynes, 1974, pp. 38–39.
10. Child, J., 'Predicting and understanding organizational structure', *Administrative Science Quarterly*, Vol. 18, 1973.
11. Beer, S., *Brain of the Firm*, Allen Lane, Penguin Press, London, 1972.
12. Cf. A. Etzioni, *Complex Organizations*, Holt Rinehart, New York, 1961.
13. Wilensky, H., *Organizational Intelligence*, Basic Books, New York, 1967.
14. Quoted in A. Pettigrew, *The Politics of Organizational Decision-Making*, Tavistock, London, 1973, p. 16.
15. Weber, M., 'Bureaucracy' in H. H. Gerth and C. W. Mills (Eds.), *From Max Weber: Essays in Sociology*, Routledge and Kegan Paul, London, 1948.
16. Hood, C. C., 'Administrative diseases: some types of Dysfunctionality', *Public Administration*, Winter 1974, Vol. 52.
17. Cf. M. Albrow, *Bureaucracy*, Pall Mall Press, London, 1970.
18. Kitchen, M., *The German Officer Corps 1890–1914*, Clarendon Press, Oxford, 1968, pp. 69–70.
19. Bailey, S. K., in J. C. Charlesworth (Ed.) *Theory and Practice of Public Administration*, American Academy of Political and Social Science, Philadelphia, 1968, p. 133.
20. Self, P., *op. cit.*
21. *8th Report of the Estimates Committee*, HC 359, 1964–1965, Non Warlike Stores for the Services, p. xxxiii, para 90.
22. *The Times*, 12.12.72 and 14.12.72.
23. Merton, R. (Ed,), *Reader in Bureaucracy*, 2nd ed., The Free Press, New York, 1960.
24. Ferris, P., *Men and Money*, Hutchinson, London, 1968.
25. Riggs, F., *The Ecology of Public Administration*, Asia Publishing House, London, 1961.
26. Kast, F., and B. Rosenzweig, *Contingency Views of Organization and Management*, Science Research Associates, New York, 1973.
27. Perrow, C., *Organizational Analysis: A Sociological View*, Tavistock, London, 1970, p. 14.
28. Blau, P. M., and R. Schoenherr, *The Structure of Organizations*, Basic Books, London, 1971, p. 347.
29. Meyer, M. W., 'Two authority structures of bureaucratic organization', *Administrative Science Quarterly*, Vol. 13, 1968, pp. 211–228.
30. Inkson, J. H., D. J. Hickson and D. S. Pugh, 'Administrative reduction of variance in organization and behaviour', unpublished paper 1968.
31. Child, J., 'Strategies of control and organizational behaviour', *Administrative Science Quarterly*, Vol. 18, 1973.
32. For example, D. S. Pugh, D. J. Hickson, C. R. Hinings and C. Turner, 'Dimensions of organizational structure', *Administrative Science Quarterly*, Vol. 13, 1968, pp. 65–105.
33. Kaufman, H., *Administrative Feedback: Monitoring Subordinates Behaviour*, Brookings Institution, Washington, 1973.
34. For example, J. Woodward, *Industrial Organization: Theory and Practice*, Oxford University Press, New York, 1965; J. D. Thompson and F. L. Bates 'Technology, organization and administration', *Administrative Science Quarterly*, Vol. 2, 1958, pp. 325–343;

T. Burns and J. M. Stalker, *The Management of Innovation*, Tavistock, London, 1962; V. Thompson, 'Bureaucracy and innovation', *Administrative Science Quarterly*, Vol. 10, 1965; J. M. Hage, 'An axiomatic theory of organizations', *Administrative Science Quarterly*, Vol. 11, 1966; P. R. Lawrence and J. W. Lorsch, *Organization and Environment*, Harvard University Press, Boston, 1967; D. J. Hickson, D. S. Pugh and D. C. Pheysey, 'Operations technology and organization structure', *Administrative Science Quarterly*, Vol. 14, 1969, pp. 378–397.

35. Tannenbaum, A. S., *Control in Organization*, McGraw-Hill, New York, 1968; 'Control in organizations', *Administrative Science Quarterly*, Vol. 7, 1962, pp. 236–257.

36. Woodward, J., *Industrial Organization: Behaviour and Control*, Oxford University Press, London, 1970.

37. Rule, J. B., *Private Lives and Public Surveillance*, Allen Lane, London, 1973.

38. Cf. Starbuck, W. H. (Ed.), *Organizational Growth and Development*, Penguin Books, Harmondsworth, 1971; T. R. Anderson and S. Warkov, 'Organizational size and functional complexity', *American Sociological Review*, 32, 1967, pp. 903–912; D. S. Pugh, D. J. Hickson, C. R. Hinings and C. Turner, 'Dimensions of organizational structure', *Administrative Science Quarterly*, Vol. 13, 1968, pp. 65–105.

39. Pugh, D. S., D. Hickson and C. R. Hinings, 'An empirical taxonomy of structures of work organizations', *Administrative Science Quarterly*, Vol. 14, 1969, pp. 115–126.

40. Starbuck, W. H., *op. cit.*, pp. 69–73.

41. Whyte, W. F., *Human Relations in the Restaurant Industry*, McGraw-Hill, New York, 1948.

42. Vickers, Sir G., 'The regulation of political systems', *General Systems Handbook*, Vol. 12, 1967.

43. Mayntz, R., 'The study of organizations', *Current Sociology*, Vol. 13, No. 3, 1965.

44. Acker, J., and D. R. Van Houten, 'Differential recruitment and control: the sex structuring of organizations', *Administrative Science Quarterly*, Vol. 19, 1974, pp. 152–163.

45. Crozier, M., *The Bureaucratic Phenomenon*, Tavistock, London, 1965.

46. Cf. S. Clegg, *Power, Rule and Domination*, Routledge and Kegan Paul, London, 1975; 'A sociological critique of an organizational theory of power' paper presented at EGOS Colloquum on Current Issues in Organizational Studies, Breau-sans-Nappe, France, April 3–5, 1975.

Chapter 9

The Limits of Control

'The techniques that are effective and efficient within a simple struc-
ture just may not be effective or efficient in a more complex case.'
R. H. Hall, *Organizations: Structure and Process*, Prentice-Hall, New
Jersey, 1972, p. 167.

In the last chapter we began to explore the second condition of perfect control
(that is, perfect effectiveness and perfect compatibility of controls) by briefly
looking at some analyses of the operation and limitations of control in
organizations. In this chapter, we will broaden the analysis of the limits of
administrative control by identifying some different types of limits or failures and
looking at some of the extra-organizational mechanisms which produce them. The
basic theme is that there is no single limit to administrative control, but rather a
multiplicity of limits of different types.

Outcomes

The first set of limits to be considered here concerns the outcomes of control.
Control processes may produce more than one type of undesired outcome. One can
distinguish inefficiency, ineffectiveness and negative effectiveness. In the case of
inefficiency, the desired effects or objectives are achieved in some degree, but at
unnecessarily high cost. There are no universal principles of efficient operation:
processes which are efficient in one context may be inefficient in another. It is
inefficient to use a bulldozer to dig a small garden, just as it is inefficient to use
spades and wheelbarrows to dig a canal.[1] Insofar as inefficiency is an administrative
limit, it is a limit of the 'economic' type — that is, control can become so costly
that it ceases to be worthwhile. For example, elaborate security measures are often
more expensive than the immediate cash value of the pilferage and the like which
they are designed to prevent. Here is a case

> '... for the first half year from September 1968, £1900 was spent in clerks'
> wages alone in checking fraudulent claims for free prescriptions in Manchester.
> 6,600 forms were checked, 43 patients were found to be not in any of the
> exemption categories, and £8 was recovered for the taxpayers.'[2]

The second type of failure is a more clear-cut limit. This is the case of
ineffectiveness, in which the desired results are not achieved at all. For example,
'matching' grants which are given by governments to local authorities or to other
organizations for the purpose of encouraging expenditure on some particular
programme may be quite ineffective if the net result of such grants is merely the

release of funds which the grantee organizations would have spent on the programme in the absence of a grant, and the diversion of such funds to other programmes. This outcome was found to be quite common by Porter and Warner in a study of the effectiveness of federal education grants in the United States.[3]

Ineffective outcomes can be subdivided into two main types. The simplest is the case where 'nothing happens' in response to some administrative stimulus. Peremptory commands which are issued from a distant headquarters with little means of 'checking up' on its out-stations are apt to meet this fate, as happened in the early days of the East India Company. As Ramsbotham remarks, the Company's head office might as well have sent out the Ten Commandments for all the effects their orders had.[4] A more recent example of this type of response was the British Industrial Relations Act of 1971—1974, which was simply ignored by the vast bulk of the British unionized labour force during its brief and unhappy life.

The other case of ineffectiveness is slightly more complicated. In this case, administrative action does evoke some responses, but these responses merely rearrange the inputs and outputs of a system with no net change, substituting one kind of activity for another in such a way that little or nothing is achieved by the authorities. The example of matching grants which was given above is a case of this type; another well-known example, mentioned in Chapter 6, is the attempt to control the growth of office building in central London in the early 1960s through the issue of permits. This measure simply resulted in rents rising sharply in central London without any appreciable effect on the outer metropolitan area or on the provinces.

After ineffectivess, the third broad type of control failure is the case in which administrative action produces results, but results which are contrary to those desired. In the second type of ineffectiveness, the administered system adjusts to restore the *status quo* in some form; but it is also possible for controls to be counter-productive in their effects. For example, before the advent of modern anti-septic techniques, hospitals were breeding-grounds for disease, with the result that most of the patients died, usually of some disease other than that for which they were admitted. Indeed, 'iatrogenic' or doctor-induced diseases are once again being increasingly discussed in the medical world, particularly in the psychiatric field, where problems such as institutionalization and drug-induced diseases are obvious even to a layman. A more directly administrative case of the problem is the device of 'clawback' of the unspent balances of grant funds at the end of an accounting period. This device can be self-defeating as a means of saving money, because it commonly encourages grantees to go on a spending spree at the end of an accounting period, especially if unspent balances will result in the following year's appropriation to the agency in question being reduced.

The Character of the Problem

Not only can controls be limited in a variety of ways in terms of the outcomes which they produce; they can also be limited in terms of the intractability of the problem involved. The basic distinction to be made here is one which has been implicit in much of the analysis of previous chapters, but now needs to be stressed. This is the distinction between, on the one hand, administrative dilemmas and, on the other hand, thresholds or non-linearities.

A dilemma is a familiar type of administrative limit.[5] It refers to situations in which it is impossible to move towards one goal without moving away from another. Clearly, many problems of control are simply dilemmas: some of the sociological analysis which we considered in the last chapter has brought out the different costs of alternative strategies of control, as in the case of red tape and bribery. By definition, a dilemma is a problem which can only be identified; it cannot be solved in any other way. We 'solve' puzzles, 'surmount' difficulties, 'identify' dilemmas and choose one problem or the other.[6]

The distinction between simple dilemmas and 'non-linearities' is the difference between those actions which unavoidably carry undesirable side-effects (dilemmas) and those actions which fail to be effective because they are applied to the wrong *extent*, such as overeating or under-eating. 'Non-linearity' problems are common enough in our everyday lives, and they seem to be particularly applicable to control processes, which seldom yield consistent results along the whole of their range. As Konrad Lorenz has pointed out, the lion-tamer's whip operates on a precarious threshold between two levels of arousal;[7] and many other control processes are only effective in a narrow range between nil effect, diminishing returns and 'reversal points', where the opposite of the desired effect is produced. Non-linearity problems differ from dilemmas in that they are not inherently insoluble. In principle, such problems can be ameliorated by 'fine tuning', although the practical difficulties of achieving delicate adjustments in most types of administrative controls should not be underestimated.

Non-linearity limits

We will explore dilemmas as a type of limit in the next main section, after exploring limits in the form of 'non-linearities'. It would be neat — alas, over-neat — to suggest that the key to understanding the limits of control was simply non-linearity: push any one of the controls of Chapter 7 too far and you will reach limits in terms of one of the outcomes which were set out at the beginning of this chapter. At first sight, an Aristotelian 'golden mean' analysis of this kind has some plausibility. There are a number of cases where control must be pitched at the right level in order to be effective. For example, secrecy in administrative operations is often necessary up to a point, but, as Wilensky has pointed out,[8] secrecy can become counter-productive at some point because of the distortions in intelligence which it produces. In other cases, the same broad analysis applies, but things are not quite so simple. Consider the process of *wastage*, which has already been mentioned in earlier chapters.

Wastage and Non-linearities

Wastage is a term which refers to the interchange of personnel between the public and private sectors or between different organizations. It is common enough for public and private organizations to be rivals in the labour market for the same professional or technical skills; and the ability of the private sector to bid successfully for talented individuals possessing valued skills is aided by the relative political inflexibility of public service pay levels and structures. Attempts to increase the attractiveness of a particular grade in the public service both tend to run into fierce pay relativity politics and typically involve much larger sums than in the private sector, with its relatively smaller units.

The simplest case of wastage is where the relevant skills straddle the public and private sectors, with the sectors competing for a relatively fixed cake of professionals. A slightly different case of wastage, but perhaps equally common, is where skills which can only be acquired in the public sector are 'saleable' in the service of the 'administered'. To take a familiar example, Thayer asserts that there are no major arms producing companies in the non-Communist world which do not have a number of high-ranking ex-military officers on their payroll.[9] The same applies in other fields. One case, explored by Mintz and Cohen, is the exodus to private industry from the ranks of the United States Food and Drug Administration. Some 10 per cent of all leavers from the FDA (apart from retirees) in the four years ended in late 1963 went to FDA-regulated companies.[10] A curious variant of this type of wastage is the growth of 'agency nursing' in Britain, particularly in London. What happens is that nurses who have trained and qualified in the hospital service are hired back to National Health Service hospitals as 'temporaries' through agencies at more than the going wage rate for permanent staff.

Of course, not all flows between the public and private sectors are one-way; for example, it is by no means unknown in the British civil service for 'gamekeepers' to turn 'poachers' and later to rejoin the ranks of the gamekeepers. Provided that the outflow of public officials is not too severe, or is matched by a comparable inflow of talent from other sectors, wastage may not seriously handicap administrative control. Indeed, up to a point wastage is often advantageous to public authorities as a control system, since the process places 'their' men in key positions in the outside world. Mackenzie and Grove, in a standard textbook on British central administration in the late 1950s, emphasized the advantages of wastage,[11] and this is a view which was often held in the past. In the field of naval contracts, Pool tells us that where ex-members of old Navy Board became associated with shipbuilding contractors, this was typically seen as evidence that the business would be soundly performed.[12]

But beyond some point wastage clearly reduces administrtive effectiveness. A well-known example of this was the experience of the British Inland Revenue Department in the 1960s. The Inland Revenue tax inspectorate is the only fully-fledged professional body arising within and confined to the civil service,[13] but so great is the demand for ex-tax inspectors in the tax avoidance industry that the number of fully-trained tax inspectors actually *fell* slightly in the 1960s, at a time when the Department's workload was greatly increasing;[14] and Mr. Roy Jenkins, when Chancellor of the Exchequer, described tax avoidance as the 'fastest growing British industry'. Professor C. T. Sandford put the size of this 'industry' at possibly as great as £250m per year in 1973;[15] and four years earlier, representatives of the Inland Revenue Department had described the situation which they were facing as follows

'If heavy additional burdens enforce a reduction in standards and relaxation in vigilance, and outside expertise runs ahead of the efforts of the (Chief Inspector of Taxes') Branch to take effective counter-measures, morale suffers, public confidence is reduced, and avoidance and fraud are allowed to flourish unchallenged.'[16]

The disease is by no means an exclusively British one: many other Western European countries face the same problem in tax administration, and it also extends to accountants and technical costs officers in other policy fields. We saw this in the contracting case: indeed, it appeared from the investigation which followed the Ferranti and Bristol Siddeley affairs of the 1960s (cases involving 'excess' profits on government contracts) that the British government was so short of such personnel that it could not adequately supervize cost-plus contracts, let alone fixed- or target-price contracts, or the investigation of sub-contractors' costs.[17]

Types of Non-linearities

Even in the case of wastage, it is difficult to identify a clear non-linearity effect. And if we look more closely at control processes, we can see that there are several types of non-linearity, or thresholds in the relation between compliance and the administrative units deployed. There is the 'critical mass' effect, the 'snowball effect' and a variety of types of negative response.

First, there is the case of 'critical mass' in some types of control. This is the idea that there is a point of effort below which controls will have little or no effect. For example, in advertizing, there is often a point below which a campaign will have nil effect, and the same applies to other types of administrative operation. The opposite case to the 'critical mass' effect is the 'snowball effect'. This effect can be illustrated in many areas of regulatory control by governments. In such cases, there is often a point at which administrative control sways the balance of advantage between evasion and compliance to such an extent that a significant number of people not merely accept control but actively help the authorities to suppress 'outlaws' in order to protect themselves against illegal competition. In this way, control can actually become self-sustaining in many cases. Obviously, the point at which 'poachers' are induced to become 'gamekeepers', to use the terminology of Chapter 7, will vary according to the logistics of the situation and to the internal divisions of the relevant community. Some administrative operations, such as the regulation of 'pirate' taxi-cabs, are much more susceptible to 'guerilla' operations than others, such as distilleries, even in cases where administrative regulation has a large degree of outside support within the regulated community. Raw alcohol is unpleasant stuff. It is dangerous and difficult to produce spirits on a casual scale, compared to the ease of turning your car into a pirate taxi-cab at night in a big city.

But in spite of different take-off points, almost any licensing situation contains very strong motivations for self-sustaining enforcement, and this is an example of administrative control 'swimming with the tide' of more general social controls which we discussed at the end of the last chapter. It has proved to be almost impossible to suppress social 'evils' such as prostitution, liquor sales or gambling, but it is relatively easy to 'channel' such activities into a controllable form by granting concessions or licences. This, of course, presents a dilemma for moralists. Many types of 'pitch' concessions are almost wholly self-administering, and the same applies to many types of taxation and regulation. Traders have an interest in suppressing tax-free or unregulated competition, and often large firms can use such schemes as a means of squeezing ill-equipped marginal firms out of the market.

This is what has happened, for example, in the bookmaking situation which will be explored more fully in the following chapter. To take a case from a different policy field, the same sort of process operates in the enforcement of fishing regulations. Fishermen are usually quick to report illegal fishing by foreign vessels within their domestic fishing limits, and indeed may take direct action against such intruders. But no such self-sustaining mechanism operates with respect to fishing regulations and restrictions on the *domestic* fleet, at any rate within groups of similar vessels (there is often considerable rivalry between fishermen using different fishing methods, particularly between longshoremen and trawlermen). Indeed, in Scotland, the advent of a government fisheries cruiser has traditionally been reported by wireless transmitter from vessel to vessel so that few infringements of the domestic fishing regulations have in fact been detected in the past.[18]

The third non-linearity is a variety of types of negative responses to control. In Chapter 2 we gave an example of controls being counter-productive as a result of the 'negative demonstration effect'. The point at which controls may become counter-productive is not necessarily the extreme point of the range. Control systems can in fact be self-defeating at both the upper and lower end of their range, as in the lion-tamer example which we gave earlier. At the lower end, a vintage illustration is the traditional process of beating Egyptian fellaheen who refused to pay the land tax.[19] This operation was in fact highly vexatious for the revenue authorities, because it became a matter of keen competition among the fellaheen as to how many blows they received before giving up their money.

This case illustrates a negative form of the critical mass effect, and there are also negative forms of the snowball effect, in that non-linearities may occur through the over-application of controls. Writers such as Gouldner[20] and Crozier[21] have pointed out the alienating effects on office and factory workers produced by 'over-organization' in the form of rigid regulations and the like, and the vicious circles which can develop between subordination and control. A larger-scale example is government interference with news media. Effective up to a point, such interference becomes self-defeating at the point where all news from such sources is automatically assumed to be propaganda lies and disbelieved, even if it is true. Effective deception presupposes a general context of non-deception if credibility gaps are to be avoided.[22]

Both of these cases belong to the category of 'negative demonstration effects'. A closely similar mechanism is the 'big stick syndrome'. Everyone knows that 'using a sledgehammer to crack a nut' is *inefficient*; but 'big sticks' may also be *ineffective* because they involve threats which are so drastic that they are unwieldy and cannot easily be used in 'marginal' situations. In Chapters 3 and 7 we have already referred to the lack of middle-range sanctions as a key weakness in many administrative control systems, and the problem is a very general one. The paradoxical weakness of the nuclear super-powers *vis-à-vis* small countries is a large-scale example: nuclear weapons are typically too devastating for their use to be an effective threat in such situations. Indeed, Herman Kahn once said that 'the closer a weapons system becomes to a Doomsday Machine (i.e. one capable of destroying all living things) the less satisfactory it becomes'.[23]

An example at a lower, more 'administrative' level, is the use of threats to withhold funds in order to enforce central government grant conditions. As we saw in Chapter 3, such threats are so drastic that officials are usually unwilling to carry them out, particularly if (as may well be the case) they punish not only the recalcitrant organization which received the grant, but also innocent third parties.[24] At a lower level still, it is difficult to punish effectively those people living at subsistence level. To take a typical problem, it is almost impossible to fine a man who is already wholly dependent on public welfare benefits at subsistence level (except in those cases where one can take away 'privileges', as with prisoners); and sending a man to prison may both reduce the chances of ever getting him off dependence on social security benefits and also may involve hardship on innocent children.

Similar problems arise, as we have already seen, in government contracting where (as so often) there is a recurrent and 'oligopolistic' pattern of supply. In such a situation, attempts to use the 'big stick' in cases such as the exercise of penalty clauses on late deliveries, may simply result in much longer delivery dates being quoted in the next 'round' of tenders.[25] Threats not to renew contracts may simply not be credible, and where they are, such threats may simply lead to the syndrome known as 'brochuremanship', in which contractors concentrate their talent on selling new contract proposals rather than in properly executing the job in hand.

As well as being ineffective, 'big sticks' may also be counter-productive.[26] Excessive harshness to captured offenders (such as prisoners of war), apart from being unpleasant, tends to encourage the enemy to fight to the death. A similar sort of problem occurs in many of the poorer countries, where governments sometimes try to weaken their own armies in order to make such armies less dangerous as potential usurpers of political power – a tactic which is often counter-productive. Again, the prescription of very heavy penalties (such as death) for offences such as smuggling, can achieve the opposite of the desired result. For example, the old death penalty for sheep-stealing in England, instead of acting as a deterrent to potential thieves, in fact seems to have deterred juries from returning verdicts of guilty on those who were accused of such offences. A case from a different sphere of operations is the use of *agents provocateurs* and informants by police authorities against subversive organizations. Such activities, intended to provoke illegal acts which will justify police suppression, may at some point be counter-productive for state security. This is because the activities of undercover agents typically help to build up subversive organizations, and the insurrectionary movements which such agents aim to provoke may weaken or even destroy the *status quo* regime.[27]

Finally, Ivor Catt has described some of the (literally) fantastic and counter-productive subterfuges and blackmails resorted to by employees of an American corporation whose personnel policy of 'new realism' (a reaction against the soft 'human relations' approach of the 1950s) was to fire employees at all levels on average every two years. The results were something like those achieved in using the 'big stick' in government contracting.[28] For example, units tended to be overstaffed, in order to protect the 'core' people within them from being fired, management tended to try to lay off the most competent rather than the least competent employees in order to prevent able subordinates from supplanting them, evidence of failure tended to be concealed until it was too late to do anything to remedy such failures and so forth.

It is not only the mis-application of a single type of control which may produce negative or ineffective results. The problem also applies to multiple-system controls. Multiple-system controls can in some cases be pushed to a point where multi-unit sub-optimization sets in, for example between administratively separate piece-work and quality controls in factories, stock control versus production flexibility and so on.[29] A classical case of the counter-productive effects of double-banking control systems is the duplication of secret police agencies, or similar cloak-and-dagger operations. For example, Waddington remarks of the Nazi police state

> 'The surveillance function was shared among the SS, SD and the Gestapo; and the resulting separation, duplication and specialization of this battery of secret police effectively prevented them from collectively recognizing the meaningful pattern from available information.'[30]

Many cases of this type are in fact on the boundary of dilemmas and non-linearities, since the basic problem is typically that one is combining controls which are incompatible. We will discuss this aspect of multiple controls shortly.

'Real Time' or Sequence of Operations

A final type of non-linearity, which limits the effectiveness of controls in a slightly different way from the mechanisms which have been discussed so far, is 'real time' or sequence of operations. We discussed this in Chapter 2 in terms of reorganization, referring to the possible disadvantages of *moving* from one position to another as opposed to the advantages of *being* in a different position.[31] It is perhaps a jargonese phrase. It is used here to denote a slightly different conception of time from the chronological concept of years, days, hours and so on. It refers to broad sequences of events, just as the odometer on a car registers the cumulative total of mileage irrespective of the chronological time which elapses between each trip.

The point is that the order in which things happen vitally affects control relationships. The combination of two elements A and B may be quite different if A has preceded B than if B has preceded A. The extreme form of real-time constraint is known as a 'Markoff process', in which every event is determined primarily by the immediately preceding event (as opposed, say, to spinning a roulette wheel, which is a case where every event is completely independent from every other event). In Chapter 2, we discussed the 'horse-shoe-nail' problem, or the small piece of grit which can foul up a large machine, and this problem can also apply to time-sequence of operations. The analogy is with a Chinese puzzle. It is not enough to discover how the pieces fit together to make the structure once it is complete. One must also discover the sequence in which the puzzle must be constructed.[32]

In Chapter 5 we discussed adaptation as a limit on administration, and here we can add two other obvious ways in which time sequence can affect administrative control in a more general sense. One is the familiar problem of credibility. That is, the outcome of a certain control will depend, among other things, on the success or failure of preceding controls.

A large-scale example can be drawn from British governments' policies towards trade unions in the late 1960s and early 1970s. After the failure of wage control in the 1960s, both Labour and Conservative governments tried unsuccessfully to strike at the structural bases of union power by industrial relations legislation; after this strategy had failed in turn, policy veered back to further attempts at wage control. It is interesting to speculate in this case how far the failure of each preceding attempt to master the problem contributed to the failure of the subsequent policy.

The other obvious way in which controls can be limited by the effect of 'real time' is the extent to which the system is 'aroused'. The term 'arousal' is a psychological one, referring to the extent to which individuals are 'awake' and therefore receptive to stimuli.[33] Arousal levels will clearly affect the degree of friction to which any control will be subject. To take a familiar example, security or safety controls typically attract a higher compliance level after an accident or a security lapse than before such an incident — hence Voltaire's famous principle of executing an admiral from time to time *pour encourager les autres.*[34] Of course 'arousal' may also have negative effects, as in the case of the negative demonstration effect.

Problems in Analysing Non-linearities

Can any overall pattern be detected in the various types of non-linearities in control which we have been exploring? The simplest hypothesis might be that the typical control system is ineffective below some point of 'critical mass' and thereafter follows some sort of proportionate relationship between compliance and administrative output between the point of critical mass and a point of marginally or absolutely diminishing returns. One might argue this by analogy from economics, where each demand curve has a different angle of slope, but all demand curves (with only a few exceptions) slope downwards.

But at least two things immediately complicate this kind of analysis. One is the empirical difficulty of relating compliance to administrative output. For example, there is the familiar problem that hiring extra policemen for law enforcement may apparently *increase* measured crime rates, because the presence of more policemen on the beat results in more crimes being detected and reported, without necessarily meaning that the number of crimes committed will be greater, smaller or approximately the same as in the period before the extra police were hired.[35] The same effect applies when police operate 'crackdowns' on particular types of crime or particular districts. Analogous effects are well known to apply in policy areas such as social work or medicine. If one relied simple-mindedly on the figures in such cases, one could produce a clear negative correlation between administrative output and compliance, but in many cases such a conclusion would be spurious.

The other complication has to do with the objectives of the system. As has been mentioned before 'effectiveness' means one thing if you are operating on engineering-type limits, another if you are operating on economic-type limits. Desmond Keeling has made the same point in his distinction of 'management' from 'administrative' systems in government.[36] A 'management system' in his terminology, aims for optimum use of resources. This implies that the objectives of such a system would be maximum compliance per unit employed. On the other hand, an 'administrative' system is not so much concerned with the use of resources as with maximum feasible compliance. A different criterion of effectiveness would therefore apply. In an 'administrative' system, controls would be considered effective until *absolutely* diminishing returns set in. A managerial system, on the other hand, operates on economic rather than on engineering-type limits, and under such a system controls would only be regarded as effective until *marginally* diminishing returns set in. The significance of non-linearity limits may therefore vary, although in practice few 'administrative' systems are totally unaffected by unit costs and it is very rare to find controls applied to the point of 'real' or engineering-type limits.

Dilemmas: Complementarity and Substitutability of Controls

Apart from non-linearities, the other way in which administrative controls can be limited, in terms of the intractability of the problem, is the case of dilemmas. In discussing the limits of double-banking control systems in the last section, we mentioned that the basic problem in some cases is that there are limits to the extent to which different types of control can be combined or substituted, and that this problem is strictly a dilemma. As we have seen, some control systems are only effective when a number of elements are coupled up. For example, we pointed out in Chapter 7 that ergonomic types of control are seldom effective on their own, illustrating the point with Newman's definition of 'defensible space' as a combination of 'ergonomic' and social characteristics, neither of which is sufficient on its own.[37] On the other hand, there are cases where the use of one type of control in effect puts another out of your reach. Such dilemmas were the second type of limit on administrative control which we identified in Chapter 2. Some incompatibilities are relatively obvious: for example, Etzioni has suggested that control by persuasion is incompatible with 'market' types of control.[38] Similarly, an administrative structure which is devised chiefly to minimize corruption among officials may be restricted in the scope of its effectiveness as a result. This dilemma can be illustrated by examining the development of structures of tax administration.

The Development of Modern Direct Tax Administration

Early forms of taxes were typically collected through intermediaries, such as barons, local chiefs or gentry, tax-farmers and so forth. But systems of this type were usually unstable, because conflicts typically arose between the administrative headquarters and the 'man in the middle', often relating to the division of the tax money between the two. Criminal racketeering organizations often display a similar pattern of conflict. Also, this type of tax administration in its crudest form was often associated with extortion by the 'middlemen'. Such extortion typically caused conflicts into which the central authorities were drawn without having profited from the original outrages. Exactly the same problems arose with tax collection through local chiefs in the overseas empires of European states in the nineteenth and twentieth centuries.[39]

The problems created by collecting taxes through indirect means led most West European countries to adopt centralized systems of appointment and promotion of tax officials several centuries ago. In classical bureaucratic fashion, such tax officials were permanently employed, entitled to pensions on retirement, and usually excluded from electoral politics. But the problems of indirect administration do not automatically disappear when direct administration is adopted. The great problem, in fact, is to devise arrangements which are reasonably proof against corruption and embezzlement by tax officials. The problems are similar to those of managing a casino — large sums of money are changing hands in a rapid and bewildering way, and the proprietor has to find ways of preventing fraud by his customers, theft by his employees and collusion between customers and employees. The last problem is a particularly difficult one. Even in the 'modern' states of to-day it haunts the field of tax administration and in some historical cases fraud and collusion by tax officials was rampant. For example, in eighteenth-century England the situation was so bad that the revenue cutters of the Customs Department were themselves an important source of contraband.[40]

The 'Fruit-machine' Model

The now orthodox way of escaping from the problem of collusion and corruption in tax administration seems to have been devised in England in the thirteenth century. This was an early type of the accounting controls which we discussed in Chapter 7. The technique is to engineer a 'matrix' of information which ramifies from the tax-payer through a number of officials and is completed only by a higher official or his staff. Most modern revenue organization and financial administration generally is now based on this kind of principle, as we saw in Chapter 7.

But a system of this type will only work effectively where some or all of the officials in the network are *mobile*. Moreover, mobility between postings has to take place within a fairly large-scale system if it is to be an effective form of control. Without effective mobility, those officials who hold the key 'combat' positions in the field (such as tax assessors) can collude with their administrative clients or with other officials to deceive the higher office. Mobility of officials is a standard feature of British tax administration, and many of the historical empires also featured rotation of officials, as well as typically preventing men from acting as officials in their native provinces.[41]

The administrative solution to the problems of collusion and corruption among tax officials is therefore to devise a regular system of rotation between the stock of officials and the stock of administrative positions at each level. In this way, the chances of official collusion with citizens or of collusion between parallel officials in a given administrative area, is reduced to a minimum. Max Weber compared the individual bureaucrat to a single cog in a giant machine, and the purpose of the fruit-machine system of institutionalized leap-frogging is to ensure that the mechanism does not depend too heavily on any one of its individual cogs at any point. This is, of course, an 'ideal' type; but the British Customs system, which reflects in large part the administrative principles of the eighteenth-century Excise super-imposed upon those of the medieval Customs organization, closely approximates to the type of control system which we have depicted.[42] Figure 3 illustrates the process.

The analogy is with a combination lock or, more accurately, with a 'fruit-machine', a gaming machine operating through three wheels, each of which turns on an individual bearing. In Figure 3, the administrative role-set consists of three sets of officials interposed between the taxpayer and the higher office; A, the officials who assess the taxes, submitting a tally to the higher office; B, the officials who audit the local units of tax assessment and collection; and C, the officials who actually collect the taxes, also submitting a tally to the higher office. With the regular rotation of officials filling roles A, B and C, the chances of officials bucking the system, or 'hitting the jackpot', in gaming terms, are fairly small. Administrative systems which do not operate controls of this type, such as police or prison administration, have a shakier grip on their field officials, and this may account for

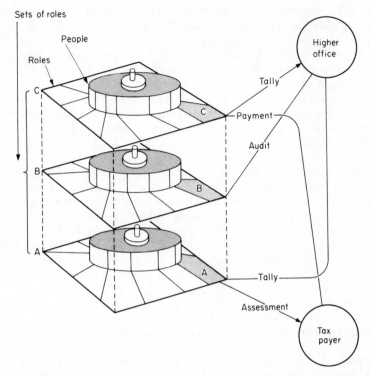

Figure 3. The 'fruit-machine' model. (In a fruit machine, each wheel spins on an independent axle with an independent timing device, but is activated by a common ratchet)

a typically far higher incidence of corruption among policemen than among tax officials. For example, the Knapp Commission on police corruption in New York concluded that in 1971 at least half of the city's police force was involved in some form of corruption.[43] By contrast, the tax administration system seems to be relatively depersonalized (although tax inspectors of the British Inland Revenue are sometimes referred to as the 'personification' of the British tax system);[44] and the same applies to other systems which combine mobility and cross-checking devices, such as the Soviet Communist Party.[45]

The Costs of Control

What are the administrative limitations of this 'classical' type of administrative control? The arrangements which we have described for separating or de-socializing tax officials have three main implications. First, they depend upon a system of written rules. Universal rules of substance and procedure are indispensable for 'standardization of parts' in a system where officials are mobile, in order to minimize discontinuities. Without a 'manual', the rotation and duplication arrangement breaks down into total clumsiness as a means of control over the population at large. Such rules are also vital as a means of control, in providing for appeal up the hierarchy concerning decision which have been made lower down; we have already discussed the technique of control through bridging devices in a hierarchy in Chapter 7. Adjudication of appeals is often the most important means of control which is open to higher officials in a ramified field administration system. To this must be added the need for standardized operations in order to prevent inequities which create discontent among the 'administered'.

But operation through standard and formally-approved procedures of this kind has costs. The growth of literacy and of written records in administration has had both broad social consequences and consequences more specific to administration. The broad consequences need not concern us here;[46] what is important for us is that operation in this way reveals the authorities' hand, compelling them to act in a formal and legalistic manner, taking account of precedent and equity. It also introduces a time-lag element into administration which may become a severe handicap. Both of these problems are by now familiar to us from Part 2.

The second implication of 'fruit-machine' control system is that when people are drawn out of their local affiliations by a control system of this kind, they are likely to develop *professional* orientations, that is, they look to the professional or occupational corps as their political and economic medium of advancement. Many authors have analysed professionalism and its growth in the twentieth century,[47] and no attempt will be made to discuss the general phenomenon here. In the specific context of administrative control, professionalism helps to create 'standardized parts' which are interchangeable in the context of mobile officials, just as professional soldiers of a given rank should be able to change places without serious dislocation.

But professionalism also has costs, particularly where it is of a strictly exclusive type. It tends to divide the administrative unit or service involved into separate horizontal boxes, creating a system plagued by demarcation disputes, with little sense of common interest and with limited ability to perform closely co-ordinated tasks.[48] Similarly, almost by definition, a professionalized structure will tend to create a scarcity of labour, since a profession is usually defined to include a large element of control over entrants to the profession and is thus self-limiting. Professionalism may also be associated to some extent with processes of wastage, which we discussed earlier, and with work-creating processes. Bertrand Russell once said that the armaments trade was the only trade where an increase in orders for one firm brought an increase in orders to others.[49] But, as we have seen, the same is by and large true of the 'administrative professions' such as tax experts and lawyers. Again, these problems are by now familiar to us.

Finally, the problems of operating a system in which no-one stays in any given job for very long are obvious enough. Apart from the more ludicrous mistakes which such a system is open to, it becomes difficult to obtain information about a local society in which the field official is by definition a 'stranger' and thereby restricted in his channels of information. For example, we will see in the next chapter that in the abortive British betting tax of the 1920s, the capability of the revenue organization in detecting tax evasion was weakened by the internal security system. This system initially made it impossible for Customs officers to make experimental bets with bookmakers and weakened the Customs' hold over small local firms (such firms had very varied types of book-keeping, which officials took some time to master) by the policy of frequent changes in local staff. Exactly the same problem applies in a military context. Military units combating guerillas and insurgents overseas typically serve short tours of duty. This has advantages in terms of minimizing contact with and possible sympathy for, the enemy, but it can severely break up the continuity of intelligence information.[50] Any system of rotating officials is very far from omniscient and depends upon routinized supplies of information. In practice, such information is almost always obtained by some of the middlemen types of control which were described in Chapter 7.

The example of tax administration shows some of the key dilemmas which can arise in dual-level control systems. This analysis of the costs of the classic 'fruit-machine' model of bureaucratic control is supported by many of the organizational sociologists whose writing we briefly discussed in the last chapter, who have concluded that such a control system in effect buys control over a ramified field structure in exchange for flexibility and intelligence capacity. So as soon as we relax the idea of perfect administration by one degree, to make a distinction between the top-level authorities and their administrative agents, the possibility arises that the imperatives of control over the officials by the top-level authorities may involve limits on the controls which can be deployed at the second stage, that is, over the populace itself. Note that the problem can apply even if we continue to assume, in a deliberately simplified way, that the top-level authorities are unitary and easy to define. In reality, of course, authorities are very hard to locate concretely.

Types of Dilemmas

We mentioned in Chapter 2 that dilemmas in administrative control could be of several types, 'horizontal' and 'vertical'. What we have just been examining are vertical dilemmas, those which arise in the chain of controls operating between the top-level command and the population at large. The large-scale dilemma of combining adaptivity with hierarchy, mentioned in the last chapter and implicit in much of the discussion in Chapter 5, is a case of this type, and it has been identified by several of the authors whom we have already discussed in different contexts. For example, de Jouvenel[51] contrasts 'attention' and 'intention' as qualities which tend to be incompatible. Blau and Scott also identify this as one of their administrative dilemmas,[52] and Stafford Beer, from the standpoint of cybernetics, makes the same point. In designing a 'multi-node', or an ultra-attentive information system, Beer concludes that such a system can only be controlled by 'politics', not by command.[53]

Apart from costs like these which are associated with the fruit-machine model of bureaucratic control, other vertical dilemmas of control can be identified. In Chapter 2, we noted that control of the public at large by violence and intimidation presents the top-level authorities with difficult problems of controlling their own henchmen, and there are also dilemmas built into the middlemen controls which we examined in Chapter 7. Judicial and bridging types of controls, too, have 'costs' in that they typically obstruct 'line' controls of administrative operations. We will return to these dilemmas in the final chapter.

The second type of dilemma is the problem of 'horizontal' incompatibility between controls. Here too, it seems that controls cannot be double- or multiple-banked at random, even outside a hierarchic setting. In discussing non-linearities we have already mentioned the multi-organizational sub-optimization which can set in when multiple controls are used: one control may pull the system one way, a contradictory control pulls it in another way. As we have already mentioned, in public administration as a whole, current fashion in styles of policy implementation implicitly contains controls which are incompatible with one another. On the one hand, there is a demand for 'corporate planning', for seeing the system as a whole and controlling it as a single unit. On the other hand, there is a tendency to multiply agencies of implementation and to operate through indirect means rather than through direct government operations. On top of that, agencies are increasingly subjected to controls based on their individual output indices, which provide powerful incentives for the export of problems between agencies. On top of all these contradictions, there is a tendency to increase the importance of citizen control in public administration, in the sense of rights of access to information and improved channels of complaint involving rights of appeal, equality and fairness — controls which inevitably work against other controls.

Taking both the vertical and the horizontal dilemmas together, many of the two types of controls which have been discussed in the preceding chapters can be placed into two broad categories of control which are to some extent substitutable, but each of which has attendant dilemmas. They could be termed the 'roadblock' strategy and the 'organizational manipulation' strategy. The roadblock strategy emphasizes the selection of easily administerable points, processes or objects on the 'bottleneck' principle which we discussed in Chapter 7. The extreme case is the type of administrative system which is built upon objects which have no close substitutes, which cannot easily be home-made or home-grown and which enter the market through relatively few channels. On the other hand, the organizational manipulation strategy emphasizes the manipulation of the role-structures within the institutions which are being controlled.

In practice, large-scale administrative systems always contain examples of both categories of control, but in principle the two strategies are alternative ways of coping with the informational handicaps of the fruit-machine type of administrative control. The 'roadblock' strategy is limited by the extent to which it is possible to 'bottleneck' social activities. To some extent, the supply of palpable 'things' or processes to administer is limited by nature. Moreover, the limits to which even the most palpable 'things' can be unambiguously defined are surprisingly narrow, as we saw in Chapter 4; and yet a rule-bound administrative system must define its operations, for reasons which we have already explained.

The other strategy, of control through latching on to the internal structures of the institutions which are being controlled, can also only be effective where the escape routes are blocked. For example, as we have already mentioned and will see in the next chapter, large firms are in general more vulnerable to taxation and regulation by both strategies than small firms, but by the same token they have more resources to deploy in hiring professionals to look for loopholes and can use threats to close down operations, and thus to create unemployment as levers at the political level. [54] In many ways, this is a general dilemma of regulation and inspection agencies, and it becomes more severe the more 'footloose' industry becomes, in the sense of firms diversifying into multi-national and multi-product operations.

The organizational manipulation strategy of control is also limited by the characteristics of the 'middlemen' type of controls which it uses as levers. The crudest way in which the process works is by the straightforward payment for information, as with the case of police informers. But in its more sophisticated forms, the control works by advantaging or disadvantaging a set of individuals to act as policemen as described in Chapter 7, merely carrying direct administrative control to the point where the 'snowball' effect of self-sustaining policy enforcement begins to operate. One of the most elegant cases of this is the situation where excise taxes create quasi-monopolies in a symbiotic relationship with governments, because a heavy tax payable in advance creates financial barriers to free competition, and the trade thus shares a common interest with the fiscal authorities in enforcing the tax and in maximizing total revenue.

Mechanisms of this type work in the case of most excise taxes, including odd ones like the tax on fixed-odds football betting and on football pools, which will be discussed in the next chapter. In cases like this, the limit to which such a process can be carried can be formally determined. In a pure monopoly situation, the point of maximum profit for the monopolist is also the point of maximum profit for the fiscal authorities (for an *ad valorem* tax on the monopolist's products), since to depart from the point at which marginal cost equates with marginal revenue is to deplete the total revenue of the enterprise. Anyone with some grasp of elementary economic theory can work this out. The maximum effective tax rate is then determined by the monopolist's lowest acceptable profit; such profit can only be appropriated by direct government production of the goods or service in question, as in the case of fiscal monopolies. The problems are very similar to those in the case of contract administration, and problems of administrative supervision have to be added to the 'pure' limits which can be identified from economic theory.

Summary and Conclusion

In the past two chapters we have been exploring limits on the operation or exercise of administrative controls, having sketched out a range of controls in Chapter 7. This has involved dismantling the final conditions of the perfect administration model — controls as unlimited in resources and limitlessly effective. As we have seen, there is no single limit to administrative control — controls can be limited in terms of the outcomes they produce, in terms of the intractibility of the basic problem, in terms of the mechanisms involved. There are 'organizational' limits on control, and limits of administrative control in a wider sense.

Some of the chief elements which we have discussed in the last two chapters are briefly summarized in Figure 4. We have seen that complementarity is needed for some of the building-blocks of Chapter 7 to form effective control systems, whereas complementarity is impossible or counter-productive in other cases. Non-linearities also play a part — the level of control intensity is a delicately balanced element, as is real time sequence. Throw in your resources too soon or use too many, and face massive retaliation — throw them in too late or too sparingly, and face defeat. And a thread running through most of these elements is the presence of a hostile environment, of a strategic enemy intelligence. The higher the overall level of hostility in the administered world, the sooner these limits will be reached. Moreover, in the past two chapters we have considered administrative control rather artificially, by largely ignoring the problems of adaptation and categorization which were treated in Part 2. In reality, of course, all of these problems interlock, as we will stress in the final chapter.

If there is no single type of limit on control, there can be no simple key to effective administrative control. But it is still all too common for writers to underestimate the limits of administration and to put forward simple doctrines based on a few observations. One example is Niskanen's *Bureaucracy and Representative Government*.[55] After a sophisticated economic analysis of bureaucratic 'output functions', to which we briefly referred in the last chapter, Niskanen basically calls for a return to a tax-farming type of bureaucracy. He mentions that profit-seeking colonels managed military supply with apparent success in the time of Louis XIV of France (when no major wars were involved); but omits to add that the British system was almost identical and that this broke down completely in the Crimean War. This is the trouble with doctrines of this kind. You can easily prove that wearing a rabbit's foot brings you luck or that dreams are prophetic − *if* you ignore the awkward cases.

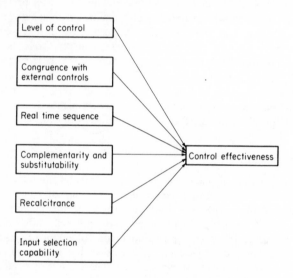

Figure 4. Some limits on control effectiveness

To conclude our discussion of control, the case study in the next chapter has already been referred to in several places and illustrates many of the points which were made in the analysis of administrative controls, as well as many problems of the type discussed in Part 2. How does one couple revenue control to an activity as elusive and dispersed as betting and gaming? Can this case be said to illustrate administrative limits, and if so, what kinds of limits? In the final chapter, we will return to our original question about the limits of administration in a general sense, coupling together all the limits which we have identified by relaxing the conditions of perfect administration in Parts 2 and 3.

Notes

1. Boettinger, H. B., 'Thinking ahead', *Harvard Business Review*, November–December 1970, p. 14.
2. Quoted from a Parliamentary reply by J. Kincaid, 'The Decline of The Welfare State' in N. Harris and J. Palmer (Eds.), *The World Crisis: Essays in Revolutionary Socialism*, Hutchinson, London, 1971, p. 60.
3. Porter, D. O., and D. C. Warner, 'How Effective Are Grantor Controls? The Case of Federal Aid to Education', in K. Boulding, M., and A. Pfaff (Eds.), *Transfers in an Urbanized Economy*, Wadsworth, Belmont, California, 1973, pp. 276–302.
4. Ramsbothom, R. B., *Studies in the Land Revenue History of Bengal 1769–87*, Oxford University Press, Oxford, 1926.
5. Blau, P. M., and W. R. Scott, *Formal Organizations*, Routledge and Kegan Paul, London, 1963, pp. 242–50.
6. Weldon, T. D., *The Vocabulary of Politics*, Penguin Books, Harmondsworth, 1963.
7. Lorenz, K., *On Aggression*, Methuen, London, 1966.
8. Wilensky, H., *Organizational Intelligence*, Basic Books, New York, 1967.
9. Thayer, G., *The War Business*, Weidenfeld and Nicholson, London, 1969, p. 305.
10. Mintz, M., and J. S. Cohen, *America, Inc.*, Pitman, New York, 1972, Chap. 7, 'The Regulatory Agencies', pp. 237–253.
11. Mackenzie, W. J. M., and J. W. Grove, *Central Administration in Britain*, Longmans, London, 1957.
12. Pool, B., *Navy Board Contracts 1660–1832*, Longmans, London, 1966.
13. Carr-Saunders, A. M., and P. A. Wilson, *The Professions*, 2nd ed., Frank Cass and Co., London, 1964.
14. Barr, J., 'The Taxmen', *New Society*, 10.4.69, p. 550.
15. Sandford, C. T., *Hidden Costs of Taxation*, Institute of Fiscal Studies, London, 1974.
16. Report of The Estimates Committee on the Inland Revenue, *Minutes of Evidence*, 12.3.69, p. 80, para 15.
17. See *Epitome of the Reports of the Committee of Public Accounts 1938 to 1969*, HC 187, 1970, pp. 497–499 and pp. 409–410.
18. Cf. *Regulation of Scottish Inshore Fisheries*, Cmnd. 4453, HMSO, London, 1970.
19. Wittfogel, K. A., *Oriental Despotism*, Yale University Press, New Haven, 1957, p. 331.
20. Gouldner, A. W., *Patterns of Industrial Bureaucracy*, Free Press, Glencoe, 1954, p. 178.
21. Crozier, M., *The Bureaucratic Phenomenon*, Tavistock, London, 1965.
22. Austin, J. L., *Sense and Sensibilia*, Clarendon Press, Oxford, 1962, p. 11.
23. Quoted in J. Maddox, *The Doomsday Syndrome*, Macmillan, London, 1972, p. 11.
24. Derthick, M., *The Influence of Federal Grants*, Harvard University Press, Cambridge, Mass., 1970.
25. *1st, 2nd and 3rd Reports from the Public Accounts Committee*, HC 166-1, 256-1, 127, 1969–1970, p. xxxvi, para 93(c).
26. For a discussion in the context of social security administration, see *Report of the Committee on the Abuse of Social Security Benefits*, Cmnd. 5228, pp. 11–12, para 38.
27. Marx, G., 'Thoughts on a neglected category of social movement participant: the agent provocateur and the informant', *American Journal of Sociology*, Vol. 80, 1974, pp. 402–440.
28. Catt, I., 'The New Reality in US Management', *New Society*, 20.11.69. pp. 814–815.
29. Cf. J. Woodward (Ed.), *Industrial Organization: Behaviour and Control*, Oxford University Press, London, 1970.
30. Waddington, P. A. J., 'The coup d'etat – an application of a systems framework', *Political Studies*, Vol. 22, 1974.
31. Penrose, E. T., *The Theory of The Growth of The Firm*, Wiley, New York, 1954, p. 2.
32. Managerial techniques such as network planning are well-known procedures for structuring operational sequences in such a way as to minimize real time constraints. See K. G. Lockyer, *An Introduction to Critical Path Analysis*, Pitman, London, 1964.
33. McGhie, A., *Pathology of Attention*, Penguin Books, Harmondsworth, 1969, p. 19.
34. Voltaire, *Candide*, Ed. O. R. Taylor, Basil Blackwell, Oxford, 1965, p. 64.
35. Cf. Marx, G., *op. cit.*; M. J. Greenwood and W. J. Wadycki, 'Crime rates and public

expenditure for police protection', *Review of Social Economy*, Vol. 31, 1973, pp. 138–151; D. Bell, 'The myth of crime waves', Chap. 8 in *The End of Ideology*, Free Press, New York, 1960.

36. Keeling, C. D. E., *Management in Government*, RIPA, Allen and Unwin, London, 1972.

37. Newman, O., *Defensible Space*, Architectural Press, London, 1972.

38. Quoted in Hall, R. H., *Organizations: Structure and Process*, Prentice-Hall, New Jersey, 1972, p. 218.

39. See, for example, *Report of Commission of Inquiry into Disturbances in the Provinces (November 1955 to March 1956)*, Crown Agents for Oversea Governments and Administration on behalf of the Government of Sierra Leone, 1956, for a classic example of this. Cf. also M. Weber, *The Theory of Social and Economic Organization* (Ed. T. Parsons) Free Press, New York, 1964, 'The financing of political bodies', pp. 310–18; and H. H. Gerth and C. W. Mills, *From Max Weber: Essays in Sociology*, Routledge and Kegan Paul, London 1948, pp. 205–206.

40. Greenwood, H. J., *Customs and Excise Essays, Historical and Technical*, H. J. Greaves, London, 1923, p. 28; cf. T. C. Barker, 'Smuggling in the eighteenth century: the evidence of the Scottish tobacco trade' The *Virginia Magazine of History and Biography*, Vol. 62, October 1954.

41. Eisenstadt, S. N., *op. cit.*

42. Crombie, Sir James, *H.M. Customs and Excise*, New Whitehall Series, Allen and Unwin, London, 1962, Chap. 4 and 13; cf. R. B. Ramsbothom, *op. cit* and N. D. Nowak, *Tax Administration in Theory and Practice*, Pall Mall Press, London, 1970.

43. *The Times*, 29.12.72.

44. *Report of the Royal Commission on Income Tax 1920*, Cmd. 615, p. 83, para 375.

45. Hough, J. F., 'Reforms in government and administration', in A. Dallin and T. B. Larson, Eds., *Soviet Politics since Krushchev*, Prentice-Hall, New Jersey, 1968, p. 33; also J. F. Hough, *The Soviet Prefects*, Harvard University Press, Cambridge, Mass., 1969.

46. Giglioli, P. (Ed.), *Language and Social Context*, Penguin Books, Harmondsworth, 1972.

47. Cf. A. M. Carr-Saunders and P. A. Wilson, *op. cit.*; T. Johnson, *Professions and Power*, Macmillan, London, 1972; W. E. Moore, *Roles and The Professions*, Russell Sage Foundation, New York, 1970.

48. Cf. H. Seidman, *Politics, Position and Power*, Oxford University Press, New York, 1970.

49. Russell, B., *Power*, Unwin Books, London, 1960.

50. Cf. F. Kitson, *Low Intensity Operations*, Faber and Faber, London, 1972.

51. de Jouvenel, B., *The Pure Theory of Politics*, Cambridge University Press, Cambridge, 1963.

52. Blau, P. M., and W. R. Scott, *op. cit.*

53. Beer, S., *Brain of the Firm*, Allen Lane, the Penguin Press, London, 1972.

54. For a notorious case, see *The Economist*, July 29, 1972, p. 67 and Cmnd. 5042, 1972.

55. W. A. Niskanen, *Bureaucracy and Representative Government*, Aldine Atherton, New York, 1971.

Chapter 10

Case Study Number Three: Taxing the Gambler

'Freak taxes . . . were irritating and mischievous and did not produce so much of revenue as of irritation and trouble.' Earl Lloyd George (HC Deb Vol 194, c.1726)

As has already been mentioned, taxation is a policy field where the problems of administrative control are perhaps uppermost, and betting taxes present special administrative problems. Betting is an attractive subject for tax (except for those who oppose taxes on 'immoral' activities) and it has often been seen as a fiscal 'philosophers' stone', because if the gross turnover figures are treated as an index of the taxable capacity of betting, it seems that it can produce a vast revenue.

In fact, the resources available for taxation are a good deal smaller than one might suppose. There are two reasons for this. One is that a large volume of betting in horse and dog racing goes into hedging bets (that is, 'laying-off' bets between bookmakers) and into professional bets. Such bets secure very low margins of profit and are thus very sensitive to small changes in price, meaning that the impact even of a low tax will be heavy on bets of this type. The other reason for betting being a more limited source of tax than it might appear is that the flow of money within the betting system is large in relation to the inflow and the outflow. Annual betting turnover is approximately ten times annual consumers' net expenditure on betting.[1] To be precise, if one assumes that the relative or absolute quantity of total consumers' expenditure devoted as 'new money' to betting (i.e. added to the sums returned as winnings) is constant, at least in the short term, the size of betting turnover at a given time is a function of the number of times money circulates between backers before being drained out of the system, which is in turn a function of the percentage 'take' times rapidity of turnover.

The economic resources involved, then, are far from limitless. But there is also an administrative problem with betting taxes. Betting does not fit easily into the 'roadblock' strategy of control which was discussed in the last chapter. As we mentioned, most other single-stage commodity taxes of a traditional kind are controlled by the roadblock strategy, but in betting the commodity itself is intangible, the contract is unenforceable (betting debts are not recoverable at law) and there are no well-defined wholesale or manufacturing enterprises apart from the retail units, so the accountability for tax has to fall at the point of direct contact with the final customer. In many ways, therefore, betting taxes present problems similar to taxes on general retail sales, but are in large part an extreme case, because even the *paiement fractionnée* method of 'peer group' control (which was discussed in Chapter 7) can scarcely be used, except in cases where remission of tax is allowed on hedging bets by bookmakers.

Early Taxes on Betting

Before betting became a professionalized and commercialized activity, but simply consisted of private transactions between individuals, it was impossible to tax bets as such. All that could be done at this stage was to tax the 'raw material', and various taxes were imposed on betting equipment before the twentieth century. Taxes on the Company of Cardmakers and the Company of Dicemakers began in England after 1660[2] (in the case of playing cards, the Ace of Spades was printed separately by the Government printing office to facilitate collection of the tax, and the penalty for tax evasion was death);[3] and there were taxes on racehorses from 1784 to 1874. Racing establishments were also taxed until 1856,[4] greyhounds were taxed at a special rate of the Dog Tax and the racecourses were subject to the (old) Corporation Tax.

State lotteries were also held in England from 1566 to 1826 and were for some of this time an important source of revenue. The tickets were usually disposed in blocks to stockholders, who acted as 'wholesalers'. Revenue from such lotteries reached a peak in 1808, but it subsequently fell, and State lotteries were abolished in 1826. One of the reasons for abolition was simply fraudulent administration; the other administrative problem was that people might bet on the draws without purchasing the official tickets, and extensive 'policy' gambling on the draws grew up, with no profit to the Exchequer.[5]

The idea of a tax on betting turnover itself began with the growth of the 'Starting Price' (SP) system with the racing newspapers in the 1870s.[6] Before this time, bookmakers made their odds individually; subsequently, bookmakers off the racecourses paid out winnings at SP odds, which are determined by representatives of *The Sporting Life* and *The Sporting Chronicle* from the odds prevailing on the racecourse at the time that a given race is begun. But the chief problem of imposing such a tax was that at this time betting in cash (in person or by post) off the racecourses was illegal, though this prohibition did not in practice apply to racecourse betting or to telephone credit betting. The strict legal position was that it was forbidden to 'resort to a place' for the purpose of betting, and thus betting by telephone or by telegraph, or with a nominally peripatetic racecourse bookmaker,[7] did not count as 'resorting to a place'.

This meant that, in effect, there was one law for the rich and another for the poor; but, absurd as the position was, it was defended by the Home Office on the grounds that the rich gambled with luxuries but the poor gambled with the housekeeping money. If the law had been effective, this argument might have had some justification; but as it was, the urban working class simply betted illegally either in illegal betting shops or with bookmakers' agents in the streets (the second method was more common in the South of England, while the first method tended to prevail in the North and in Scotland). In many cases, the enforcement of the law was not very serious, being confined in many areas to annual police raids or rota systems of prosecution, often resulting in the imposition of minimum fines in magistrates' courts.[8] In Scotland, the law was frequently used as a means of raising revenue rather than of suppressing illegal bookmaking, since, in contrast to the English system, Scottish Burgh Court fines were paid into local authority funds, and thus annual police raids were in fact used as a kind of licensing system, through court fines and the confiscation of moneys found in illegal betting houses.[9] But in spite of half-hearted law enforcement, the police control system was not totally ineffective. It tended to hamper the growth of large-scale bookmaking businesses, because illegal cash betting depended on bettors being personally known to bookmakers' agents (both in order to be sure that casual bettors were not plain-clothes policemen and because no written receipts were given). So illegal betting was largely conducted by small firms and by local agents – a system particularly difficult to tax. The only exception to this rule was the case of cash betting by post, for which there were a number of large firms in Scotland.

In the face of this administrative problem, British Customs officials worked on the 'middleman' control system of turning poachers into gamekeepers, and, following this approach, asked for off-course cash betting to be legalized when carried out in licensed premises.[10] Licensees would protect their own interests, the Customs officials thought, by informing on the activities of illegal bookmakers, and by this process the business would become concentrated into fewer, larger firms, a system which would be much easier to tax. The officials thought that the introduction of betting shops was the linch-pin of any effective control system for a betting tax; but this measure was outside the limits of what was politically possible at the time. The proposal of a betting shop system was opposed by a curious alliance between Free Church interests (using the argument that 'dirty money' should not be taxed),[11] the Home Office (taking the view that the working class should not be encouraged to gamble) and credit bookmakers and racecourse interests who feared that legalization of off-course betting would damage their trade.[12]

After a long period in which proposals for a betting shop system had been frustrated by these forces, Winston Churchill, as Conservative Chancellor of the Exchequer in 1926, was attracted by the concept of a betting tax. To put it negatively, since 'to tax and to please is not given to man', Churchill judged that such a tax was the one out of two or three alternative schemes of taxation which was least likely to find serious opposition within the Conservative Party. Churchill therefore decided to go ahead with a tax on legal betting turnover without legalizing or taxing street betting.[13] This was a politically attractive compromise and Churchill thought that such a tax would be feasible because at that time it was estimated that about 85 per cent of bets (by value) placed with bookmakers were legal and it seemed that a large revenue (perhaps £6 m on a 5 per cent tax) could be had by taxing only the legal type of betting.

The Customs officials opposed this plan as administratively dangerous, but the Chancellor reasoned that it would be as easy as the Stamp Duty on Stock Exchange transactions and that there would be little transfer of clientele: middle-class punters would not suddenly take to surreptitious cash transactions on the streets in large numbers. He would thus ignore the unremunerative and elusive field of street betting. Even so, the options remained open: illegal betting could be tackled later on. Churchill carried the day, and accordingly a tax of 3½ per cent *ad valorem* on bets made with bookmakers (with a preferential rate of 2 per cent for racecourse betting and tax remission on hedging bets by bookmakers) was imposed in the 1926

Budget. The tax liability fell on bookmakers, who were licensed, together with their premises, and it was payable either in advance by the purchase of official revenue tickets or in arrear on the basis of returns after suitable bond had been given. The tax began inauspiciously (owing to bad weather, illness of the head of the Betting Duty organization, industrial depression and a 'run on the book', with horses running persistently to form) and the Customs officials lacked such basic administrative information as how many bookmakers there were, much less the details of their business. This was perhaps an omen for the future course of this ill-fated tax: 40 years later Sir James Crombie described the failure of the tax as 'written on the Customs' heart'.[14]

Definitional Problems

A set of definitional problems, of a type familiar from our discussion of categorization in Chapter 4, immediately arose. Take, for example, bad debts — a fairly obvious problem in the betting business, particularly since betting debts are not legally enforceable. It might seem reasonable enough to allow remission of tax on bad debts, but serious administrative difficulties would lie in determining when an unpaid debt becomes 'bad' and how it is to be shown that the debt was contracted and/or not paid. Betting in 'clubs' presented a similar definitional problem, and as will be seen below, the definition of 'clubs' sprang a serious leak in the tax in 1928. The tax applied to bets made with bookmakers, not to bets between private individuals, but the distinction between the two forms of betting broke down in the case of betting 'exchanges'.[15] In some clubs (such as the Victoria Club) bets took place between bookmakers, or between bookmakers and private individuals, as well as between private individuals themselves.[16] Bets of the first two types were legally taxable, but not the last type, and there was an obvious risk of evasion in such clubs, particularly in the social clubs in the North of England.

A problem of the same type arose with double and accumulator bets. A 'double' is a stake of £x on horse A to win event Y and horse B to win event Z. An 'accumulator' is a stake of £x on A, and the proceeds staked on B if A wins. An 'any to come' bet is £x on A and some (a proportion or a fixed sum) of the proceeds staked on B if A wins; and all of these types have almost infinite variations (such as 'up and down' betting). The legal and administrative problem is, how many taxable transactions are involved in such bets? The Customs treated accumulator bets and doubles as single transactions, but treated 'any to come' bets as two or three or more transactions and counted each draw in football fixed-odds betting as a separate transaction.[17] This largely corresponded with the practice of the trade on commission rates, but hard cases kept gritting up the administrative machine, and it was in fact decided later to treat 'any to come' bets as single transactions.

As a final example of this type of problem, the Finance Act required bookmakers' agents and branches to be separately licensed. But the 'sub-cells' of the trade differed considerably in their degree of autonomy from the parent body, and in practice it was impossible to draw a firm line between 'mere assistants' (telephone operators and other human 'conduit pipes') and employees acting in a more or less independent capacity. The Customs officials publicly held that such a distinction could be drawn, but this led them into innumerable tangles which only admitted of arbitrary solution, such as the position of the agencies and of the racecourse representatives of the 'Blower', the racing wire service (this is used by off-course bookmakers as the means of laying off bets with bookmakers on the racecourses and thus altering the racecourse odds which are the source of SPs).

The Course of the Tax and the Problems of Control

Table II summarizes the history of the tax.[18]

There was a considerable difference between the ease of policing the tax on the racecourses and the problems of controlling off-course betting. One of the reasons for this is that it was possible to apply the 'poachers-turned-gamekeepers' model of control on the racecourses. Recognized permanent 'pitches' exist on racecourses on a semi-hereditary basis, administered by racecourse executives and bookmakers' committees, and the system is policed by bookmakers themselves, which makes clandestine operations and casual bookmaking almost impossible, except at very minor meetings, point-to-point races and unenclosed racecourses. On top of this, enclosed racecourses were relatively easy to police for 'ergonomic' reasons, and the Customs were able to cover racecourse betting with four flying squads of specialized officers who attended all important race meetings. The tax worked surprisingly smoothly, with most course bookmakers paying tax on the basis of returns; and there was relative uniformity over the treatment of the tax, with most course bookmakers deducting six pence (d) in the pound from winnings.

The only substantial method of tax evasion for course bookmakers was to falsify their books, and a process of mutual adaptation developed, of a kind which was discussed in Chapter 5. That is, a running battle developed between the Revenue and its intended victims, in which closure of loopholes simply evoked more sophisticated evasion and louder complaints (both from tax evaders and from the innocent bystanders who were trampled in the process) as to the proliferation of ever-more-minute bureaucratic controls.[19]

At first, bookmakers 'fudged' their field books either by altering them or by presenting another set of figures in a new book to the verifying officials. The Customs countered by requiring books to be stamped on the racecourse by the Betting Duty officers, who also noted certain bets and passed the details on to Station Officers (these are the general field officials of the Customs) who verified the returns.

Table II. Betting duty statistics, 1926–1931

Year	£m Estimate	£m Receipts	Prosecutions
1926–7	1.5	0.6	
			Oct. 1926 to Oct. 1927 : 738
1927–8	6.0	2.7	
			Oct. 1927 to Oct. 1928 : 1,700
1928–9	2.0	2.2	
1929–30	0.3	0.28	
			Not available
1930–31	0.02	0.01	

Bookmakers parried by using loose-leaf books from which pages were easily removable without trace, altered bets other than those noted by the racecourse officials, forged stamps and initials, or kept records in pencil or in coded symbols. The officials responded by stipulating intelligible records to be made in indelible ink in books containing at least 100 numbered pages, glued and stitched, to be stamped by both the Station Officer *and* the Racecourse Officer.[20] Even so, forgeries continued, and the Betting Duty officers were urged to note bets secretly; but it was difficult for them to hoodwink the bookmakers in this way and unattached officers, unknown to the racecourses, had to be imported for the purpose. This move (in 1928) was thought to be a check-mate. Evasion by betting 'on the nod' and on a 'homomorphic' principle (that is, a bet of £60 might be recorded as £6 and so on) continued to some extent, but was limited by the fact that both methods depend for success on prior arrangement and fair dealing, and also bookmakers acted as informers. Indeed, the enforcement of licensing and taxation became so strict that it was said to have driven 'welshers' (fraudulent bookmakers) off the racecourses.[21]

No such happy administrative outcome was achieved either off the racecourses or at greyhound racing stadia. The advent of the electric hare and greyhound stadia in the cities was a betting 'boom' in the 1920s, comparable to bingo in the 1960s,[22] but established racecourse bookmakers were not drawn in to this market because of relatively low profits to be made in dog-racing and the opportunity for 'fiddles' in the early days of the sport. The result was a highly competitive bookmaking market on the dog-tracks, with bookmakers, many of them part-time., operating on very tight margins. This provided a strong incentive to evade the tax, and it was easier for bookmakers to conceal their activities in the crowds at greyhound racing stadia than in the rings on horse-racecourses. As a result, the Customs did not obtain effective information from the trade, and the tax remained precarious in this field, particularly when, later on, tax-free totalizators operated by the stadia companies came into competition with the bookmakers.

On the off-course side, things were even worse. At first the tax had gone relatively well, though the Customs had had to relax their control procedures at a number of points. For example, the normal Excise rules governing 'entry' of premises to facilitate Revenue control (this is an 'ergonomic' control technique involving, for example, no internal communication with other premises and use only for the business for which 'entered') were in fact unworkable in this case. This was because bookmakers' offices were often in the back of shops or in shared office buildings with common staircases. Similarly, the Customs had to accept penalties less than those strictly adequate for bond in order to encourage bookmakers to pay tax on a returns basis. The very diverse nature of the accounts kept by bookmakers also presented serious problems, in view of the frequent changes in local staff (part of the 'fruit machine' security mechanisms described in the last chapter), which made it harder for the organization to learn effectively about the accounting idiosyncracies of particular 'clients'.

Among wholly legal bookmakers little tax evasion was thought to take place. The big firms could not falsify their accounts without placing themselves at the mercy of their clerks (a feature of administrative control which we discussed in the last chapter), and among the small firms the amounts involved were small; in any case tax evasion was relatively easy to detect in this case owing to the localized character of such office business. But things were quite different in the case of illegal betting. At first, the policy had been not to tax illegal betting, on the Churchill argument which has already been described, and Excise prosecutions were only added to police prosecutions in second and subsequent offences for illegal betting. This was an application of the principle of *de minimis non curat fiscus*, which has already been discussed; but a snag quickly began to appear in this policy in the case of betting.

The snag arose from the fact that Churchill's argument about the unlikelihood of bettors transferring their business applied only to punters, not to bookmakers. There was little danger of the well-to-do telephone backers, who formed the backbone of the credit betting market, transferring their custom to street book-makers except in the case of very small bets (in the one to ten shilling range). But the possibility that *bookmakers* might switch from legal to illegal business had not been foreseen by the Customs, though it had been foreseen by the Home Office. Indeed, the tax had been devised on the assumption (carefully fostered by *soi-disant* 'legal' bookmakers) that the legal and the illegal bookmaker were separate persons. This was true only of the biggest bookmaking firms; but it later appeared that nearly half of the bookmakers licensed by the Customs carried on both legal and illegal business. This at once opened up a new vista of unforeseen oppor-tunities for evading the duty, since telephone credit bets might be recorded on the slips which were used for street betting.

Although at first even wholly illegal bookmakers had taken out certificates and paid tax in large numbers (such bookmakers were very willing, in fact, to discuss their illegal practices), the duty on illegal betting and indeed on all betting in the 'mixed' business, rested in practice on a purely voluntary basis. As this came to be realized, subscriptions dropped steadily, since Customs Officers, inspecting the books on which the total transactions of mixed firms were recorded, had to accept the bookmakers' unsupported word as to which of these transactions were legal and therefore upon which they elected to pay tax.

The position was obviously impossible, particularly when the big Scottish cash postal betting firms' tax payments started to fall off (these payments were a major bulwark of the tax). The Customs finally began a serious attempt to tax illegal betting, particularly in 'mixed' firms, after a High Court action in 1927 which ruled that bets made illegally were liable to duty. The Customs in fact brought this action because of the reluctance of Churchill to change his 'legal betting only' policy, and had also tried to find ways of circumventing the betting laws in order to discover a method by which postal cash betting might be legal — an experience in tax legislation being perhaps an ideal apprenticeship for such an exercise. But this official attempt to circumvent the law was unsuccessful, and the problem also had a multi-organizational dimension. The Home Office was reluctant to countenance the legalization even of postal cash betting on the grounds that such a move would obliterate the distinction between cash and credit betting upon which the whole precarious logic of the general betting law was at that time erected, and could lead to irresistible demands for further relaxations in the then existing restrictions on betting — a Gadarene slope leading speedily from cash bets by post to cash betting offices, advertizing, gaming houses and 'mischievous automatic gaming machines' (a diagnosis, incidentally, which has proved to be perfectly correct).

Since the law could neither be changed nor made nugatory by circumvention, the only remaining possibility was to suspend it by relaxing enforcement. The Home Office would not contemplate such a step, but the Scottish Office, in whose domain the bulk of the postal cash betting lay, was more amenable and virtually suspended the law by instructing Procurators Fiscal (Crown servants) to report all postal betting cases before taking action on prosecution. Even so, this suspension was not complete and prosecutions later restarted under pressure from anti-gambling interests; but only cash-by-post bookmakers of ill-repute with the Customs were in practice selected for sacrifice. After the 1927 High Court decision, the Customs made a special effort to control illegal betting, with surprise visits and mass raids at carefully chosen hours on bookmakers suspected of evading tax.[23] The work of inspecting bookmakers' offices in large towns was also centralized into specialized units in the hope of building up more expertise than could be expected from the general field officials of the Customs.

Special inspections were also carried out by headquarters staff, and the result of all these measures was an increase in the number of prosecutions to a rate of about 20 per week, which created a major 'traffic jam' in the Customs Solicitor's Department, and caused objections by local magistrates to double prosecutions of illegal bookmakers by the Customs and by the police. Such special inspections, especially one in 1927, were effective but costly, and merely indicated the in-security of the grip on the trade afforded to the Revenue by the prescribed routine checks, which amounted in fact to little more than checking arithmetical totals and samples of ticket counterfoils or returns against ledger accounts,[24] although later cheque counterfoils and bank pass books seem to have been inspected as well.

The Customs could hardly insist on the issue of tickets for illegal bets and accepted slips or Day Book entries for verification purposes, but bookmakers often destroyed these, since such records furnished evidence for prosecution if discovered by the police (note the multi-organization problem: the Customs were prosecuting bookmakers for *destroying* betting slips, whereas the police were prosecuting them for *keeping* them). Police activity in some places often necessitated frequent changes of trading addresses as well, causing great inconvenience for the Revenue.

In their campaign against tax evasion by illegal bookmakers, the Customs also began test bets by *agents provocateurs*, though such bets were confined to credit and postal betting (a nice legal point: it was illegal to *receive* postal cash bets, but not to *send* them), and the top officials were unhappy about the prospect of Customs officers opening accounts with bookmakers, because of the risk of corruption. Rewards were also granted to officers showing special zeal or ingenuity in detecting betting tax offences and in obtaining convictions; indeed, almost the only possible strategy to which the Customs did not resort was tapping bookmakers' telephones.

But, in spite of all these expedients, the officials did not succeed in turning the corner leading to the poachers-turned-gamekeepers situation for which they hoped. The 'mixed' businesses did not turn informer, since this might prejudice their own position; and those firms whom it would have benefited to give information about tax evasion (the large, wholly legal, bookmakers) either were not in a position to obtain useful evidence, or might thereby lose custom from some of the smaller bookmakers, for whom they acted as clearing-houses for hedging transactions. Thus, although the Customs received a large amount of information from bookmakers as well as from the police (who sent in about 600 to 700 reports per month), much of it was useless and it was not sufficient to reach the pitch of self-sustaining enforcement, that is, the point at which revenue officials have sufficient 'grip' on the trade to make traders more likely to benefit from exposing tax evaders than from joining them.

Recoupment of the Duty

One of the reasons why the pressures to evade the tax were so strong was the problem which arose concerning the manner in which the tax was to be collected from the punter, who was intended to be the true bearer of the tax. No specific method was laid down by law, apart from the percentage of betting turnover which was liable to tax. Racing and bookmaking interests would have much preferred a winnings-based tax to a tax on turnover. The Customs' stock reply to this was that the difference between a winnings-based tax and a turnover tax would be small, since 95 per cent of all stakes were returned to backers via winnings, but this missed the point. The bookmakers correctly foresaw that a turnover tax, without a mandatory form of recoupment, on a competitive industry facing a falling market, would lead to a 'concession war' over the tax and the strongest pressures for evasion.

This is precisely what did happen; but the Customs refused to change to a winnings basis of tax, for several more or less 'technical' reasons. First is the fact, already mentioned, that Starting Prices are fixed in an unofficial (though customary) way and bookmakers are under no obligation to pay out at such odds. It would therefore be possible for bookmakers, by colluding with backers, to falsify SPs or to declare different odds to the Revenue from those at which they actually paid out winnings. This would lead the Revenue into disputes about the appropriateness of bookmakers' odds, which would be both undignified and difficult to settle. Second, betting debts are not recoverable at law,[25] which would make the legal basis of a tax on winnings doubtful.

Third, a ticket system of tax collection could not be so easily enforced for a winnings tax. There were two reasons for this. One was that the variety of stakes were adequately covered by ten denominations of revenue tickets, whereas the variety of sums paid out as winnings is infinite. This would mean that all bookmakers would have to pay on a returns basis and give bond, which would be likely to force the smaller firms out of legal business altogether. The other reason was that punters had a common interest with the Revenue in securing official receipts for *stakes* as proof that bets had been placed (in case of disputes when collecting winnings). No such self-interest could be harnessed for fiscal profit in the case of a tax on winnings, because punters and bookmakers would have a common interest in under-declaring the sums paid out.

Any mandatory form of recoupment of tax is likely to excite the voluble opposition of that section of the trade which is disadvantaged by it, and it is therefore standard Excise procedure not to specify the form in which duties are to be recovered from the general public. But in this case the Customs' veto of a tax on winnings excluded perhaps the only method of tapping the betting industry which might have avoided a concessions war and the consequent pressure for tax evasion.

Tax Havens and Totalizators

As already mentioned, the decision to tackle 'mixed' businesses in 1927 did not prove to be the turning-point which the Customs had expected. It was a reciprocal learning situation, and bookmakers responded to the Customs' attack either by going over to wholly illegal business or by separating the legal from the illegal side of their businesses and paying tax only on the former. Where they did not do so, bookmakers laid themselves open to be outflanked by their own street agents, some of whom had taken the opportunity of becoming principals of rival businesses paying no tax.

The High Court decision at least temporarily saved the revenue from the large cash postal businesses, but here too the Customs were not dealing with a passive environment, and in 1928 the big legal bookmakers began to transfer business to nominees in Belfast. The Customs officals had realized from the start the possibility that Belfast, the Isle of Man and the Channel Islands might act as 'tax havens', and they had become more apprehensive when they realized the danger to be more that of British firms moving abroad (artificially) than that of the transfer of business by punters to unknown foreign bookmakers. There was no power in the Westminster Parliament to impose a betting tax on Northern Ireland,[26] and this was one of the few fiscal matters at that time in which the Stormont government did not follow Westminster. Moreover, the Customs never secured sufficient Parliamentary time to pass a bill prohibiting betting with a bookmaker outside Great Britain (this could not be included in a Finance Bill, since it was not a purely financial measure; one attempt to do so by the Customs had been ruled out of order by the Speaker of the House of Commons).[27] The 'Belfast problem' later became serious, although there was no similar problem with the Irish Republic, since the Irish government had introduced a betting tax in 1926.

Thus by 1928, the Revenue's control over the situation was weakening. The 1928 tax receipts were over 10 per cent smaller than those of 1927,[28] in spite of the growing popularity of greyhound racing. Apart from the problems of illegal and hybrid businesses and the threat of tax havens, the tax received another serious blow from a decision by the Court of Appeal in 1928 (*Attorney-General v. Luncheon and Sports Club Ltd.*). This ruling, which reversed an earlier High Court decision, was that bets on a totalizator machine (a mechanical form of *pari-mutuel* betting, at that time new to the UK) were not 'bets with a bookmaker' and therefore were neither illegal nor taxable. The House of Lords upheld this judgment.

In Chapter 4 we noted the possibility that quibbles over categorization or definition could cause administrative 'dams' to break; and this court decision was a minor case of such an event. As a result of the Court of Appeal judgment, greyhound stadia companies installed totalizators and 'tote' clubs grew up off the racecourses (the growth of such clubs was one of the major reasons for the appointment of the 1933 Royal Commission on Betting and Lotteries).[29] Many *pari-mutuel* and totalizator companies, perceiving that the Customs were now merely bluffing and had no longer any legal basis for taxing them, escaped from the Betting Tax as a result of this decision. More important, there was no longer any legal basis for taxing the totalizators of the Racecourse Betting Control Board, a quasi-government body set up in 1928 (in the face of fierce opposition from the bookmakers) to operate totalizators on horse racecourses and to devote the profits to the racing industry.[30]

The combination of all these 'leaks' meant that the tax was administratively a failure. The idea of taxing only legal betting turned out to be unworkable, but the administration of the duty was not hindered so much by the law in itself as by the proliferation of small bookmakers which the legal regime in effect protected. Some 'street bookmakers' were merely agents of larger firms, and this kind of transaction in fact presented few problems because bets taken illegally on a commission basis appeared in the accounts of the 'captive' large firms who were acting as master bookmakers. The real problem was the existence of so many localized entrepreneurs whose market was in effect protected from penetration by the big firms through its illegality, which necessitated essentially personal relations with clients in order to escape suppression by the police. Only the institution of betting shops since 1960 has enabled large fiscally vulnerable cash betting businesses to take over the former preserves of the street bookmakers.

But, in spite of its unhappy administrative history, the Churchill tax was in fact finally abolished for political reasons. The bookmakers had proved to be as divided as the legendary cats of Kilkenny in deliberations about possible changes in the tax. For example, the larger bookmakers (plus the sporting press, which depended upon their advertizing revenues)[31] made much of the widespread evasion and transfer of business to street bookmakers and 'social clubs' which the tax had provoked, with the illegal bookmakers growing rich on trade stolen from the respectable office firms who were facing ruin. They therefore argued that a flat-rate tax based on graduated licence fees, and therefore simple to administer, should be substituted for the turnover tax; and such a change would clearly have advantaged the larger firms against the smaller ones. But the street bookmakers denied that their trade had been affected by the Duty or that the middle classes were betting in the street, and preferred the turnover tax to any alternative. The loyalty of such bookmakers to a turnover tax was no doubt partly because such a tax was easier for them to evade than any licence duty, and they were thus in a similar position to the bootleggers who supported Prohibition in the United States.

In spite of these divisions, straight abolition of the tax was a proposal which commanded some degree of consent; and thus the curious alliance between Free Church and racing interests (which has already been mentioned in connection with the outlawing of street betting) contrived to defeat the tax. The Labour Party, using the Free Church argument that it was 'immoral' to tax betting,[32] pledged itself to repeal the tax, and the bookmakers therefore lent their support to Labour candidates at by-elections. In some cases this support was considerable; for example, bookmakers produced over 100 cars at the South Battersea by-election of 1929 in order to help get out the Labour vote.

In spite of the absurdity of this situation, Churchill was forced to compromise. For reasons of credibility, he did not want to abandon the principle of a betting tax altogether (having been defeated over the issue of the Paraffin Duty in 1928),[33] but he cut the rates of tax to 2 and 1 per cent in 1928.[34] Later the Customs relaxed their enforcement of the tax, by cutting down on prosecutions and raids and dropping the pressure for payment of outstanding duty in several cases. Finally, the turnover tax was wholly abandoned in 1929, with the declared intention of introducing a simple capitation-type tax on bookmakers' exchange telephones, plus a licence fee, after the general election.[35] Originally, a more ambitious scheme had been proposed, and indeed any licence tax which would have been worthwhile from a revenue point of view would have had to begin at about £50, but many of the small bookmakers had difficulty in raising the £20 which was needed for the licence and entry certificate under the earlier tax system. Another scheme for a payroll tax on bookmakers' employees was rejected because it would have had to apply to wholly illegal as well as to 'mixed' businesses; and there would have had to be arrangements for refunds and transfers of licences and days of grace (as for the Male Servant Licence Duty) which might well launch a thousand tax-evasive gambits, since they would create problems similar to that of distinguishing agents and 'conduits'. On the other hand, telephones were tangible and traceable and did not involve records. So a highly scaled-down and relatively unremunerative scheme was adopted, which would have brought in less than £½m per year.[36] But in the event, all these concessions were in vain, since the Labour Party (without the help of the bookmakers) won the 1929 election and the capitation tax was never introduced.

Stings in the Tail

But the licences for bookmakers and bookmakers' premises were not abolished for another 18 months after the demise of the tax itself, and the Customs continued to prosecute defaulters, *pour encourager les autres*, in spite of the evident absurdity of prosecuting people for not having a licence for an activity which was illegal and of registering them for a tax which had been abolished.[37] In fact the bookmakers did not press for the abolition of these licences, but after the repeal of the tax they concentrated on a campaign against the Racecourse Betting Control Board's totalizators, reminding the new Chancellor, Philip Snowden, that he had promised in Opposition to disfranchize the Board on the grounds that it was subsidizing 'racing millionaires' (a later Labour Chancellor, Hugh Dalton, exempted the 'tote' from the Betting Tax of 1947 on the grounds that subsidizing horse-racing was not 'private profit' and therefore deserved exemption). If Snowden would not prohibit the tote, the bookmakers urged at least a 5 per cent tax on the machines in order to prevent (they said) the ruination of 'millions' of honest bookmakers and clerks, who would be unable to compete with a machine taking only 6 per cent of turnover.

In this, they had been very largely hoist by their own petard, because at the time that the establishment of the totalizator was being considered by the Jockey Club in 1927, the bookmakers had been arguing against the Betting Duty on the grounds that they worked to a very small margin of profit to turnover (3 per cent). Indeed, the Racecourse Betting Act of 1928, which established the 'tote', had included a provision allowing racecourse executives to charge extra admission fees to bookmakers in order to give the tote a 'fair chance'. In fact, the Customs had estimated that racecourse bookmakers aimed at a profit of 20 per cent on turnover, but had not seen fit to mention this in the official deliberations about the appropriate rate of deduction for the totalizator. Bookmakers' complaints about the tote fell on deaf ears at the Treasury, and the bookmakers were thus wholly defeated on the only issue upon which they were relatively united, whereas they had won the battle of the Betting Tax more or less by default.

Post-war Offensives

After the fiasco of the Churchill tax, no further attempt to tax betting was made until 1947. In the 'austerity' years after World War II, the arguments for taxing betting were pressed once again and the Chancellor, Hugh Dalton, considered a betting tax in 1946. But in 1947 he announced that he had decided against it, because it seemed unlikely that such a tax would be more successful than before.[38]

The Customs' attitude to this, as revealed to the 1949–1951 Royal Commission on Betting, Lotteries and Gaming, was identical to that of the Customs officials in 1923.[39] For administrative reasons, they did not want to attempt another general betting duty unless off-course cash betting was legalized. But, as in 1926, a more limited scheme which would skirt the political problem of changing the general law of betting, was in fact adopted. The football pools, which had been in their infancy in 1926,[40] had become so large and centralized by the late 1940s (partly through the wartime paper shortage) that they could not by then escape a tax.[41] A 10 per cent tax on the turnover of football pools and greyhound totalizators was accordingly imposed in 1947, but bookmakers were excluded because they were thought to be too difficult to tax. Similarly the Horserace Betting Control Board, denounced by Snowden in 1927 as a subsidy to the rich, was excluded from the tax.[42]

The greyhound tote tax proved to be a poor revenue-raiser for economic reasons, namely the relative decline of the sport from its post-war peak. But the football pool tax has been raised steadily since 1947, and indeed has something of the character of an unofficial state lottery. The pools are a lottery insofar as one can only win a large prize if the results are quite different from those which might be expected on the basis of form (in fact the Pools had their big push after World War II with the invention of the 'Treble Chance' in which the odds against success – and therefore the prizes – are very large); and a heavy tax payable in advance helps to consolidate the semi-monopoly of the Pools Promoters, and can be raised to the point where only such monopoly management is profitable. We explained such arrangements in the discussion of control in the last chapter. Even giant bookmaking firms like Hill's and Ladbrokes cannot break into the football pool market because of this tax.

By the 1960s, the pools were being threatened by a tax-free competitor, fixed-odds betting on football matches, a form of betting which was growing in popularity. Fixed-odds betting on combinations of football results is the equivalent of ante-post betting on horses, whereas football pool betting is on the *pari-mutuel* principle, that is, the odds against a given set of results are determined automatically by the weight of money staked and the bookmaker cannot lose in any event. The growth of fixed-odds football betting presented the Customs with an administrative challenge, insofar as to protect the pools revenue, fixed-odds betting would also have to be taxed. At this time the Customs officials were still very nervous about betting taxes; but they thought that, though a tax on credit betting could be evaded, there would be far less difficulty in enforcing a tax on fixed-odds football betting, where every bettor has to supply a coupon.[43]

It also seemed possible to apply the same control strategy to the fixed-odds business as had been applied to the pools, namely to use tax as a kind of 'tariff' to protect established firms. Although the *amplitude* of the profit-loss cycle in football betting is similar to that of horse-racing (where unbacked, long-priced outsiders come in on average every eleventh race) the *period* of the cycle is longer and therefore the business requires a capital 'float' larger than that needed for horse or dog bookmaking, where losses can be more quickly recouped and it is easier to lay off bets. This is because, although there is a 'normal' long-run proportion of Home Wins, Away Wins and Draws similar to the 'normal' long-run proportion of horse-race favourites to 'skinners', there are only about 36 days of betting per year, as compared to horse-racing which takes place almost every day and thus produces the norm more frequently. Any tax would therefore raise the 'entry fee' into the market as it did for the pools, and would favour large firms like Hill's, Ladbrokes, Coral's and Littlewoods, who were then engaged in a concession war with smaller firms over the odds offered in the 'nothing barred' lists.[44]

The General Betting Duty, 1966

But the final stone in the edifice of betting duties did not come until a general betting duty was reintroduced in 1966. The way for this had been paved by the legalization of off-course cash betting in licensed betting shops in 1960.[45] This change had been recommended by a Royal Commission some nine years previously,[46] but had been delayed, chiefly because of the divisions within the racing and betting fraternity, many parts of which were strongly opposed to the introduction of betting shops (racecourse interests and bookmakers, large credit bookmakers and illegal bookmakers in the Midlands and South of England).[47] Accordingly, to sweeten the pill of betting shops to racing interests, a statutory levy on off-course bookmakers was introduced, to be collected by a quasi-government body (the Horserace Betting Levy Board) and to be spent on the racing industry.[48] This levy reconciled racing interests with betting shops, showed the shops to be a 'soft touch' and eroded former convictions that bookmakers were untaxable. Moreover, the advent of legal off-course betting shops caused pressure for a general betting duty from greyhound totalizator operators, who now had to face tax-free competition not only from the bookmakers on the tracks (there was in fact a licence tax on greyhound track bookmakers, strictly graduated according to the rings in which they worked) but also from the betting shops off the course, which could stay open until 6.30 p.m. and thus cover part of the evening dog races.[49]

A new general betting duty was accordingly introduced in 1966. This was procedurally very similar to the 1926 duty, being paid on monthly returns or by pre-paid Betting Duty sheets, but it was at a uniform rate of 2½ per cent, which included greyhound totalizators but not football pools or fixed-odds football betting, which continued to be taxed at the old rate. The tax was copied in almost every detail by the Northern Ireland government, which thus removed at least one of the problems of the earlier tax.

The recoupment problem of the 1920s, however, remained, and for the same reason. The tax could only be made relatively automatic and invisible to the punter by shortening the SP odds, but, as in the 1920s, this did not happen, because ante-post racecourse betting is very largely 'on the nose' (win only) and therefore adjustments in SP odds or place odds could not benefit the racecourse bookmakers who make the SPs. As a result, the tax was collected by shortening the place odds to $^1/_5$ and deducting varying amounts from the returns (winnings plus stakes). Such deductions are relatively invisible to cash bettors, but not to credit bookmakers' customers, especially those with large accounts, and this caused friction over who should bear the tax, since the balance of tax due may exceed the balance of winnings over losses in any credit period.[50]

The method of recovering the tax, in fact, was the subject of fierce argument, as it had been in the 1920s. In some places, including Scotland, there was agreement over recoupment, and indeed bookmakers were accused of deducting the tax twice over (this also happened in the 1920s). But in other places, particularly London, there was considerable concession warfare over the tax.[51] At first many betting shops swallowed the 2½ per cent tax in its entirety, apart from alterations in place odds; but this laid them wide open to an increase in the tax, which was doubled in 1968, and subsequently such shops had to make deductions from winnings to cover the tax.

In 1969 the tax rate was expected to rise again, but it was in fact left at 5 per cent lest another increase might damage the revenue. But the racecourse trade (the Tote, racecourse companies and course bookmakers) had been pressing for a tax differential in favour of on-course betting, as had happened in the 1920s. The reason why there was strong pressure for a differential rate of tax was partly to make the declining racecourses more attractive to the gambling public, but chiefly for a more technical reason. Racecourses are still the source of SPs, but the double taxation of bookmakers' hedging bets in 1966 penalized off-course firms from 'blowing' their covering money on to the racecourses to change SPs. This meant, of course, that the odds on the racecourse might not reflect the 'true' odds represented by the weight of off-course money, and that it was possible to 'fix' an SP favourite, particularly at minor meetings or in bad weather, by heavy betting on the racecourse such that the form favourite (=the horse or dog most likely to win the race) started at very long odds. The coup was then made by betting at the same time with off-course bookmakers, backing the true favourite at rigged SP or Tote odds.[52]

In spite of the possibilities of 'rigging' markets in such a way which had been increased by the tax, the Customs refused to exempt or differentiate in favour of racecourse betting or of hedging bets up to 1970 for fear that they would thereby open the door to tax avoidance measures. As a result, the Chancellor in 1969 gave the sickly racecourse trade an 'Irishman's rise'[53] in the form of an extra tax on betting shops at three times their rateable value. This tax was estimated to yield £7m and to give on-course bookmakers an advantage of 1 per cent on turnover; very probably another motive was to counter local evasion of Betting Duty by driving many small shops out of business, since they could not evade this type of tax.

The Rateable Value Tax 1969–1970

The rateable value tax in fact was a *debâcle*. It was (allegedly) designed to prop up the racecourse betting market, but in fact it merely further undermined other weak sections of the betting industry — the Tote and small betting shops — which were already suffering from the turnover tax, and reinforced the strength of the most powerful. Strong protests came from small bookmakers,[54] and local authorities also opposed the tax on principle (surcharges on rateable values are a threat to local revenue, because they are a strong inducement to firms to reduce their rate liability).

More important, there was a 'multi-organization' problem. It appeared that the Horserace Totalizator Board (the successor to the Racecourse Betting Control Board) would be bankrupted by the tax. British racing takes place for a few days each year on a large number of racecources (about 62), which means that, compared with other countries, far less betting is done on racecourses and that the operation of totalizators carries far higher overheads. Higher overheads mean higher deductions, and in spite of the bookmakers' fears in the 1920s, British tote odds are often uncompetitive against bookmakers' odds. The financial burden of the extra rate bill could not be met by the Tote Board, and much was made of the absurdity of the Government raising taxation to the point at which it was driving its own betting enterprise out of business.[55] Subsidizing the tote was politically unthinkable, so the Customs finally had to agree to bend the rule and to accept the rateable value tax in monthly instalments instead of twice yearly.[56]

This defeated the object of the tax to some extent, and certainly displeased the larger firms, who were looking for a 'clean up'; and after a High Court decision, the policy of monthly instalments was attacked by the Lord Chief Justice, who reproached the Chancellor for allowing the Commissioners of Customs to collude with bookmakers in breaking the provisions of the 1969 Finance Act.[57] But the tote was still (illegally) allowed to pay tax on a monthly basis.

After this chapter of accidents, the rateable value tax was abruptly repealed in 1970, after only six months of operation. The differential in favour of racecourse betting was more firmly established by exempting on-course hedging bets from tax altogether (the *paiement fractionnée* system) and by another 'Irishman's rise' in the form of an increase in the general rate of duty for off-course bets to 6 per cent, while the on-course rate remained unchanged at 5 per cent.

Revenue and Managerial Control

Table III indicates the history of the general betting duty over its first five years; it is worth comparing this with Table II.

The features of interlocking taxation and internal control systems in betting-shop chains have already been briefly mentioned in Chapters 7 and 8. As the betting shop chains grow larger, so they have to depend increasingly on techniques of 'remote control' through foolproof mechanized accounting systems. Such systems were virtually unknown in the 1920s, when betting transactions depended entirely on the spoken word, though 'clock bags', which provided a check on the time that bets were made, were beginning to be used for bookmakers' agents at that time. The development of such remote-control techniques inevitably make taxation easier as well as securing a greater measure of control over employees for firms. Thus the large firms which provide the overwhelming bulk of the revenue are more or less unable to escape the tax illegally, and no significant leaks have been sprung in the tax by the use of tax havens. But there is a large, if diminishing, number of small or family businesses surrounding the big firms (in the late 1960s, almost 70 per cent of bookmaking firms declared a profit of less than £2,000 per year),[59] who are able to evade the tax by passing less than the full total of their transactions through the official books. The Customs' only effective weapon against evasion of

Table III. Betting duty statistics 1966–1971[58]

Year	Estimate £m	Receipts total £m	General betting duty £m	Prosecutions
1966–7	52	50.1	10.8	12
1967–8	70	67.9	30.2	267
1968–9	100	99.7	54.4	367
1969–70	109	119	58.9	435
1970–71	120	117	76.0	450

this kind is the use of test bets by officers who are not known in the neighbourhood. In addition, there is a good deal of illegal betting outside betting shops, in public houses, factories and clubs, which can escape tax, even if it is done on a commission basis.

Even so, the revenue loss from such marginal operations was not sufficient to jeopardize the financial success of the tax. But the Customs did not adopt a *de minimis* policy with the 1966 tax and regularly prosecuted illegal bookmakers and small bookmakers or betting shop managers who under-declared their turnover.[60] The pursuit of the 'marginals' both pacified the Revenue's regular tax-paying clients who were anxious to see tax evasion by competitors stamped out, and it was also necessary because the effect of the tax, at least in the early years, was to strike harder at the middle-sized firms than at the one-man businesses or at the big chains.

The reason for this was that the effect of the tax, plus other overhead costs like the levy, compulsory insurance, clerks' wages and so on, was to raise the minimum viable turnover of a betting shop in a chain and thus advantaged the very large against the middle-sized firms[61] (because it was a proportionate charge on turnover, whereas in bookmaking profit on capital employed tends to rise more than proportionately to turnover owing to the Statistical Law of Large Numbers). Similarly, the fact that hedging bets were taxed twice over before 1970 disadvantaged the smaller bookmakers.

On the other hand, a one-man business, without many of the overheads mentioned above and with the less rigorous standards of accounting which are possible in such a situation, could make a profit on a betting shop taking much less per week than would be viable if such a shop were a member of a chain. The result was that a large number of one-man betting shops survived alongside an increasing number of very large betting shop chains, and thus the Customs did not entirely escape the problems of the 1920s in terms of tax evasion by small firms 'cooking the books'.

Gaming

Revenue control of gaming, which was included in the general betting duty of 1966, presented problems similar to the control of bookmakers. In 1960 gaming in private houses and in private social clubs was permitted, though 'commercialized' gaming was still prohibited. But the distinction between 'commercialized' and 'private' gaming was another of those legal definitions which collapse under pressure. 'Commercialized' gaming was defined as gaming in which the chances of winning were not equally favourable to all the players. This was circumvented by gaming establishments by charging for gaming sessions and mounting games like *chemin de fer* (where the bank passes from player to player) and modified roulette in which players were given the opportunity to take the bank if they wished (this was in fact of very little value to players, since the bank's statistical advantage applies only in the long run in roulette). Also the distinction into 'private' and 'commercial' gaming failed to distinguish commercially operated clubs from members' clubs, and by 1967 1,000 gaming clubs and 3,000 bingo clubs were in existence, either avoiding or openly defying the law.[62] Although this was an unwelcome surprise to the Home Office, at least it offered an opportunity to the Treasury, and in 1966 a rudimentary form of taxation, a surcharge on rateable values, was imposed on bingo halls and casinos, together with an annual licence tax on gaming machines.

There was evidence at this time that the British gaming boom was attracting criminal associations, including overseas criminal interests, which the locally-based control system for casinos (licensing by local authorities) was incapable of preventing.[63] So in 1968 the technique of control by 'canalization' which had been applied to betting shops was applied to gaming clubs, which were severly restricted in number and confined to 30 approved areas. People seeking to run such clubs had to be approved by a Gaming Board, a central quasi-government body which was given extraordinarily wide legal powers and established a corps of 26 inspectors. Many of the controls on gaming clubs were very similar to the Customs requirement for 'entered premises', and it may be that the exercise was a curtain-raiser for an eventual excise tax on the bank profits of gaming. This would be a more profitable basis of tax than a surcharge on rateable values, which in any case invites tax avoidance: many gaming clubs responded to the tax by splitting into several operating companies and charging a *pro rata* amount for rent and rates to those providing non-taxable services (food, bar and so forth).[64] To some extent, the process was begun by discarding the rateable value tax on bingo halls in 1968 and replacing it with a more profitable turnover tax on stake money; and control would also be facilitated by the Gaming Board's restriction of permitted games to roulette, craps, blackjack, baccarat, chemin de fer and punto banco under specific rules approved by the Board.

Conclusion

The case of the betting duty, and the contrast between the failure of the 1920s and the relative success of later taxes, is an interesting example of the growth of an administrative control system in an apparently unpromising area. This might be contrasted with the United States, where some sample surveys indicate that in gross turnover, gambling is the largest national industry.[65] But until recently 90 per cent of it has been illegal,[66] and the Federal 10 per cent excise tax on gross turnover has in the past produced a derisory sum, being far outweighed by the 'ice' paid to police officials, sometimes with criminal protection rackets as intermediaries. But several states have now gone over to a licensed betting shop system on the poachers-to-gamekeepers model.

The problem, however, is not wholly an administrative one. Even in the 1920s, much of the problem was political — Churchill's attitude to illegal betting as 'forbidden fruit'. Where the liability was clear, large illegal betting firms paid tax, and in fact the important administrative distinction was not so much between legal and illegal betting as between large firms and small entrepreneurs. There was no real administrative difficulty in obtaining betting tax from the large street bookmaking firms, and the Inland Revenue had the same experience with Income Tax. But gaming would be an even greater administrative challenge to the Customs than horse or dog betting, because in gaming very large sums of money change hands very quickly without any written record, and therefore it is by no means so easy to control as the more leisurely and mechanically-documented system of horserace betting in shops.

Other administrative difficulties encountered in this case were problems relating to incompatibilities in levels of control – note the unease in the 1920s over allowing Customs officers to make test bets and the frequent changes of local staff, which weakened the Customs' power over the local firms. The permanent flying squads on the racecourses were more successful in 'learning' but also faced 'counter learning' in the same way as the local police. Off the racecourses, the large firms, unable to evade tax, also developed counter-learning capacity in tax avoidance – note their use of tax havens, the demolition of the law over *Pari-mutuel* betting, the splitting up of gaming clubs in 1966 and similar operations by 'hybrid' bookmakers after 1927.

The process of reciprocal learning is also clearly identifiable in the general law of betting and gaming. In gaming, the difficulties which emerged after the 1960 Act were such that the British government was obliged to abandon the attempt to control gaming by means of coherent and equitable rules 'without regard to persons', and has reverted very largely to the basis of *raison d'État* which was in fact the unofficial method of control by the local police before 1960. A similar example is the attempt to curb the greyhound racing boom of the inter-war period by local authority licensing of greyhound tracks and limits on the number of days of racing per year and per week on each track, which was introduced in 1934. This was circumvented by licensees in adjacent licensing areas, such as greater London or the West Riding of Yorkshire, arranging licensing days so that one of the tracks in the locality was open on the days when the others were closed, and vice versa.[67] This meant that greyhound betting facilities were almost continuously available within a locus of convenient travelling distance in such places, contrary to the intentions of the authorities.

It is interesting that the 1966 betting tax has not apparently been seriously affected by this type of reciprocal learning. But in spite of the happy administrative ending (so to speak) of this story, the economic constraints on betting taxation remain, and many influential public figures do not seem to understand why the gross turnover of betting cannot be taxed at a very high rate to produce a huge revenue,[68] apart from the obvious pressures for tax evasion which such a rate would produce. One possibility which has been put forward by those who think in these terms is the idea of a government tote monopoly on the French or Soviet model. Such a monopoly, *if* effectively enforced and *if* the total volume of betting remained constant, would obviously increase the share of the 'betting fund' available for the Treasury, since the element of bookmakers' profits would be eliminated. Such a monopoly could probably be enforced on the racecourses for 'ergonomic' reasons, but it is doubtful if such a monopoly would make much money if restricted to the racecourses, because the great bulk of British betting takes place off the racecourse. On the other hand, the administrative problems of implementing a tote monopoly for off-course betting would be overwhelming. Government tote monopolies are unenforceable for off-course betting in most countries where they exist (such as France): even the Soviet authorities encounter this problem, and in Moscow illegal bookmakers seem to operate on the racecourse in competition with the government tote,[69] in spite of government attempts to suppress such activities.

Notes

1. See Appendix III, *Minutes of Evidence to the Royal Commission on Betting and Lotteries 1933*, 20th Day 15.12.32 (Statement of Evidence by J. M. Keynes), pp. 492–497; *Report of the Royal Commission on Betting, Lotteries and Gaming 1949–1951*, Cmd. 8190, pp. 16–17, paras 64–65.
2. Dowell, S., *A History of Taxation and Taxes in England from Earliest Times to the Present Day*, Longmans, London, 1884, Vol. 4, pp. 325–327.
3. Olmstead, C., 'Analyzing a pack of cards' in R. Herman (Ed.), *Gambling*, Harper and Row, New York, 1967, p. 139.
4. Dowell, S., *op. cit.*, Vol. 3, p. 297.
5. *Report of the Royal Commission on Betting and Lotteries*, Cmd. 4341, 1933, pp. 6–8.
6. Kaye, R., and R. Peskett, *The Ladbrokes Story*, Pelham Books, London, 1969, p. 26 and p. 262.
7. *Report of the House of Lords Select Committee on Betting*, HC 114, 1902, p. 31.
8. Cmd. 8190, *op. cit.*, p. 65, para 221.
9. Royal Commission on Betting and Lotteries 1933, *Minutes of Evidence*, p. 93, para 1212.
10. *Report of the House of Commons Select Committee on Betting Duty*, HC 139, 1923, p. xv, para 16.
11. *Ibid* Qs 2003 and 6141.
12. *Ibid.*, Qs 3359–64; Royal Commission on Betting, Lotteries and Gaming 1949–1951, *Minutes of Evidence*, 3rd Day 10.10.49, pp. 80–85.
13. HC Deb Vol 196, c. 505.
14. Crombie, Sir James, *H.M. Customs and Excise*, New Whitehall Series, Allen and Unwin, London, 1962, p. 121.
15. HC Deb Vol 196, c. 2005–2006.
16. Cmd. 4341, *op. cit.*, p. 37, para 128.
17. Customs General Orders, GO 86/1926, 13.11.26; GO 103/1926, 28.2.26.
18. Source: Customs and Excise records, annual reports and HC Deb Vol 222, c. 1938.
19. Cf. O. Stanley, *A Guide to Taxation*, Methuen and Co., London, 1967, pp. 121–131 and *passim*.
20. Public Notice by HM commissioners of Customs and Excise, 24.6.27 and Customs General Order GO 58/1928, 4.7.28.
21. HC Deb Vol 613, c. 995.
22. Royal Commission on Betting and Lotteries 1933, *Minutes of Evidence* 5th Day, 15.9.32 (Statement of evidence by Lord Askwith for the National Greyhound Racing Society of Great Britain) pp. 108–110.
23. Customs General Order GO 81/1927, 26.9.26.
24. Customs General Order GO 90/1926, 22.11.26.
25. Chenery, J. T., *An Introduction to the Law and Practice of Betting and Bookmaking*, Sweet and Maxwell, London, 1961.
26. Cf. Government of Ireland Act 1920. 10 and 11 Geo 5, Ch. 67, Sec. 21(1).
27. Cabinet Papers 48(26) 2.
28. *Report of HM Commissioners of Customs and Excise*, Cmd. 3435, 1929, p. 106, Table 88.
29. Royal Commission on Betting and Lotteries 1933, *Minutes of Evidence* 2nd Day, 1.7.32, Q.585, 5th Day 15.9.32, p. 112, para 35–36.
30. HC Deb vol 220, c. 647–771.

31. Cf. *The Sporting Life*, 19.9.27.
32. HC Deb Vol 227, c. 661.
33. HC Deb Vol 216, c. 1590—95.
34. HC Deb Vol 220, c. 420—1 and c. 959—71.
35. HC Deb Vol 227, c. 49.
36. HC Deb Vol 229, c. 89.
37. HC Deb Vol 231, c. 835.
38. HC Deb Vol 736, c. 78—9.
39. Royal Commission on Betting, Lotteries and Gaming 1949—51, *Minutes of Evidence*, 2nd Day, Q. 709.
40. Gulland, J., *Football Gambling from 'Pontoon' to 'Pool'*, National Anti-Gambling League pamphlet, 1936.
41. HC Deb Vol 420, c. 98—9; Vol 422, c. 68; Vol 427, c. 1482.
42. HC Deb Vol 444, c. 405—7.
43. Kaye, R., and R. Peskett, *op. cit.*, p. 200.
44. *Ibid.*, p. 182.
45. HC Deb Vol 613, c. 904.
46. Cmd. 8190, *op. cit.*
47. Cf. C. C. Hood, 'The development of betting taxes in Britain', *Public Administration*, Vol 50, Summer 1972, p. 184 and p. 191.
48. *Report of the Departmental Committee on a Levy on Betting on Horse Races*, Cmnd. 1003, 1960.
49. HC Deb Vol 558, written answers, c. 32—3 and 65—6; Vol 570, written answers, c. 97; Vol 596, written answers, c. 78—9; Vol 787, c. 666; *The Licensed Bookmaker*, May 1963, p. 2.
50. *The British Bookmaker*, September 1966.
51. *The Licensed Bookmaker*, February 1967.
52. Kaye, R., and R. Peskett, *op. cit,*, pp. 224—225.
53. HC Deb Vol 783, c. 379.
54. *The Sporting Life*, 26.8.69; *The Licensed Bookmaker*, June 1969.
55. *The Economist*, March 14, 1970 'Backing a loser', p. 75; Oct. 4, 1969 'Tottering tote', p. 87.
56. *The Times*, 12.9.69.
57. HC Deb Vol 793 c. 206.
58. Source: Annual Reports of H.M. Commissioners of Customs and Excise.
59. *58th Report of H.M. Commissioners of Customs and Excise*, Cmnd. 3490, 1966, Table 58, p. 120.
60. Cf. *59th and 60th Reports of H.M. Commissioners of Customs and Excise*, Cmnd. 3873 and 4256, p. 18 and p. 25 respectively.
61. Cf. M. Rolfe, *The Sporting Life*, 13.9.68.
62. Cf. *New Society*, Vol 15 No. 393, 9.4.70, 'A gamble', p. 587.
63. *Report of the Gaming Board for Great Britain*, HC 208 1970, p. 14 para 26, and p. 15, para 28.
64. Rubner, A., *The Economics of Gambling*, Macmillan, London, 1966, p. 145, fn. 1.
65. Scarne, J., *Scarne's Complete Guide to Gambling*, Simon and Schuster, New York, 1961, p. 94.
66. Kennedy, R. F., 'The baleful influence of gambling' in R. Herman (Ed.), *Gambling, op. cit.*
67. Cmd. 8190 *op. cit.*, p. 27, para 99 and p. 103, para 142.
68. Cf. John Grigg, *The Guardian*, 16.1.68; Woodrow Wyatt (from National Association of Bookmakers Files of Evidence to the 1967 Benson Committee on Racing); the late Sir Gerald Nabarro, HC Deb. Vol 672, written answers, c. 84; Vol 675, c. 1162—3; *The Economist*, May 19, 1962, 'Twist or bust', p. 662.
69. Scarne, J., *op. cit.*, p. 94.

Chapter 11

Summary and Conclusion:
The Limits of Administration

'... an ineffective administration is probably the least implacable obstacle which a government has to face.' C. G. Moodie, 'The political aspects of the strategy of development', *Public Administration and Economic Development*, OECD, Alcala de Henares, 13–25 September 1965, pp. 81–82.

And now to draw the threads together. Like Sir Josiah Stamp's tax problem, which was mentioned in Chapter 4, it is not easy to reduce the contents of the preceding chapters to the level of a 'pill advertisement'. Besides, there are probably too many 'pill advertisement' theories of administration as it is. But in this chapter we will attempt to show how the pieces fit together.

Implementation as a Problem

It is by now a commonplace that policy 'implementation', 'execution' or 'administration' is a class of problems which need more analytic attention than they have received in the past. Several writers have drawn attention to the lack of balance in the standard administrative and business literature between the emphasis on planning and decision-making on the one hand, and the lack of a systematic discussion of implementation processes on the other hand. Control and policy execution, it would sometimes appear, is a matter of mere *fiat*. Gordon Tullock, for example, expresses his surprise that there has been so little serious discussion of

'... the inherent limitations that organizational and administrative constraints place upon the choice of policies.'[1]

Gross, another of the critics of the dominant approach, has put it this way

'Many people think of administration as a small-a affair involving nothing but staff tools and formal structures rather than a large-A affair involving the guidance of complex systems in difficult environments.'[2]

Pressman and Wildavsky, as we have seen, have made a similar point, noting the almost total absence of serious writing on what Gross terms 'the nastier problems'[3] which have to do with persuading, manipulating or coercing people to act in accordance with decisions that are (somehow or other) made. Pressman and Wildavsky have offered one type of analysis of this problem, and economists like

Tullock have offered another type of analysis, using economic-type arguments which have made a distinctive contribution to administrative theory. 'Organization theory', a multi-disciplinary body of literature on organizations which is drawn largely from sociology, offers yet another approach to the problem. We have briefly reviewed all of these approaches in the preceding chapters.

In fact, the general problem of policy implementation has probably received more attention from academics and practitioners outside rather than inside the academic public administration and political science fraternity. For example, the bitter experiences of development economists with administrative snarl-ups and unforeseen political developments upsetting economic forecasts has led to attempts to include 'political and administrative variables' into economic planning models. Practitioners such as the World Bank actually use concepts of a 'coefficient of administrative friction' for project appraisal. The World Bank's coefficient is based on the average discrepancy for any given economic sector between the original costs, benefits and time of construction estimates on the one hand and, on the other hand, the actual benefits, costs and time taken.[4]

Our general criticisms of the existing 'models' of implementation problems is that they are one-sided and insufficiently systematic. There are more kinds of administrative problems than are dreamt of in their philosophies. As we discussed in Chapter 8, the traditional sociological explanations of administrative problems in terms of red tape and bribery are far from adequate as explanations of ineffective implementation. Such explanations exclude some of the key processes by which projects administered by honest and intelligent officials can be self-defeating.[5] Again, we have seen that Pressman and Wildavsky's theory of inter-agency bargaining is not altogether satisfactory as a general theory of implementation problems. It is an elegant and lucid analysis of one important class of such problems. But it will not do as a *general* theory. There are important problems which it omits. It would be interesting to explore how far the particular 'angle' which Pressman and Wildavsky have taken towards the problem is conditioned by the special characteristics of the type of policy field which they were investigating and how far it is conditioned by the general institutional context of government in the United States, with the federal structure making inter-agency bargaining a central problem in every type of policy implementation. But only systematic research could answer questions about the relative effects of difference in type of policy field and differences in overall administrative/political systems as determinants of particular implementation problems.

Similarly, the World Bank's concept of 'administrative friction' is not broad enough to encompass all of the administrative problems which we have discussed in this book. Certainly, 'friction' is one kind of administrative limit. But such limits are not always expressed in terms of drag, leakage or friction. In some cases, as has been pointed out in Chapter 9, administrative processes can produce results which are quite the opposite of those desired by the authorities. An example of this, which we briefly mentioned in Chapter 9, was the British Industrial Relations Act of 1971–1974, the stated object of which was 'to promote good industrial relations'. Over most of the policy areas which the Act sought to control, it was simply ineffective. Pre-entry closed shops for union members, for example, apparently continued as before, although such practices were formally outlawed by the Act. Where the Act was not ineffective, it was counter-productive in that its operation provoked industrial unrest, notably a national dock strike in 1972, which arose out of the working of the Act in one famous case, the 'Midland Cold Storage' case. It is true that part of the problem lay in the inherent contradictions between the various objectives which the Act was intended to promote. For example, the Act was intended at the same time to strengthen the control of central union officials over local militants (using a 'middleman' strategy of control), and at protecting the individual from union power in general. But nevertheless much of the explanation for the Act's failure lies in the hostile political environment in which it was implemented, creating a 'negative demonstration effect'.[6]

Administrative Limits

Our approach to analysing implementation problems began by asking 'Are there administrative limits to policy outcomes?'. This initial question was perhaps child-like. It was too bald. In our analysis of 'perfect administration' in Chapters 1 and 2, we quickly discovered that there are several possible types of limits. For example, there are absolute limits, quasi-administrative limits, referring to those limits which are derived from strictly external contraints; and economic-type limits, referring to points at which some balance of advantage shifts. Similarly, there are *limits* and *failures*. 'Limits' only apply where recurring failure is either expected or experienced.

Probably one cannot speak of pure and absolute limits to administration. The degree of hostility in the environment is the key factor. To a large extent, recalcitrance is the *raison d'être* of administration, as we have already pointed out: one 'administers' because there is or may be resistance in the system. But recalcitrance is also a limiting factor, indeed *the* limiting factor in many cases. The more that the authorities try to prohibit or to enforce activities that a significant proportion of ordinary people do not feel to be wrong or right, respectively, the more administrative difficulties they will encounter.[7]

Recalcitrance, of course, cannot explain every single case of administrative failure. Some versions of the 'horse-shoe-nail' type of problem are clearly an exception to the rule. In some operations, particularly in the context of what Thompson has called 'long-linked technologies' (that is, a process combining a number of serially independent acts)[8] one small mistake, or the combination of several small mistakes, may lead to disaster without any strategic enemy intelligence being involved. A well-known example is Captain Scott's Antarctic expedition of 1912, the failure of which was caused by a combination of small errors — too little fuel for the stoves, the use of ponies and man-hauled sledges rather than dogs, and the miscalculation of the quantity and type of food which is needed to keep men fit in Antarctic conditions.

'Economic-type' Limits

Not much can be said in a general way about economic-type administrative limits, because the nature of such limits is by definition dependent on policy priorities. Policy priorities differ from one situation to another, and moreover priorities typically shift over time, causing the limits to which it is worthwhile to enforce compliance in any administrative operation, to change as the 'heat' goes on from one issue to another. All that can be said in a general way about this type of limit is that even if we could do everything, we could not do everything at once. This is partly a question of simple economic resources: even in a wealthy society, there are sharp limits to the amount of men and money which can be devoted to administration. Moreover, there are structural incompatibilities which would make it impossible to do everything at once.[9] So even in an 'ideal' situation where overall priorities are stable and unambiguous, 'crackdowns' typically have to be done on some sort of rota basis for simple reasons of capacity.

Quasi-administrative Limits

In Chapter 1 we distinguished 'objective' administrative limits from what we called 'quasi-administrative' limits. Quasi-administrative limits refer to situations where administrators are given an impossible job because of high policy decisions, or situations in which we are deliberately putting more weight on administrative systems than we can afford to pay for. The first type of limit proved elusive. If we were looking for 'Great Administrative Impossibles', analogous to the Great Scientific Impossibles (such as perpetual motion, anti-gravity, trisecting the angle, magic carpets and so forth), we have been largely disappointed. Administration rarely if ever seems to be a 'critical' limit to policy outcomes in this pure sense.

Most of the problems which were revealed by the case studies were quasi-administrative limits. One cannot help noticing from such studies how often governments exhibit what in an individual would be symptoms of brain damage, i.e. hyper-activity, inconsistency, emotional lability and distractability.[10] In none of the cases which we have studied was an administrative 'failure' divorced from political manoeuvering, though in many cases it is administrative factors which serve as the flywheel for such manoeuvering. This can happen in two ways. First, it is relatively easy to secure the change or the abolition of some disliked policy measure if such a measure has proved to be administratively unsuccessful or it has not had a chance to become firmly established. Downs calls this the 'initial survival threshold' of policies or agencies.[11] The Land Tax illustrates the point. Pressure by the Land Union, the Conservative Party and other groups for the abolition of the Lloyd George tax was obviously helped by the operational failure of the tax. The political power of these groups was not sufficient to secure the abolition of the more successful Mineral Rights Duty, which continued after 1920. The same applies to the Conservative abolition of the development charges system in 1953 and of the Betterment Levy in 1970.

The other way in which administrative factors may act as a 'flywheel' on political manoeuvering is by making political concessions expensive in terms of administrative control. For example, in the Betting Tax case in the last chapter, there were several problems, over which the politicians were quite willing to give ground in order to placate sections of the racing and betting industry, but were constrained by considerations of administrative control. Cases of this were the refusal to exempt bad debts from tax, the refusal to base the Betting Tax formally on punters' winnings or to refuse Excise licences to defaulting bookmakers. In both of the last two cases, the revenue authorities wished to avoid having to underwrite the decisions of unofficial and unaccountable bodies, that is, the Sporting Press and Tattersalls Committee, respectively. Similarly, there was the Treasury's refusal to earmark the Betting Tax for the benefit of the racing industry, resulting in the eventual resort to a separate taxing authority for these purposes. There were other, more 'technical' cases where the administrative machine failed to mesh with the organization of the racing and betting industry and to adopt the strategy of 'swimming with the tide', or adopting controls which are congruent with the built-in-structure of control in the institutions subject to taxation.

One of these examples could in fact be argued the other way as well. By refusing to tax punters' winnings, the Customs authorities in a sense rely on controls built in to the situation, because a tax based on stakes gives punters an interest in co-operating with the tax machinery by offering a means of proving that bets have been placed, whereas a tax based on winnings would give punters a common interest with bookmakers in evading the tax. Thus it may be that administrators sometimes have to choose between contradictory alternative built-in control systems. The Land Tax situation is simpler in this respect. No system has yet been devised (up to 1974) which has not given both seller and buyer in private transactions a common interest in underdeclaring the true purchase price of a site, and as a result any tax has to rely heavily on the cumbersome machinery of official valuation. The same problem also crops up in the 'open-ended' British drugs purchasing system which was discussed in Chapter 3. No-one outside the health ministry has any real interest in keeping costs down.

Social Structure and Contingent Limits

Some social scientists, particularly those in the Marxist tradition, might argue that there is a deeper level at which one might speak of quasi-administrative limits on implementation than the level of policy objectives. This is the level of social structure in a broad sense. In particular, it might be argued that, even if policies are sincerely pursued, many administrative problems are intractable because they are rooted in the nature of a class society.[12] Administrative structures are not autonomous from class structures in practice, so administrative 'tinkering' in the face of class power will be futile.

This view is perhaps attractive, if only in the sense of grand simplicity, and, as we have intimated above, a case can be made for the view that there is no such thing as a purely administrative limit to policy outcomes. For evidence to support this position, one could point to the fact that many of the administrative tangles which have been explored in this book have to do with the legal complexities which surround the ownership of property, the inherent difficulties of equitable action in the context of an unequal society, whether in the distribution of cash benefits, taxation or the regulation of business or of trade unions. These problems are typically exacerbated by the ability of the private sector to employ experts or ex-officials and to 'buy time' through cumbersome legal appeal procedures.

There are two possible lines of counter-attack against this approach. One is that it does not tell you very much about the precise circumstances in which administrative measures will fail. Clearly, all administrative actions do not fail in the same way or to the same extent. Some even succeed. To attribute all cases of administrative failure to class struggle and to the power of one class or another is to argue by a process of definition, and it is difficult seriously to maintain this analysis in the face of cases like the Betting Duty or some of the cases which we examined in Chapter 2. Capital is not the only form of power (unless you define all forms of power and authority as 'capitalist') and in any case 'capitalist' or 'worker' power will be more effective in some cases than in others. At the least, some sort of strategic, middle-level theory is needed to take account of different circumstances.[13]

The other line of counter-attack is similar. Would there be no administrative problems in a classless society? The conventional Marxist position is that a classless society would be very simple to administer ('every cook shall learn to govern'),[14] and that the administrative problems which remained after political conflicts had disappeared would by implication only be trivial ones. But there are sources of inequality which would arise independently of inequalities in income and wealth and which would still create administrative difficulties. For example, consider differences in age, sex, beauty, fertility, intelligence and location. In principle, it could be argued that such differences only cause administrative difficulties in the culture of a capitalist society, but this argument is far from convincing.

The argument can be examined from the aspect of real-world experience as well as from *a priori* reasoning. Most of the great political revolutions have uncovered classical problems and limitations of administration. For example, there are the ancient problems of how to divide up functions and territory, how to control field officials, whether to use 'professional' or elected officials, or a temporary versus a permanent administrative machine. Anti-bureaucratic experiments in government by elected, temporary officials were conducted in both the French and Russian revolutions and were quickly abandoned in both military and civil administration. There are also more general problems of control at the level of surveillance of the population at large, in particular the difficulty of devising effective controls for the rationing of food and other materials — a characteristic post-revolutionary problem.

The control systems which have been devised under such pressures have typically constituted a return to what Edmund Burke called 'that long roll of grim and bloody maxims which form the political code of all power'[15] which proceeds by constraint rather than by consent. Very often the authoritarian means which are used to control the population at large at the same time make it harder for the top-level authorities to control the administrative machine. It is these experiences which have led to views about an 'iron law of bureaucracy', meaning that the administrative 'superstructure' of a country can remain essentially the same as under the former regime, while the social basis of the system changes, as has happened in France, Mexico and, to some extent, Russia. As Finer has pointed out, such processes present something of a paradox for Marxist theory.[16]

'Perfect Administration'

In an attempt to construct a middle-level strategic approach to implementation problems, we began in Chapter 1 by imagining a fairytale world of 'perfect administration'. Perfect administration was seen as a rough analogue with the economic idea of perfect competition, and other writers have used the same sort of analysis in closely related fields, as with Rule's idea of 'total surveillance' or Bauman's notion of 'perfect planning', which involves conditions such as perfect information, perfect rationality by the planners, no conflict of interest in the society and perfect administrative control.[17] The remainder of the book has explored the problems which arise when one relaxes the various conditions of perfect administration.

In Chapter 1 we saw that perfect administration requires both extra-administrative conditions and internal conditions. We have concentrated on the internal conditions and the limits which arise when they are not fulfilled, leaving aside the external conditions and some of the ambiguous cases which are not easy to classify as 'internal' or 'external', such as administrative impossibility as a form of rhetoric, the 'politics of bureaucracy' and power-plays within bureaucratic systems. Even with the internal conditions of perfect administration, we have not dealt in any detail with the 'horse-shoe-nail' problem or with the problem of incompatible objectives. We have largely focused on the simple problem of securing compliance, since in a hostile environment the limits of administration are the limits of control. Hence the importance of the discussion of controls in Part 3 and the exploration of the other aspects of the compliance problem in Part 2. Control and coercion must have a central place in any theory of administration as we have defined it.

In exploring administrative control in Chapters 7, 8 and 9, we have stressed that it is frequently a multi-faceted thing, difficult to boil down usefully to a single 'principle', and often requiring several elements to be in combination in order to take effect. For example, from the contracting cases of Chapter 3 we can observe the limits of purely procedural change in overcoming cost-over-runs, or the uselessness of banking controls on top of one another when they are all built upon a single (and shaky) accounting basis; indeed, this tactic can be counter-productive in some cases, as we pointed out in Chapter 9.

If we feed into this what we discussed in Chapters 4 and 5, we notice that the problem is additionally complicated when we begin to analyse the impact of space and time on administrative operations. In the case of 'space', we saw in Chapter 4 that physical categorization is limited to a single dimension in most cases, though it is in principle possible to have multi-dimensional categorization. On the other hand, analytical categorizations, by using language, can more easily be multi-dimensional. But there is the problem of mutually incompatible categorization, which in some cases is the basis of 'multi-organizations'. This is a typical administrative 'funny story' theme, which we have touched upon in several places. Moreover, analytical categorization is just as vulnerable as physical categorization (probably more so) to the difficulties of 'lumpiness' and 'slippage', particularly when facing a hostile environment.

Chapter 4 can thus be seen retrospectively as an elaboration of one of the 'costs' of the standard 'fruit-machine' model of administrative control which we sketched out in Chapter 9. Given a desire to operate on the basis of equity and written documentation rather than on the basis of 'gun law' and of arbitrary decisions, problems of the type discussed in Chapter 4 are bound to arise. Some are quite inescapable. And the time dimension creates further difficulties. We rarely start from scratch. We are *usually* operating in a 'real time sequence', with all the possibilities of theoretically correct moves producing absurd and counter-productive consequences such as those discussed in Chapters 2 and 9. Besides, we are *always* operating in a chronological sequence. In some such sequences, 'timing' may be everything, with the possibilities of small errors producing ineffective or self-defeating outcomes. We noted that this problem is particularly applicable to cyclical processes.

Quite apart from the 'timing' problem, the learning situation which is faced in most administrative operations is the case of reciprocal learning. As we saw, public administration is often disavantaged in this type of learning process by its structural characteristics, such as multi-organizationality, elaborate legal checks and appeal procedures, uniform pay and grading structures which make the system vulnerable to 'wastage' of key people and so on.

All of these problems represent successive relaxations of the conditions of 'perfect administration'. When all of them are added together, a would-be administrative controller may have little idea of which buttons to press or which levers to pull. Some of these controls may only work in combinations (which he may not understand). Some will produce no effect at all. Others will produce the reverse of what he intends. Worse, any given course of action will not necessarily produce the same results when it is repeated on another occasion. This may simply arise because so many variables are involved; for example, in football, if team A beats team B in September, and B beats C in October, we cannot say for certain whether A will beat C in November.[18] To this must be added the effect of reciprocal learning processes. It is not merely the problem of driving a vehicle with very difficult controls through a highly complex landscape; it is as if the landscape were deliberately moving about to resist the efforts of a driver to steer his vehicle.[19]

The problems which we have identified by relaxing the conditions of 'perfect administration' give us a 'check list' of things to look at in case studies of administrative processes. It has often been remarked that 'public administration is a subject matter in search of a discipline'.[20] Whereas it is not claimed that the analysis offered in this book amounts to the 'systematic and empirically based theory of administration in the public sector' which some authors are looking for,[21] it does at least offer a check-list; and check-lists are badly needed in so concrete and contextual a subject.

Both of our tax case studies brought out the gaps between what is politically desirable and what is administratively feasible. The Land Tax case in particular shows some of the complexities which can arise when one tries to put into effect what seems like a simple and clear-cut principle. Valuation raises problems of the kind which were discussed in Chapter 4, in particular the 'back garden' cases which clog up the machinery when one tries to prevent tax evasion by the fragmentation of properties through some device of legal fiction. There are also difficulties of effective enforcement, particularly those difficulties which are created by the 'two-price' system. The Betting Tax case is in many ways similar, but it also shows how a type of administrative control mechanism has grown up from unpromising beginnings.

The contracting cases in Chapter 3 bring out almost all of the administrative problems which we have discussed. For example, there are 'horse-shoe-nail' problems, such as the foul-ups in putting Rolls-Royce engines into US Phantom aircraft after the decision to scrap TSR-2 in 1965. Similarly, there are incompatible objectives at the heart of many contracting problems, such as the extreme case of producing aero engines to be immediately dismantled again after World War I. So far as general compliance problems are concerned, contracting produces cases ranging from the 'nit-picking' accounting problems which have to do with specification of terms, wastage processes and so on, to broader strategic control problems, such as the problem of controlling sub-contractors — the key, but elusive, element in many procurement cases. There are also adaptation problems — 'moving landscapes' of a variety of types; and finally there are grand policy dilemmas such as the apparent choice between the international business competitiveness of industrial sectors in a second- or third-rank industrial country versus effective control mechanisms for domestic governments to operate in such industrial sectors.

Few conceivable case studies would be 'perfect' on any point on our list of the characteristics of perfect administration, and the case studies which we have actually chosen fall very far short of this. But they vary in their scale positions for each item. For example, problems of adaptation appear in all three cases, though for different reasons. Problems of incompatibilities between controls at various 'levels' arise in the cases of betting and of contracts, but much less so in the case of land. Catagorization problems are more obvious in the case of betting and of land than in the case of procurement, but procurement and land taxation contain more problems of multiorganizations than betting. Overall objectives are typically clearer in the tax cases than in the procurement cases, perhaps partly because the land and betting systems are more isolated from general economic management and from the international economy than is the contracting system.

Some Dilemmas of Administration

Having identified some key types of administrative limits and some of the mechanisms which are involved, the next stage of analysis is to trace out a little further what mechanisms involve what kinds of limits and why administrative capacity is more limited in some cases than in others. No comprehensive theory of administrative limits can be presented here, and we have certainly found no single magic key to the problem. At least two broad elements are involved. These are administrative dilemmas and non-linearities, which were distinguished in Chapter 9.

So far as administrative dilemmas are concerned, our hypothesis can perhaps be most easily grasped if it is set out in the form of a diagram, and Figure 5 accordingly summarizes some of the main arguments of this book by coupling together the various systems or elements which have been discussed in the previous chapters. The diagram is intended to identify a chain of alternatives (each of which has costs) at various logical stages. At each stage there are two or three possibilities, and the choice of one of these possibilities switches the chooser on to the next set of dilemmas or consequences. Diagrammatically, the horns of the dilemmas point downwards, with consequent dilemmas branching off below. Figure 5 is thus crudely similar to the form of a computer programme or of a decision tree.

First, it is almost axiomatic that the more recalcitrance is to be found in a system, the more there will be a need for control and coercion in administrative processes rather than simply for voluntary co-operation. This has to be central to any theory of policy implementation. Following from this, there are two very broad types of control system which we identified in Chapter 9. On the one hand, there is direct administration; and on the other hand there is administration by proxy, a device which relies on the various types of 'middlemen' which were discussed in Chapter 7 and which are only sketchily represented in Figure 5. The distinction between these two broad types of controls is an analytic one, but, as we have noted, in practice direct and indirect controls are apt to be combined in a

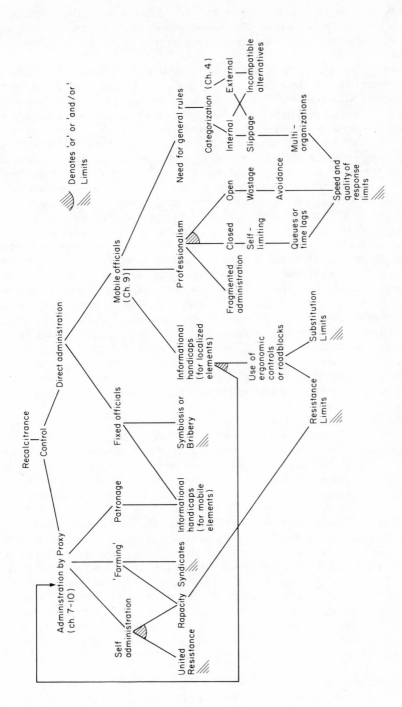

Figure 5. The limits of administration

variety of ways in modern administration. Also, 'direct' administrative structures which do not incorporate any of the classical 'fruit-machine' procedures which we discussed in Chapter 9, will not in practice be very different from 'indirect' administration.

What are the costs of these two broad types of control? Both of these types, mobile direct administration and indirect localized administration, suffer from informational handicaps. But they are 'blinkered' in opposite ways. As we have seen, the mobile type of system cannot easily pick up information relating to highly localized activities, as happened with the Customs officials in the 1920s in the Betting Tax case described in the last chapter. On the other hand, a localized system, though more capable of handling this particular problem, is less capable of handling the wiles of more mobile elements, such as gypsies, multi-national companies, people with scattered property-holdings. For example, we have noted in Chapter 4 the difficulty of operating a parish-based income tax structure in the context of a more 'national' and monetized economy, and Rule discusses exactly the same dilemma in the context of surveillance systems.[22] A localized structure is also much more likely than a mobile one to succumb to bribery by, or sympathy with, its 'clients'. In the Betting Tax case, compare the role of the local police with that of the Customs officials in the 1920s — the localized police frequently 'in the know' about illegal bookmaking activities, but often bribed by or lenient towards, street bookmakers; the mobile Customs officials zealous but relatively ignorant. As we have noted, the same dilemma also applies to military operations. To avoid infiltration by, or the growth of sympathy with, the 'enemy', one keeps soldiers in barracks and moves them about between different tours of duty, at heavy costs in terms of intelligence. Jean Blondel sees this as a very general dilemma for controlling agencies: the further such agencies are from the object of control, the more independently they can act, but the less they can understand the thing which they are trying to control.[23]

As we have discussed in Chapter 9, a mobile 'fruit-machine' system can handle its information problem in two broad ways. One is by the 'ergonomic' or quasi-ergonomic means which we described as the 'roadblock' strategy. Our simplest model of this was the use of a gate or turnstile as a control device, and in fact this is far from trivial as an administrative technique. Factory gates, for example, are typically used for surveillance and control in a manner similar to the gateways of walled towns in the middle ages. An extreme case is the British Royal Mint, where the basic technique of controlling employees operates through the 'gate'. Employees can be searched at the gate as they go in and out of the premises, and to make this control effective, employees have to leave their money at the gate and to purchase plastic tokens which are the only form of 'money' accepted at the Mint's canteen (ironically, money is not 'legal tender' at the Mint). But, as we saw in Chapters 7, 8 and 9, the 'gate' is only the simplest type of this kind of control. Other bottlenecks or 'roadblocks' have 'social' characteristics, and at the margin this type of control is scarcely distinguishable from operation through middlemen. But it is fairly clear that attempts to control the activities of a large group of people in some detail for unpopular purposes without resort to such a technique will tend to fail.

Two striking examples of such failures can be quoted. One is the attempt made by some of the state governments of the United States in the 1880s to levy annual taxes on the watches owned by individuals. By contrast, the 'roadblock' strategy would suggest taxation of such items on a once-for-all basis at point of sale or of manufacture. The economist R. T. Ely was told at this time (jokingly) that 'There are not ten men in Savannah who own watches'; and in Philadelphia, the 'official' number of watches owned by individuals was less than 20,000 — in a city of a million inhabitants.[24]

The second example is a similar sort of case. This is the attempt by the English Parliament to support the fishing industry in the sixteenth century by commanding the entire English population to eat fish three times per week, on days which were called the 'Fish Days'. This measure, like the American watch taxes of the 1880s, turned out to be impossible to enforce, since it involved administrative supervision of the whole population in their private lives. The Fish Days were later replaced by measures which channelled aid to fishing on a 'bottleneck' basis, in the form of subsidies to companies and subsidies on the weight of fish landed at ports.[25]

In Figure 5, two elements have been identified as limiting the effectiveness of the roadblock strategy. The first is the availability of substitutes for the goods or activities being controlled, and the second is a more or less political limit, the point at which control exerted through the bottleneck will provoke open resistance. As we have noted, the smaller the first type of limit the more important the second type will tend to be. It is those who are unable to resist administrative control *sub rosa* and who are therefore caught in a roadblock, who must logically turn to methods of open resistance to the authorities. In the field of taxation and of regulation, as we have already explained, large firms frequently have no option but to take the course of open resistance, whereas small firms or sub-contractors can more easily evade control. This applies both in the case of the large bookmaking firms of the 1920s, who spent large sums in a political campaign to change the tax, and of the Roche drug prices row in the contracting case. We noted that the other problem with the roadblock strategy is that social bottlenecks have a habit of being by-passed or opened up in the course of social development, and the problem of the controlling agencies becomes one of 'un-de-bottlenecking' the social processes upon which their control depends.

The other main strategy which can be employed by a mobile fruit-machine administrative system in obtaining information is by reliance on informers of some kind. But informers must be paid, blackmailed or otherwise privileged in some way. So this strategy amounts to a kind of administration by proxy and to a large extent it therefore shares the problems of 'proxy administration', which will be summarized below.

The adoption of the classical mobile system of control involves 'costs' or dilemmas which have already been discussed fully in Chapter 9, as well as the problems which were discussed in Chapters 4 and 5. These costs are diagrammatically represented in Figure 5. A mobile system of control has to be a system of interchangeable parts. Hence the stress which we have laid on the importance of written laws and procedures, the development of systems of administrative law for the public service and of other 'appeal court' systems of control. Apart from the strength of the legal profession, much of the reason for the relatively underdeveloped state of administrative law in Britain compared to most continental European countries probably lies in the fact that the technique of government through local gentry and through other 'local notables' was abandoned relatively late in Britain, and therefore the problem of controlling a ramified bureaucracy did not appear in Britain until some centuries later than in the Continental European states with an absolutist tradition of government. But with the expansion of British bureaucracy in the twentieth century has come a parallel growth of administrative tribunals and formal channels of complaint.[26]

Delays and problems of adaptation apart, all might be well with a control system of this kind if it were not for the problems of categorization which were discussed in Chapter 4. As it is, these problems create further difficulties both at the level of control by officials over the public at large and at the level of control over the officials by the authorities. For example, Continental European administrative law text-books are full of cases where the law is 'vague' in one or other of the ways which were discussed in Chapter 4, and such cases thus raise knotty questions about *pouvoir discretionnaire* and legal review.[27] We can add to this the problems of administrative 'osmosis' (permeation of boundaries) which are created by wastage in situations where professions or key occupations straddle the boundary between the administrative apparatus and the administered. Such osmosis may also have an international or inter-jurisdictional aspect, as with the case of tax havens, flags of convenience, gambling paradises, havens for criminally- or politically-gained money, and all the other opportunities for this kind of international 'blackleg' activity in a world of proliferating small states.[28] We saw this international dimension to the wastage problem in the bookmaking case, and almost any other tax case would have brought out the same process, probably in a more extreme form.

The next step in Figure 5 is to trace the implications of the learning and adaptation problems which were discussed in Chapter 5. These appear in the bottom right-hand zone of the figure. We saw in Chapter 5 that adaptation problems are likely to be aggravated both by the multi-organizations which are created by imperfect categorization and by the shortage of staff which are created by a closed professionalized structure, particularly for public authorities.

These problems apply mainly to the particular problems of adaptation which take place in the ruse and counter-ruse of day-to-day administrative warfare. This was our fourth type of learning system in Chapter 5. But there are also cases of cumulative learning, as illustrated in our case studies. In both the Betting Tax and Land Tax cases, the loss of the early battle and consequent retreat resulted in a change of tactics when operations were resumed. Thus the development charge system of the 1940s, faulty though it was as a control system, was less so than the approach of 1909–1920. The Betterment Levy of the 1960s in turn avoided some of the pitfalls of the development charge system (both changes, significantly, represented a steady retreat from pure Georgist doctrine). The 1974/5 land taxation scheme in turn avoids some of the pitfalls of the betterment levy by placing land acquisition and physical planning powers (nominally at least) in the same local authority hands. The same thing obviously applies to the slow and pragmatic re-imposition of duties on betting after the fiasco of the Churchill tax in the 1920s. But a 'hard core' of problems remained in both cases.

Administration by Proxy

Apart from devices of direct bureaucratic control, the other major type of administrative control is 'administration by proxy'. We explored some specific cases of this in Chapter 3, and discussed it in more general terms in Chapters 7 and 9. Pressman and Wildavsky, in discussing the general strategy of 'going outside the bureaucracy', consider that this is an administrative device which creates more problems than it solves, mainly because of the loss of political thrust from the centre which is involved.[29] Others have come to broadly similar conclusions, as we saw in Chapter 3. An example is 'Altensetter's paradox' of government by grant in the field of health programmes, which we referred to earlier. It is quite possible to argue that the follies of bureaucratic operation can easily be matched by the follies of administration by contrast.

The specific problem in such a system is the old dilemma of how to control the middleman. This is partly a levels-of-control problem. The stronger the middleman's ability to deliver useful goods or services to the authorities, the harder it will be to control such middlemen. On the other hand, the weaker the position of the middleman, the less effective he is likely to be as an agent of the authorities. Closely similar dilemmas lie in the rewards and sanctions which must be deployed if such a system is to be effective. If the sanctions, rewards or powers devolved to intermediaries are too small, proxy administration can break down for lack of incentives (or of 'negative incentives'); but the greater the powers which are allowed to an intermediary, the greater the possibility of rapacity and extortion. These dilemmas are real for any trade union boss to-day; and they were a persistent feature of colonial administration, particularly in the former British empire, where government through some sort of tribal chief or head man was always attractive because it was relatively cheap.

Non-linearities

Some writers (such as Charles Perrow for example)[30] would have it that all the sins which are generally ascribed to bureaucratic processes are 'dilemmas', like the branching alternatives which are set out in Figure 5. For every 'good' feature there is inevitably a 'bad' feature. Take the case of police organization. In the past, British policemen in cities walked round their 'beats', a system which had advantages in terms of intelligence, but which was labour-intensive and which also gave individual police officers opportunities for corruption, arbitrariness and petty tyranny. Now there are motorized police patrolling much larger 'beats', and there are complaints about lack of 'community involvement'. You cannot have it both ways in cases like this (though it is true that police authorities have tried to do so by appointing 'community involvement officers'). But are *all* administrative problems like this?

In Chapter 9, it may be recalled, we noted that many items in the collection of administrative failures and horror stories which have been discussed at various points in the earlier chapters, cannot simply be explained as dilemmas or as responses to confused or incompatible external demands. We suggested that 'non-linearities' must be introduced as the other broad element which is involved in administrative limits. Non-linearities add another set of items, which are less tightly constrained by each other than are the branches of the tree in Figure 5, impinging on control in a more processual and free-floating way. These are the elements which appeared at the bottom of Figure 4 in Chapter 9 in relation to the discussion of the effectiveness of administrative control: that is, real time sequence, congruence with outside social controls, level of hostility in the environment and level of control in terms of administrative output.

Several of these elements are closely related to one another, particularly level of control, recalcitrance and 'congruence'. They are also closely related to many of the problems which were discussed in Part 2. The more recalcitrance there is in a system, the greater the likelihood that adaptation between controller and controlled will take the form of strategic opposition rather than of symbiosis or of learning systems of the second or third type discussed in Chapter 5. Likewise, recalcitrance lies behind the deliberate manipulation of ambiguity in familiar symbols (the process of 'slippage' which we discussed in Chapter 4), whereas even in circumstances of high 'objective' uncertainty, clear communication can be achieved by goodwill and fellow-feeling. It is often remarked that a surprisingly high degree of mutual understanding can be achieved by sign-language between people with no language in common, whereas it is easy to engineer deliberate misunderstanding even within the context of a shared language.[31]

Any theory of administrative limits would therefore have to incorporate both a broad model of ramifying dilemmas and a series of more 'contingent' factors which produce non-linearities in control. The 'contingent' factors are harder to represent diagrammatically than the dilemmas, and so do not appear in Figure 5. The result is a more complicated and less easily verifiable answer to our opening question about administrative limits than we would like. But, as we explained in Chapter 1, we did not set out to identify precise limits to administrative processes, only some of the mechanisms which operate such limits. To borrow Oakeshott's formulation, we did not set out to predict which horse will win the Derby, but to sketch out the general considerations which should be explored before making an intelligent bet.[32] Also, to say that the pattern is complicated is not to say that there is no pattern at all and that one can do no more to analyse administrative limits than to list administrative 'funny stories' in a fashion analogous to the 'unending catalogues of human idiocy' as compiled by writers such as Flaubert or Pareto. Complexity, of course, is one of the penalties of middle-range theorizing: one can always simplify by greater abstraction. There are 'levels' of meaning, each of which can be defended; but there is much to be said for the 'middle level', something which goes beyond mere description but which is not too far away from problems which are recognizable in ordinary discourse.[33]

A Last Word

In this book we have deliberately ignored or evaded some key questions about policy-making. We have not discussed what *ought* to be the limits of administration, or the moral limits of state action. We have not discussed the legal limits of administrative authority; nor how social objectives actually come to be chosen. We have largely ignored the 'politics of bureaucracy', assuming for the most part that there are 'authorities' with 'objectives'; and we have also ignored the effects of variations in overall constitutional arrangements (democracy, dictatorship and so on). These questions are not unimportant: they are the classical problems of political science. We have simply left them on one side in order to explore policy implementation.

Clearly, we cannot question everything at once, and our approach can be defended as an expositional device. All the same, it may be, as Graeme Moodie implies in the epigraph to this chapter, that the questions which we have begged are ultimately more important than the administrative limits which have been discussed in this book. Specifically, Moodie is suggesting that administration is seldom the 'critical' limit on policy outcomes, and we have come broadly to the same conclusion. Even if all the administrative problems in the world disappeared overnight, many social problems would still remain. But nevertheless, to dismiss administration as the 'least implacable' obstacle faced by governments is a bit like saying that deafness is the least implacable obstacle faced by a man who is also blind and paralysed.

Moreover, in the contemporary world, there seems to be an obvious tendency for the political demands which are generated by mass democracy to push administration to its limits, both by pursuing incompatible goals simultaneously and by stretching administrative resources too far. The disease of basing grandiose social programmes on slim or non-existent administrative resources is only too familiar to those with any experience of policy execution. Abraham calls this the 'King Canute syndrome':[34] governments are easily pushed into promising things which they cannot possibly deliver. For example, in Britain one can observe central government steadily expanding the tasks which local authorities are expected to perform and the standards which they are expected to meet, while at the same time tending to squeeze local authorities financially. Moreover, as we mentioned in Chapter 9, the same sort of doublethink is at work in the current administrative fashion, followed in a number of contexts, to pursue overall strategies which require a high degree of cooperation between agencies or sub-units; and at the same time to evaluate the performance of each agency or sub-unit by separate output criteria. Mass education may also have an effect: an increasingly educated public-at-large is also an increasingly querulent public-at-large, and a growing 'complaints industry', both through formal institutional channels and through direct action taken against both the public and private sectors in western countries, inevitably results in slower and creakier administration.[35] We are no longer in the militarized, hierarchical, deferential world of Max Weber's early twentieth-century Prussian bureaucracy.

Indeed, in the contemporary scene, there is a certain paradox in the coexistence of 'anti-bureaucratic utopianism', an impatience with any kind of administration, with demands for goals such as greater social equality which imply a more organized society. Anti-bureaucratic ideas come at several levels of 'fundamentalism'. Perhaps the least serious is simply baiting the bureaucracy as a game – a favourite pastime in countries such as Britain and France where it is not dangerous. The next level is to attack bureaucracy as an inefficient (or worse) means of policy implementation. We have discussed this level of argument in earlier chapters. For example, a number of American writers consider that the shift to 'honest' and 'expert' administration has worsened the position of the poor in American cities compared to the older style of city government by corrupt party 'machines'.[36] Perhaps this is merely a roundabout way of attacking the goals of politically dominant forces in the society. At the third and most serious level, are to be found those who value communalism and syndicalism as ends in themselves and who therefore question the idea of one man or group 'administering' another, no matter how efficiently or for what good end.[37] Such attitudes provoke counterblasts from those pro-bureaucratic writers like Charles Perrow, who assert that there are inherent difficulties in the concept of administration which is responsive, effective, decentralized and 'participative' at the same time, for all the classical reasons. H. G. Wells put this case succinctly: you must have bureaucracy, he said, because you cannot settle a railway timetable or make a bridge by public acclamation.[38] But anti-bureaucratic ideas are deeply rooted and have a long history, and the argument goes round and round.

Many contemporary 'administrative' problems lie basically in schizophrenic social and political attitudes of the kind which have just been discussed. It is not the purpose of this book to make any moral judgments about administrative processes, or to preach sermons about social attitudes. But, in case the analysis of this book seems too negative, too inclined to look for problems rather than for solutions and to dwell unduly on a catalogue of failures, mistakes and lost causes, it is worth pointing out the payoffs of the analysis. Approaching administration in terms of its limits can be defended on at least two grounds. One is that in some circumstances, the perception of a problem may be all that is needed for a 'cure', as with cases where incompatible objectives are being pursued. Freudian psychoanalysis, of course, proceeds largely on this basis, and there are analogous procedures for promoting 'attitude change' in organizations. The second defence relates to the administrative dilemmas which were discussed in Chapter 9 and which implicitly appeared elsewhere. In a dilemma, there can by definition be no wholly satisfactory solution: but to know that there is no answer is itself an 'answer' of sorts, if only as a discouragement to naive hopes. There is no point in trying to 'fine tune' in such cases. Finally, 'limits' and 'possibilities' are merely the opposite sides of the same coin.[39]

Notes

1. Tullock, G., *The Politics of Bureaucracy*, Public Affairs Press, Washington, 1965.
2. Gross, B. M., *Action Under Planning*, McGraw-Hill, New York, 1967. For a more recent statement of the same theme see D. S. Van Meter and C. E. Van Horn, 'The Policy Implementation Process', *Administration and Society*, Vol. 6, No. 4, 1975, pp. 445—488.
3. *Ibid.*
4. Seers, D., and M. Faber (Eds.), *Crisis in Planning*, Chatto and Windus, London, 1972.
5. Niskanen, W. A., *Bureaucracy and Representative Government*, Aldine Atherton, New York, 1971.
6. Thompson, A. W. J., and S. R. Engleman, *The Industrial Relations Act; A Review and Analysis*, Glasgow Social and Economic Research Studies, Martin Robertson, London, 1975.
7. Wilensky, H., *Organizational Intelligence*, Basic Books, New York, 1967.
8. Thompson, J. D., *Organizations in Action*, McGraw-Hill, New York, 1967.
9. Cf. R. M. Cyert and J. G. March, 'A Behavioral Theory of Organizational Objectives', in M. Haire (Ed), *Modern Organization Theory*, Wiley, New York, 1959, p. 82.
10. McGhie, A., *Pathology of Attention*, Penguin Books, Harmondsworth, 1969.
11. Downs, A., *Inside Bureaucracy*, Wiley, New York, 1967.
12. One cannot really speak of a distinctive Marxist tradition of administrative studies. One fairly recent book claiming the mantle of Marxism for technology-based contingency theory is W. L. Zwerman, *New Perspectives on Organization Theory*, Greenwood Publishing Co., California, 1970.
13. Chapman, R., and A. Dunsire (Eds.), *Style in Administration*, Allen and Unwin, London, 1971.
14. Cf. the theme of administrative simplification in V. I. Lenin, *State and Revolution*,

Progress Publishers, Moscow, 1965; R. F. Miller 'The new science of administration in the USSR', *Administrative Science Quarterly*, Vol. 16, 1971.

15. Cf. Burke, E., *Reflections on the Revolution in France*, Ed. W. B. Todd, Holt Rinehart and Winston, New York, 1968.

16. Finer, S. E., *Comparative Government*, Allen Lane The Penguin Press, London, 1970.

17. Bauman, Z., 'The limitations of perfect planning' in B. M. Gross, *op. cit.*

18. Griffith, G., and M. Oakeshott, *A Guide to the Classics*, Faber and Faber, London, 1936.

19. A metaphor used in the context of development planning by Emil Rado of Glasgow University.

20. Waldo, D., in *Theory and Practice of Public Administration*, Ed. J. C. Charlesworth, American Academy of Political and Social Science, Philadelphia, 1968.

21. Wamsley, G. L., and M. N. Zald, *The Political Economy of Public Organization*, D. C. Heath, Toronto, 1973, p. 84.

22. Rule, J. B., *Private Lives and Public Surveillance*, Allen Lane, London, 1973.

23. Blondel, J., *Comparing Political Systems*, Weidenfeld and Nicholson, London, 1972, p. 138.

24. Ely, R. T., *Taxation in American States and Cities*, T. Y. Crowell, New York, 1888, pp. 166–167.

25. *Report of the Committee of Inquiry into the Fishing Industry*, Cmnd. 1266, 1961.

26. Wraith, R. E., and P. G. Hutchinson, *Administrative Tribunals*, Allen and Unwin, London, 1973.

27. For example, Stassinopoulos, M., *Traité des Actes Administratifs*, (Preface de Rene Cassin) Athens, 1954.

28. Cf. Grundy, M., *Tax Havens*, Establissement General des Instituts Financiers, Vaduz, 1969.

29. Cf. Pressman, J., and A. Wildavsky, *Implementation*, University of California, Berkeley, 1973.

30. Perrow, C., *Complex Organizations*, Scott Foreman, Glenview, 1972.

31. Cf. R. Hoggart, *Speaking to Each Other*, Chatto and Windus, London, 1970.

32. Cf. Griffith, G., and M. Oakeshott, *op cit.*

33. Cf. Mackenzie, W. J. M., 'Political science', *New Society*, 25.7.74.

34. Abraham, N., *Big Business and Government: The New Disorder*, Macmillan, London, 1974.

35. Cf. K. Friedman, 'Complaining', paper presented to the conference of the Canadian Political Science Association, Montreal, August, 1973; R. Wright, *The Day the Pigs Refused to be Driven to Market*, Hart-Davis MacGibbon, London, 1972.

36. Among those who have attacked the equation of good government with honest government are Fred Riggs, Gordon Tullock, E. C. Banfield and W. A. Niskanen.

37. Cf. Albrow, M., *Bureaucracy*, Pall Mall Press, London, 1970, p. 78. The so-called 'New Public Administration Movement' in the USA emphasizes syndicalism and participation as elements of key importance. See F. Marini, *Toward a New Public Administration: The Minnowbrook Perspective*, Chandler, New York, 1971; D. Waldo, *Public Administration in a Time of Turbulence*, Chandler, New York, 1971; V. Ostrom, *The Intellectual Crisis in Public Administration*, University of Alabama Press, 1971; P. Savage, 'Dismantling the Administrative State' *Political Studies* Vol. 22, 1974.

38. Wells, H. G., 'A paper on administrative areas read before the Fabian Society' (1903) and A. Maas (Ed.), *Area and Power*, The Free Press, Glencoe, 1959.

39. Cf. J. Child, 'Organization: a choice for man' in J. Child (Ed.), *Man and Organization*, Allen and Unwin, London, 1973.

Index

212